MW01144278

# CROSS CULTURAL CHRISTIAN

## A Christian theology of world issues, cultures and approaches to mission

Stuart Buchanan

Designed by David Payne

Published by St John's Extension Studies
Bramcote, Nottingham NG9 3RL

© St John's Extension Studies 2010
ISBN 978-1-900920-18-6


Images © iStockphoto.com

Other than as permitted under the Copyright Act 1956, no part of this publication may be photocopied, recorded or otherwise reproduced, stored in a retrieval system or transmitted in any form by any electronic or mechanical means without the prior permission of the copyright owner.

Printed in Great Britain by B&B Press Ltd, Rotherham

# CONTENTS

Who this book is for?

How to use this book

# WHO THIS BOOK IS FOR?

This workbook replaces the two previous Faith for Life workbooks *Entering Another's World* and *The World Christian* that were compiled and edited by Robin Thomson and Margaret Wardell twenty years previously. Both were excellent resources, but world issues, cultures and approaches to mission change and some material had become dated; the original books form the inspiration for much that follows.

I like book titles that are ambiguous; they encourage you to think what the real meaning is. This book is written with different purposes in mind that are included within the ambiguity of the title:

- As the **cross-cultural** Christian - it is aimed at those who go as Christians from one culture to another and also for those who remain within their own culture but find themselves amongst people of different cultures;

- As the **Cross** cultural Christian - it is a reminder that Jesus was sent by God to bring all creation back into a full relationship with God the Father, so that we might have life in all its fullness; that his life, death and resurrection were intended to redeem all cultures; that the Cross redeems all cultures;

- As the cross cultural **Christian** - we draw awareness to the fact that it is easy to confuse Christianity with culture and that insights into other cultures help us to distinguish gospel from culture. As Paul writes in Ephesians 2 'he has made both groups into one and has broken down the dividing wall that is the hostility between us.' Try looking at an object with just one eye; you can see it, but you lose the perspective gained by using both eyes. Looking at Christ through different cultural eyes provides us with the perspective that enriches our understanding of who Christ is, and what he wants of us.

- Finally, and slightly tongue in cheek, as the cross **cultural-Christian** – it is a reminder that if you end up as a cultural Christian, who sees Christianity only through the lens of a single culture then, when you do engage with Christians from different cultures or come across their ideas, you can quite easily become angry, or cross!

# USING THIS BOOK

This book doesn't pretend to have the final answer on any topic that is covered, but is designed to begin to get you thinking about issues and encourage you to explore more deeply those issues that excite you and that will particularly enable you in your cross-cultural experiences.

It is a workbook. There are plenty of questions and exercises for you that are intended to get you thinking about the different issues that it introduces you to. Of course, it is possible to ignore these and just read the text but, as with most things in life, the more that you put into it the more you will get out of it. If you do the exercises you are likely to come to conclusions that are yours and that you believe in, rather than just taking on board the views of the contributors in the text that follows.

The book can be used by individuals, or you may find others who wish to work with you as a group in reflecting on the exercises. If you are going to work or live as a Christian in another culture, you will be seeking prayer support from your church; prayer support is more effective if it is informed. You may wish to use some of this material with people from your church as a way of helping them to reflect upon the issues that you will be engaging with, so that they better understand the issues that you will be facing and can be better informed in praying for you.

As well as the questions and exercises that appear throughout the text, there is also the option of registering with St John's Extension Studies and be given more challenging assignments, have tutorial support and have your assignments marked and commented upon. Your work can then be credited as part of a broader course.

# The beginning

Where do we find the first example of cross-cultural Christianity in the Bible? Reading the first chapters of the book of Acts we know that the early church was made up of those who were culturally Jewish and it continued within that culture. The choosing of the seven deacons to serve the 'Greeks', in Acts 6, refers to those who were Jews from the Greek Diaspora; despite some differences they were basically culturally Jewish.

One of those deacons, Philip, finds himself witnessing to Samaritans and, immediately afterwards, in the desert with an Ethiopian official explaining that Jesus is the suffering servant of Isaiah, but neither narrative provides us with any deep cross-cultural issues.

The first real example of Christianity engaging with a different culture is in the story of Peter and Cornelius in Acts 10.1 - 11.18. Reading this narrative will highlight some of the issues that need exploring in order to be a cross-cultural Christian.

*Read Acts 10.1 - 11.18 and note some of the issues that strike you about this story.*

We will look in more detail at sections of this paragraph later in this workbook but some of the key issues can be placed within the following topics:

- **Culture**
  - o The factors that shape Peter's understanding of the scriptures
  - o Peter's understanding of the food taboos
  - o Peter's and the other apostles' worldview; their initial and subsequent understanding of God's purposes and the place of the Gentiles within these

- **Living and lifestyle choices**
  - o Peter's decision to go against cultural norms and offer hospitality to Cornelius's servants
  - o Peter accepting hospitality from Cornelius
  - o Communication
    - § God communicating with Cornelius
    - § Jesus communicating with Peter
    - § Peter and Cornelius communicating with each other
    - § Peter communicating with the apostles in Jerusalem

- **Faith**
    - o Cornelius's original worldview
    - o Cornelius and his household's conversion
    - o The change in Peter's faith
- **Church**
    - o Peter's accountability to God
    - o Peter's accountability to the wider Church
    - o Peter's interpretation of what was necessary for baptism
    - o The potential for the Church to split into a Jewish Church and a Gentile Church
    - o The potential for the Church to split into those who accept Gentiles as Christians and those who don't
- **Mission**
    - o It is God's mission
    - o The Holy Spirit initiating, directing and overcoming human barriers
    - o Peter sharing the Good News of Jesus
    - o Peter and the Church learning more about God's purposes and mission by being involved in God's mission.

These five headings give the framework for what follows.

# The end or a new beginning

The final section of the workbook is designed to be used after you complete your cross-cultural experiences. It is aimed to help you reflect upon your experiences and identify some of lessons learnt and how they can be applied. As such, this should not be the end; it should be the beginning of the next stage of your Christian life and ministry.

# The Material

This book includes:

- original material written, complied or edited by Robin Thomson and Margaret Wardell
- material that has been adapted by the editor from original material
- new material from named contributors
- new material written by the editor

I am deeply grateful to all of those who have contributed to this workbook and to Gordon Molyneux of SIM International (UK) and Clare Amos and Alyson Barnett-Cowan of the Anglican Communion Office for reading and commenting upon certain sections. The mistakes remain mine alone.

*Stuart Buchanan*

# SECTION ONE: CULTURE

## PURPOSE

This Section will help you to understand what culture is and how we are all shaped by the underlying values of our culture and help you to survive and thrive within a cross-cultural situation.

## CONTENTS

# Learning Objectives

By the end of this section, the learner will be able to:

- Describe what is understood by 'culture' including different inter-related aspects of it and how it is shaped
- Identify some of the aspects of culture that vary in different societies and the impact that they might make upon those cultures
- Understand some of the issues that cause cultures to change and what impact they have upon culture
- Identify aspects of their own culture and how they have been shaped by their culture and be able to compare their culture with another culture
- Understand the concept of ethnocentricity and derive a strategy to avoid it
- List the different phases of culture shock and consider strategies to minimize its impact
- Reflect upon how culture impacts upon the way that we interpret different parts of the bible and gain some skills in separating culture from gospel

Peter, in his dream (Acts 10.14) believes that he is not allowed to eat certain foods as they are forbidden by the Jewish food laws. His Jewish culture also means that he should not be offering hospitality to Gentiles (10.23) and certainly not receiving hospitality from Gentiles (10.48 and 11.2). His culture would also have meant that he would be more likely to want to avoid contact with Gentiles than share his faith with them (10.45).

We know that Cornelius and his relatives and close friends do not take on Jewish culture after their conversion, but we can assume that their own culture will change in different ways.

---

*Before reading the first unit, write down:*

*How you would define culture;*


*What you think shapes culture; Some of the ways that you think your culture has changed since your (a) grandparents and (b) parents were your age;*


*Think of a specific culture, other than your own, that you know something about. Write down advice that you would give to a person from that culture visiting your own culture for the first time.*

---

# WHAT SHAPES CULTURE?

**SECTION ONE**

**CONTENTS**

# WHAT IS CULTURE?

includes material from *Entering Another's World*

Two definitions of culture are:

- an integrated pattern of human knowledge, belief and behaviour that depends upon the capacity for symbolic thought and social learning

- the set of shared attitudes, values, goals and practices that characterizes an institution, organization or group.

These definitions help make the point that culture is:

- **Shared** – People cannot hold a culture in isolation; culture is owned by a group, or community, or nation and although the rules of a culture are not usually written down they are known and owned by the whole community. Cultural values will be embedded within institutions.

- **Learnt** – People of a culture are not born knowing what the rules of the culture are but learn them in their families, in school and communities. Cultural values will be reflected in how language has developed and how it is used. There will be clues in the words that are there and in the words that are not there, or are not used. Because people of a particular culture learn that culture over a period of time, the person going fresh into that culture is going to take time to fully understand the culture and is likely to make mistakes.

- **Environmentally shaped** – If a climate is hot and dry, life will be lived outside of the home far more than in a climate that is cold or wet. If the sun rises and sets at the same time every day and there is as much daylight as darkness, then patterns of life are likely to be different from an environment that has far less daylight in winter than in summer. Abundance of water, or other commodities, might make culture different from cultures where some things are in very short supply.

- **Integrated** - The different aspects of culture are interdependent upon each other and don't exist in isolation. Sometimes, when people of a particular culture move to a different place, they find that one aspect of their own culture doesn't apply in the same way; it could mean that the new culture will feel strange and they might need to modify their viewpoint to continue to be integrated. If life has been lived in a hot rural environment with much outdoor living, how will it feel in a small high-rise flat in a cold country? If you are used to knowing and trusting all of your immediate neighbours, because life is lived out amongst them, how will life feel if you travel a long distance to work and spend little time in your home? If you are used to fasting part of the year until sunset in a country where the sun always rises and sets at the same time, how will it feel in a country where times of sunrise and sunset change with the seasons?

Because we are so familiar with our own cultural norms, we take them for granted and are not explicitly aware of their operation or even of their existence. We become aware of them only when we encounter someone who breaks them and behaves differently.

We live in a global village. With television and the internet we can view almost any part of the world at the flick of a switch. We can communicate instantaneously by phone, email or SKYPE all around the world. We can find those of other cultures living just a few seconds or a few minutes away and actually cross the world physically in a matter of hours.

But although we all live together in one world, it doesn't take long to discover that we actually live in many different worlds. In one way, people are all the same underneath. We share our common humanity. But in hundreds of other ways we are very different.

## Seeing the Difference

Sometimes it is obvious. We are likely to be able to find people in our own country, let alone other parts of the world, who have a different culture from us. Sometimes it will be obvious and we will expect it, but we can be surprised. The people down my street, or even next door, may live in a different world from me. We have the same kind of houses; go shopping in the same supermarket. But we may have been brought up with different relationships in our family, different ways of eating, different attitudes to older people, different ideas about what is good, different beliefs about life, different attitudes to death, family rituals, stories told us by our parents...'

We live in different worlds because we have different cultures or different faiths. Whether the differences are obvious and visible or subtle and hidden, they are very real. And if we want to communicate with people of another culture or faith, beyond the most superficial level, we need to understand those differences. We need to enter their world. Otherwise we will not be able to communicate.

# Four layers of Culture

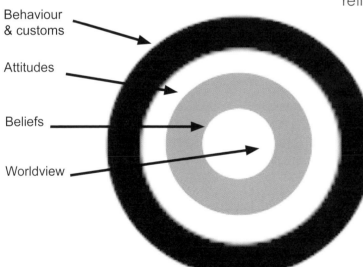

Behaviour & customs
Attitudes
Beliefs
Worldview

**Behaviour and customs** - When we first go into any culture, the first things we notice are the behaviour and customs of that culture; the ways in which things tend to be done. As we get to know the culture better we become aware of what is shaping behaviour and customs. Discovering a culture is like peeling the layers of an onion. As we get beneath the surface, we find the next layer; in this case it is the attitudes that produce the behaviour and customs.

**Attitudes** - Often the attitudes will have influenced the language. I gather that in Urdu there is no word for describing a friend of the opposite gender. I remember visiting a married couple in Pakistan, both of whom I had known individually before their marriage, but the wife was now unable to describe me, to her language teacher, as her friend but only as her husband's friend. In Kiswahili, there is no verb 'to have'. You cannot describe yourself as 'possessing' an object but only as 'being with' an object. You can begin to imagine the impact this has upon the idea of cross-gender friendships in Pakistan and upon attitudes to possessions in parts of East Africa.

Attitudes can also influence institutions. In Britain we hear references to 'institutional racism'. This does not mean that individuals are trying to be racist but that a whole structure has been set up based upon attitudes and assumptions that can lead to racist behaviour.

**Beliefs** - Attitudes do not just happen, they are shaped by the next layer of our onion. They are the result of beliefs. If a culture has attitudes which are racist or sexist, this reflects beliefs that certain ethnic groups or one of the genders is inferior. If a society puts an emphasis upon relationships as more important than achievements, this will reflect what people believe in that culture.

**Worldview** - Digging deeper, we need to work out what it is that determines the belief system. This is what is known as a worldview. A worldview is an understanding of how everything comes to be and how the relationships between everything have been arrived at. It is shaped both by the society that we live in, but also by our religion or philosophy. We will return to the impact of society later in this unit, but start by considering the impact of religion or philosophy.

For Christian and Jewish believers the first eleven chapters of Genesis explain how creation happened and how it was good before it was corrupted by sin. Such a worldview shows that creation has the potential to be good again.

*The first 11 chapters of Genesis give a narrative about the different relationships between God, humanity (both man and woman) and the rest of God's creation. Write down your understanding of these relationships and what is happening within this narrative. We will return to this in Section 5 on Missiology.*

and has a purpose in his actions. The narratives found in other parts of the region are based on the gods arguing and causing the flood by accident showing a lack of trust in the divine.

I know of a couple of different African creation narratives that begin with God living very close to his people, being positioned just above them. In both narratives God moves away, in one case because a woman lights a fire to cook a meal and the smoke annoys God, in the other it is the a woman pounding yams who keeps banging the ceiling of the world, which is the floor of heaven, with her stick that annoys God. In both narratives, God moves away from his creation and becomes distant. Do you notice any similarities with the Genesis narrative? Yes. The woman gets the blame each time!

The Christian and Jewish worldviews have common starting points but further developments in these two faiths lead on to other differences. Those who claim to have no faith or philosophy still have a worldview. If you believe that life came about with a big bang and that there is no God and no overall purpose to creation, then your belief system will reflect this. If you believe that absolute truth is unknowable and that all values are relative, this influences your beliefs, attitudes and behaviour. As mentioned, our individual worldviews are not only formed by our religious belief but are further shaped by the society that we live in and our personal histories, including the events that were going on at key periods during our lives. These change and so do our worldviews.

In the novel *The troublesome offspring of Cardinal Guzman* by Louis de Bernières a priest describes an alternative worldview. His world is created by Satan. Adam and Eve are angels who have been tricked by Satan and trapped within the mortal bodies that he has created. With this worldview all creation is seen as flawed or evil and flesh is seen as wicked, so that all we can do is await death as an opportunity to escape back to heaven. It is easy to imagine how such a worldview might influence beliefs, attitudes and behaviour. His characters believe that God is powerless to redeem such a fallen world; they have a fatalistic and pessimistic attitude and make no attempt to improve fallen behaviour.

Many geologists have acknowledged that the flood referred to in Genesis 7 was a historical fact; it is also referred to in the narratives of other people from that region. The narrative found in Genesis tells of a God who cared for his people

# QUANTIFYING CULTURE

## SECTION ONE

**CONTENTS**

# Hofstede's personality traits

In 1968 and 1972, Gerard Hendrik Hofstede carried out a huge survey of 116,000 employees, from 72 countries, in one multi-national company. This helpful research, revised in 1994, quantified certain personality traits within different cultures. He explored five different measures:

- **Power Distance** - the extent to which the less powerful members of organisations and institutions accept and expect power to be distributed unequally

- **Uncertainty Avoidance** – the extent to which a culture expects its members to feel comfortable in unstructured situations

- **Individualism versus Collectivism** – the degree to which individuals are supposed to look after themselves or remain integrated into groups

- **Masculinity versus Femininity** – the distribution of emotional roles between the genders

- **Long Term versus Short Term** – the extent to which members of a culture accept delayed gratification of their material, social and emotional needs.

Hofstede produced a table, based upon his research, which quantified different cultures. Given that all who took part in the research were working for a multinational company, it is difficult to assess how valid the research is generally for those societies, but it does offer us helpful indicators in reflecting upon different cultures.

# Kohls' five core values

In 1981, Dr L Robert Kohls identified five core values found in any culture, with three choices of the dominant strand. These are:

**Human Nature** – what is the basic human nature?

- Evil
- Mixed
- Good

**Man-Nature** – what is the prevailing relationship between mankind and nature?

- Subordinate – mankind subordinate to nature
- Harmony – mankind living in harmony with nature
- Dominant – mankind dominating nature

**Time Sense** – what dominates our understanding of time?

- Past – society is dominated by the past and keeping past traditions and practices
- Present – society is lived out and fulfilled in the present age
- Future – society looks to the future and sacrifices present day fulfilment for what might be achieved in the future

**Activity** – what is the best mode of activity?

- Being – with an emphasis upon relationships
- Becoming – an emphasis upon how potential can be fulfilled
- Doing – achieving and goal orientated

**Social Relations** – what is the best form of social organisation?

- Hierarchical – certain individuals having privilege based upon status
- Collateral – individual's causes being promoted for the good of the whole community
- Individual – egalitarian with all individuals having equal rights

Both the above can be useful in identifying certain aspects that vary in different cultures, but neither gives a full view of the differences.

*Since the Enlightenment, Western cultures have compartmentalised different aspects of life; we keep the religious and the secular separate; we view health as consisting of physical, mental and spiritual aspects. These are generally still considered integrated in non-Western societies.*

*Consider your own culture and a culture very different from it that you have some information about. Consider how they differ based upon both the five measures used by Hofstede and the five measures used by Kohls.*

# Cultural identities

Globalization, and particularly international travel and access to the internet, means that increasingly people have come across aspects of other cultures. Often, in some areas of life, some aspects of a different culture can be taken on board and we can assume that cultural differences are not as great as we first assumed which, of course, can cause more confusion at a later stage. Sometimes these cultural changes are just a role that is adopted within a particular aspect of life. Globally, an example of this might be professional workshops that are run in a Western style and reflect Western culture, whereas the rest of life reflects the traditional lifestyle and culture. Nearer to home, we may find that we, or other Christians that we know, function differently when with different people. Is your behaviour, your attitudes and the choice of language that you use different when you are with other Christians compared with when you are with non-Christian friends? Increasingly we speak about the clash within cultures, rather than the clash between cultures. As with many issues, it is sometimes easier to identify this in other people than in ourselves!

I was with a group of Christians in the Middle East. Through a friend we ended up being invited for a meal with a Muslim family. As well as a lovely meal they thoughtfully provided cutlery for us visitors, so that we didn't need to use our hand to eat. We washed our hands before eating; I am used to eating with my right hand, and know that Muslims and other people, in parts of the world that have been influenced by Islamic culture, will use the right hand for 'clean' activities such as eating, the giving and receiving of things and waving or greeting. In contrast, the left hand is only used for unclean things; I happily got on with eating with just my right hand. After a while I realised that my hosts were using both hands to eat.

I felt like explaining to them that they hadn't read the right books about culture and should have known that they should only use their right hand! Instead I learnt the lesson that , despite what you read and hear, cultures vary and the only way to really learn what applies in a particular place is to ask and learn from the local people whose culture it is.

Write down any examples of your behaviour, use of language and attitudes that vary according to the people that you are with.

How deep within the layers of the onion do the differences go?

What is happening for you at the levels of beliefs and worldview?

# CHANGING WORLDVIEWS AND ETHNOCENTRISM

## SECTION ONE

**CONTENTS**

# Changing worldviews

But a worldview is rarely static; it is affected by changes that are going on in the world and our reflection on, and reaction to, these.

*Look at the changes in culture that you identified between when your (a) grandparents and (b) parents were your age and now. What changes to worldview do you think caused these changes?*

Although the following examples come from Britain, most of the points will be valid in many other parts of the world. Assuming that your grandparents were your age about sixty years ago, some of the changes that have happened in Britain since they were your age are as follows:

- **Post modernism** – has been defined as 'incredulity towards meta-narratives'. The modern era began with the Enlightenment. Within modernity there was an assumption that all truth was knowable so that there was one answer to any question, or one story to tell (this is what a meta-narrative means) and that this answer or story needed to be controlled so that any other answers or alternative stories would be dismissed and marginalised, by use of the law or violence if necessary. Looking back at history we need to accept that with wars it is nearly always the winner who writes the history and other versions of events are dismissed. Post modernism has affirmed the value of asking questions rather than just accepting the narrative and has valued different narratives that result in different views. It has been said that 'Post modernism doesn't so much reject the concept of absolute objective truth but rather has grave doubts about the human capacity of human reason to grasp that truth.'

  Within modernity and its meta-narratives was the assumption that we had the answers to all of the world's problems and only needed time to solve them. The history of the Twentieth Century with the massacres of the Great War followed by economic recession on a global scale, Second World War and the Cold War undermined the assumption behind modernity. Many other cultural changes have their roots in post modernity and the move away from the 'meta-narrative' to give value to different narratives and views.

- **Multi-cultural society** – although Britain had 'ethnic minorities', these were quite small and their contribution to Britain wasn't at all recognised. Britain was more of a mono-cultural society with minorities that were expected to try to integrate, rather than having their gifts and values appreciated. Curries, kebabs, burgers and pizzas were seen as 'foreign food' rather than part of British heritage. Local and national football and cricket teams were white not mixed.

- **Racial equality** – although prejudice is still found, it has diminished and there are many laws that try to establish equality and good community relationships;

- **Pluralism** – very few people would have known someone from a religious faith other than Christianity. The views of those of other faiths weren't taken seriously. Other cultures were looked down on and so their worldviews couldn't be taken seriously either. Not only have the views of the major faiths been taken more seriously and been included into religious education curricula, but people have taken a serious interest in a whole range of new spiritualities.

- **Youth culture** – post-war economic development turned young people into serious economic consumers in the nineteen-sixties so that their desires were taken on board. Pop music being just the beginning of an era when young people's views have been represented and their views taken more seriously than before, leading to young people feeling that they have their own identity and culture.

- **Sexual liberation** – the nineteen-sixties saw the Pill, and other contraceptives become freely available. Without the fear of unwanted pregnancies, increasing numbers of couples cohabited without marrying. With such cohabitation becoming more common, the need to marry before having children diminished and the stigma of babies born out of wedlock has vanished in many parts of society.

- **Sexual equality** – women being able to be sexually active without producing children was one change that led first to Feminism and then to a greater equality amongst the sexes without the strong Feminist agenda that can be the symptom of the struggle towards any equality. I am not suggesting that full equality has yet been allowed to develop throughout society but, like racial equality, there is far greater equality of opportunity compared with sixty years ago.

- **Sexual identity** – a widely held scientific understanding of sexuality being genetically determined, rather than a lifestyle choice, together with the decriminalising of homosexual acts and a number of legal changes related to discrimination, has taken away the stigma of homosexuality in much of society and allowed more individuals to be open and honest about sexual orientation.

- **Teaching to learning: didactic to discovery** – when there were meta-narratives, that is just one understanding of truth, then the task of the teacher was to explain and pass on this understanding. Post modernism encourages the exploration of different understandings; educational research shows that we are more likely to remember things that we discover ourselves, rather than what we are told or what we read.

- **Rights rather than responsibilities** – every narrative and view being equally valid has put a far greater emphasis upon individuals and their stories, rather than seeing ourselves as part of the bigger story. This in turn leads to an emphasis upon our individual rights, rather than the part that we should be playing within, and our responsibility to, society, nation and the world.

- **Blame culture** – a consequence of people focusing upon their rights, rather than their responsibility, is that some people no longer take personal responsibility for their lives and the lives of their families; increasingly there is the need to identify an institution or individual as the person who is responsible for our misfortune and, if possible, sue them for compensation.

- **Christendom to Post Christendom** – by 337 AD Christianity had become the official religion of the Roman Empire. As the Empire became replaced by nation states, Christianity remained the national religion within most of Europe. There was the assumption that everyone was Christian and the Church had a privileged place in society and a close relationship with the state; Christian views and values underpinned society, its laws, institutions, places of education and course content and national values. In much of Europe this influence has long gone and only a small minority really understand the Christian message; the position of the Church, and often of Christian views, has become marginalised.

- **Secular society** – society seems to be shaped by not just an absence of emphasis upon a Christian heritage and Christian values but an increasingly strong anti-religious agenda which, although aimed primarily at Christianity, also attacks the other major faiths.

- **Political correctness** – although a product of post modernity, actually contradicts the assumptions underlying post modernity. Political correctness is the new meta-narrative that affirms every view apart from those that used to be meta-narratives! It affirms that every view and story is valid except those that were dominant in the past. It is a reaction against modernity that then uses the tools and instruments of modernity to control.

Other changes include:

- **End of the Empire** – maps of the world from sixty years ago show a third of the world in pink, indicating these countries were part of the British Empire. Britain has needed to negotiate new relationships with these and other countries in the intervening period. Britain's role upon the world stage has diminished and other countries' perception of Britain has changed.

- **Fall of Communism** – the end of the USSR and the Eastern Bloc meant that Communism and Socialism, built upon common ownership, lost its credibility leading to a redefining of left wing politics. As international politics seems to depend upon an 'us and them' scenario, 'them' appears to have been redefined in new ways including both countries that are not seen as democratic and also certain Islamic countries. Some political attitudes seem to need to demonise those who are classified as 'them'. On the world stage there can be both the tendency for the West to demonise certain other world players, and for those countries to demonise the West.

- **Collapse of local community** - the Second World War, and the time of post war rebuilding, were times when people knew their neighbours well and there was a strong sense of local community; not only were there street parties to celebrate the end of the war, but also for the coronation of Queen Elizabeth II. Nowadays fewer people will know their local neighbours. This is a result of people moving away from family homes, more people moving because of work and people working at a distance from home. 'Community' still exists, but often at a distance. Entertainment is found at home through technology, rather than going to the theatre, cinema or dance hall; Christians often worship at a distance, at a church that they feel suits them better than the local church. Many people now find their sense of community in different ways; often it is 'virtual' community, found through internet, email, mobile phone calls, text messages and social networking sites rather than face to face contact.

- **Economic change** – the post war rebuilding of the nineteen-fifties was followed by a technological revolution in the sixties that further expanded both the economy and people's expectations of economic growth and personal wealth. Since then there have been periods of growth and periods of recession. Expectation of continued economic growth has fuelled a culture of borrowing and debt and this section is being written during a period of global recession that has seen banks collapse, shares plummet and increased unemployment, all of which shape the way that we view society.

- **Travel** – one cost that has not increased with inflation is the cost of flights. Airline travel has become far more common and more people are not only flying to nearby countries and experiencing those cultures, but there is an increase of long-haul travel so that people are experiencing a tourist's impression of other cultures both directly and also through the tourists coming to their own country.

- **Global warming** – a consequence of increased air travel and economic development has been the increased use of fossil fuels leading to an increase of 'green house' gases and global warming. We stand at a watershed in our history where either we make drastic changes to our lifestyle and economic expectations or we face an irreversible impact on our environment. Both will influence the shape of our future society, but in different ways.

- **Food, health and self image** – simultaneously, our news reports are full of two extremes. The combination of a lack of exercise with an increased dependency on 'fast food' has led to increased levels of obesity. At the other end of the spectrum the fashion industry has coined and promoted the term 'size zero', and encouraged extreme slimness. Both extremes are bad for health and both can undermine self image.

- **Cult of celebrity and reality television** – there has been a much increased interest in the lives of celebrities so that in certain sectors of the media their everyday lives are presented as being far more important than events that impact upon hundreds or thousands of people in other parts of the world. The interest in celebrity lives and their impact as role models often borders on idolatry. The knock-on effect of this interest in celebrities has been the growth of so called 'reality television' where ordinary people see an opportunity to become celebrities. One possibility from appearing on such programmes is celebrity status but the more likely outcome is humiliation. If being publicly humiliated and psychologically bullied on television are being seen as acceptable, then we should not be surprised if there is increased humiliation and bullying going on in society.

- **Communication** – post has always been slow and telephones were expensive and not widely owned in many parts of the world. The development of, and public access to, fax, mobile phone, internet, email accounts and social networking websites has, and continues to, radically change communication. A consequence is that face to face meeting is used far less than in the past. Emails are usually written in a very different way to letters, 'twitter' limits you to a maximum of 140 characters and texting has produced a new shorthand for words and phrases so that the nature of communication is completely different from in the past.

- **Globalisation** – there has been an ongoing process by which regional economies, societies and cultures have become more interconnected and integrated; although this is often economic it also embraces technology, language and culture.

The above list is by no means comprehensive and I am sure that you can add to it.

*Consider three of the above changes that impact upon worldview, or changes that you have identified, and consider how these changes might impact upon beliefs, attitudes, behaviour and customs.*

We will return to these impacts on worldview when we consider Gospel and culture in Unit 4

# Ethnocentrism

*Look back at the five core values found in any culture identified by Kohls then read the following statements. Write down which core value you think has led to each comment, the value of the person making the comment and value of the person or people being commented on.*

1 *I find it so frustrating trying to get things done here. Meetings never start on time as people are always late for meetings. They say that they met someone on the way to the meeting and spent ages talking to them instead. When meetings do begin, there is so much time spent on general chit chat about how people are, rather than getting on with the task in hand.*

| core value |
| --- |
| value of the person making the comment |
| value of the person/people being commented on |

2 *I was really shocked. I knew that human rights were very poor there but I expected that this was the result of an oppressive government. I didn't expect to find that my colleagues didn't think that human rights were important.*

| core value |
| --- |
| value of the person making the comment |
| value of the person/people being commented on |

3 *It is all very well for people in their country to talk about the future and the need to reduce our carbon footprint or we will make global warming worse in the future. Our country has been crying out to reduce poverty for decades. If we don't develop our industry now, we won't have a future anyway.*

| core value |
| --- |
| value of the person making the comment |
| value of the person/people being commented on |

...continued overleaf

4 *I find him so rude, he is always in such a hurry to get things done that he never has time to stop and speak and find out how people are and what really concerns them. I am afraid that all of his hard work will come to nothing if he doesn't spend some time trying to understand people and what makes them tick and what their aspirations are and what gifts they have to share in getting things done.*

| core value |
| --- |
| value of the person making the comment |
| value of the person/people being commented on |

5 *It is a strange country with strange values. They speak all of the time about their own rights and about human rights, but they seem to have lost sight of what is good for society in general. Should whole groups people of people live in fear and have their lives ruined because of the so called human rights of one individual who doesn't care about anybody else?*

| core value |
| --- |
| value of the person making the comment |
| value of the person/people being commented on |

6 *They don't understand it is our past that has given us our heritage, shaped who we are and given us our sense of values and self worth. If you take away our heritage we will be nothing and will lose our sense of values and of self esteem.*

| core value |
| --- |
| value of the person making the comment |
| value of the person/people being commented on |

As indicated in the previous unit, our culture is like an onion comprising different layers. At the centre is our worldview, then our beliefs, then our attitudes and then our behaviour and customs. Because the different layers all fit together neatly for us, our culture will appear to us to be the natural and right way for any culture to exist. If our starting point is our worldview, then the beliefs that flow out of this worldview will be the ones that we hold. If we try to impose someone else's beliefs onto our worldview, then they won't make sense and won't fit. Other attitudes won't sit neatly with our beliefs and other behaviour and customs won't seem appropriate if our starting point is our attitudes. This is why, whatever your culture is, it will appear to you to be the right culture; any other culture will not match up to it and will seem inferior. The term for considering that your own culture is best is called ethnocentrism.

Those from Western cultures can be very arrogant in assuming the superiority of their culture. If you look back at the factors that have changed in your society and impacted upon worldview and culture in recent decades, then there can be a Western assumption that not only are all these factors progress but also the assumption that such changes will be followed, in due course, by other cultures. The implication can easily become that other cultures, that have not reached these assumptions, are 'backward' rather than accepting that they are based upon different values.

All cultures can be guilty of Ethnocentricity. Many cultures will look at my Western culture and see the negatives and dismiss the positives. What one person perceives as progress, another sees as moral decline. It is an interesting phenomenon that although we are prepared to be critical of our own society, culture and history with others from our culture, we can get very defensive when those from other cultures are critical of our own society, culture and history. Particular aspects of ethnocentrism are to be dismissive of whole groups of people because of their race or religion. All cultures including our own are valid, but imperfect, ways of life. There can be a tendency when living in a culture that has been influenced

by Christian values to assume that it is a Christian culture. There is no such thing as a Christian culture. History has shown that those cultures that assume that they are based upon religious values have often been some of the most repressive, intolerant and least Christian. It is sobering to remember that it was the 'Christian' nations of Europe that massacred each other in the First World War and recent atrocities in other parts of the world have often occurred in countries that had considered themselves as Christian. Jesus came in order that we may have life in all is fullness. All cultures are fallen, but Jesus came to redeem all of creation including all cultures.

To avoid the trap of ethnocentricity you need to be able break down the barriers of 'us' and 'them'. Reading books and listening to those from your own culture who have lived within that culture can be a starting point, but you really need to get to know people and make friends with those of other cultures. When you accept people as friends, you accept the whole person and find it easier to cope with difference. There is the need to really listen and seek to understand people's starting point and think yourself into their situation. If you can begin to understand their worldview, it will be much easier to understand their beliefs, attitudes, customs and behaviour.

Many people find it helpful to write a journal when they arrive in a different culture; it particularly helps to make a record of your feelings and thoughts as well as what you do. These thoughts and feelings can be offered to God in prayer. Look through the psalms; you will see that the writers of these were comfortable offering their anger, anxieties and frustrations to God in prayer as well as their praise and joy. Re-reading your journal entries, just a few weeks later, can be a real opportunity to reflect upon your cultural understanding and any ethnocentrism and how it is changing.

Identify those who can offer you prayer support; those who you can be honest with and you can share your negative thoughts with. They won't be able to pray for you effectively on this issue, or any other issue, if you pretend that you are not having problems.

*Before reading Unit 1, you wrote down advice that you would give to a person from a specific different culture visiting your own culture for the first time. Look back at what you wrote. In the light of what you have learnt from these two units, is there anything that would you like to change in your comments?*

*Draw up your own strategy, or plan, to try to avoid ethnocentrism.*

# CULTURE SHOCK

It is likely that Peter would have felt quite ill at ease when he was invited in by Cornelius to receive Gentile hospitality. It is usual for your feelings to go through different stages when you go into a different culture. At first everything is new and feels exciting and stimulating and you feel positive but, after a while, the novelty wears off and you feel less positive. As time goes by you can feel more and more frustrated, and homesick and can feel quite low, but eventually you adapt and learn to look at things differently and your feelings level out again.

Interestingly, when I was involved in sending people for two-year placements we reckoned that the whole cycle took two years to work through but I have found that groups going for just three weeks take three weeks to work through this cycle. It seems that working through the process, and the extremes of the feelings involved, do vary with your own understanding of how long the experience will last for.

## SECTION ONE

### PURPOSE

This Unit will help prepare you for the unnerving feelings surrounding Culture Shock, and will suggest some ways of dealing with it.

### CONTENTS

Symptoms of stress
15 ways to cope with your feelings

# Symptoms of stress

*You may have had experience of living in, or visiting, another culture; try to get back in touch with your feelings about that experience. Try to write a letter or email to a close friend (think of a particular one), telling him or her what you are experiencing and how you are feeling.*

**from *Entering Another's World***

When we enter another culture our reinforcement mechanisms are taken away. The stable home culture which helps us to deal with stress is not there. Our initial response to living in a different culture may be excitement at travel, seeing new sights and observing strange customs. But this soon wears off and it is necessary to confront the daily reality of living as a stranger in a strange land.

There are various reasons why different people are affected in different ways.

- The quality and length of preparation for the change. Also how much control you have over circumstances once you are there.

- Personal characteristics, such as age, extent of previous travel, language skills, resourcefulness, expectations, personality type, tolerance levels, extrovert or introvert.

- Biological factors, such as one's overall physical condition, special medical or dietary needs; how one's body copes with stressful disruptions in routines; the way in which one reacts to fatigue and to meeting members of other groups.

- The extent of the difference between the home and the host culture.

- Obvious factors like length of stay, climate and accommodation.

Other factors that vary have more to do with the job we may be doing:

- Expectations from project colleagues, for example that the new 'expert' will solve all problems overnight. We may have to deal with their disappointment when they find this is not so.

- Our job experience may be different from what local people expect of us. Job descriptions are difficult to write and tend to emphasise the positive.

Here are some of the ways in which we may feel stress. You may not feel all of these – or any of them! But they are all symptoms which different people have felt as indications of their stress.

- We feel we want to withdraw from the local culture because trying to adapt is so stressful. Local people may interpret this as pride or a feeling that we are critical of their country and culture. That can make us feel worse.

- A tendency to want to 'do' to justify being there, because we feel guilty about our weaknesses and ineptness, especially in a hot climate.

- We feel inadequate as we compare ourselves with others. They seem able to do more.

- Because we experience a conflict of values or identities, we feel incompetent in conversations.

- We experience a sense of bereavement, loneliness and loss because we have been deprived of familiar relationships, objects and surroundings, and the emotional support which our status or our job gave us. We feel we have been shaken to the roots.

- We feel overwhelmed by lack of privacy.

- We feel as though we are in a goldfish bowl where local people stare at us or appear to be watching our performance.

- The need for conscious adaptation causes fatigue.

- The feeling of being a baby in the new culture passes into 'a teenager' stage when we try to give the impression that we know it all, yet we are all inexperience and insecurity underneath.

- We find it difficult to cope with our domestic life – limited fuel or water supplies, lack of gadgets, coping with local help for cooking and cleaning.

- We feel confused, even distressed, because of the difference in senses of humour.

- We feel confused about our role, role expectations and self-identity.

- We feel under pressure to be constant and positive in our witness to local people, especially if friends at home write asking such things as 'Has anyone been converted yet?'

# 15 ways to cope with your feelings

Positive attitudes and the willingness to observe and listen lead eventually to rapport and empathy with the culture. Negative ones lead to withdrawal and alienation. Which path will you choose to follow?

1. **Secure help and answers from insiders**, when potentially stressful situations come up. Those who keep apart get an outsider's answer to an insider's situation.

2. **Do share real pain with others**, but don't grumble.

3. **Plunge right in** and experience life from the insider's perspective; avoid the temptation to run away psychologically and physically and create a mini-culture with family or other expatriates. If you do this you cut yourself off from the people of the new culture.

4. **Set realistic goals** and reduce activities if necessary. Don't compare yourself with others; your personality and gifts are unique.

5. **Make it plain that you want to learn** and admit your needs and confusions to local friends. People help people in need.

6. **Make cultural adjustments -** this includes relating to expatriates of other nationalities.

7. **Relax**. Take breaks if you can't cope with more tension. Don't feel guilty about it.

8. **Have a hobby** and make time to relax with it; this should be different from your usual work. Look out also for interesting cultural activities

in your new environment. Keep up your world interest through the internet. If you don't have internet access, get a friend at home to send you a good magazine regularly.

9. **Expect** a more authoritative form of supervision than you were used to in your own culture. Adjust to the authority of the Christian leaders in the new culture. If their style of leadership is different from what you have been used to, it does not mean that it is inferior.

10. **Be patient!** Make every effort to understand the local cultural system rather than trying to make changes in the way things are done.

11. **Seek to understand** others and their situation. Avoid worrying about the impression you are making.

12. **Develop a positive attitude**. Praise God. Laugh with people. Laugh at yourself!

13. **Be sensible** about maintaining your health – physical, mental, social and spiritual. Don't be so anxious to identify with the local culture that you endanger your health. The details will vary according to your situation. To be careless about avoidable risks to your health is irresponsible.

14. **Make friends in the new culture**. Join a local church where you can call on people for any urgent assistance or just for a friendly chat. Christian friends in the new culture can become our closest friends. One of the best ways to cope with emotional stress and other problems is to have a support group you can call on in your host culture. But don't associate only with Christians or you will find you have been cut off from the wider society which you have entered and want to get to know. Look for friends from other backgrounds as

well. You can also arrange a support group at home with whom you correspond.

15. **Forgive yourself** when you make mistakes.  Don't mope over failures.

**modified from *Entering Another's World***

# GOSPEL AND CULTURE

**SECTION ONE**

## CONTENTS

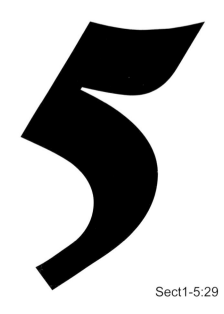

# How many cultures?

People sometimes think that in order to communicate effectively with another culture, you just need to know your Bible and that culture. Some missionaries have assumed that their task is simply to bring 'the gospel' to 'another culture'.

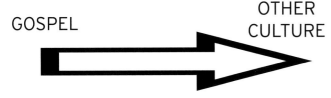

GOSPEL             OTHER CULTURE

They do not realise that their experience of the gospel is the gospel in their culture. Unconsciously they pass on that form of the gospel to the other culture. This especially happens when we assume that our culture is 'Christian' or better than another.

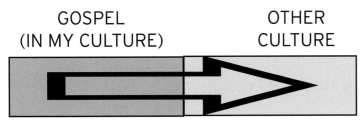

GOSPEL (IN MY CULTURE)       OTHER CULTURE

We need first to understand our own culture in order to see how it has affected our understanding of the gospel (and how the gospel has affected our culture). Then we can look for ways to relate the gospel to the other culture as well. So two cultures are involved, both in relation to the Bible and the gospel. Some would say three cultures, because the Bible itself comes out of another culture.

MY CULTURE     GOSPEL     OTHER CULTURE

We must also realise that the Bible is definite about many moral issues and these principles remain the same in any culture. We must not compromise these and throw out the baby with the bath water. For example, the Ten Commandments apply to every culture. Jesus was the unique son of God and repentance and faith in Him are the only way to eternal life.

However, some Biblical customs such as greeting one another with a holy kiss are inappropriate in a culture where any touching between opposite sexes is regarded as immoral behaviour. When Paul encouraged the believers to do this he was speaking from within the culture in which he lived. When we have managed to eliminate, as far as we are able, overtones of culture in the gospel we present, we can then show the unchangeable values of Christianity that apply in any culture.

**from *Entering Another's World***

Turn to I Corinthians 7.17-19 and Matthew 22.17-21. Each of these passages has obvious cultural features. Take each in turn and decide what three cultures the message moves through. Define the principle being illustrated and the commands being taught in each case. Show how the features of the respondent's culture have been selected and adapted to the situation in question and how the message has been applied in this context.

How do you explain the fatherhood of God in a matriarchal society?

Must a polygamist divorce all his wives except one before he is baptised?

Are the local rites of honouring ancestors a matter of reverence or worship?

Can you suggest other examples of practices (in your culture or another culture) which may be difficult to adopt?

# Is 'Western' Christian?

from *Entering Another's World*

> *I think it is significant that today's image of the Christian missionary from the Asian point of view is an image of comfort and privilege. Hence, Asians tend to reject the Western Christian and misunderstand his message.*
>
> *(A Korean missionary)*

Not only do many missionaries confuse the gospel with culture, local Christians may be similarly confused in cultures where Christianity was introduced from the outside.

## Three Mistakes

Some are under the misapprehension that because Western culture has been Christianised, this is the only form it can take anywhere. Some think that the development of certain art forms in the West is necessarily part of the gospel. A third mistake is to think that since Western culture developed in part from Christianity, this is a perfect expression of Christianity in society.

Many West Indians who migrated to Britain in the fifties and sixties expected that what they looked on as their 'mother' country would show them what living as Christians was really like. Most of them expected immediate acceptance in Britain because both home and mother country were 'Christian'. They were bitterly disappointed to meet rejection and racial prejudice.

## Non-Christians Too

People who are not from a Christian background may be similarly confused. One day two Christian women were queuing for a bus in a multi-racial area of Britain. One was English, and one Indian. The Indian Christian turned to a fellow Indian woman behind her and began to talk to her about Jesus. 'Oh!' said the woman, 'Do you worship Jesus?' 'Yes,' said the Christian. 'So you are not an Indian then?' the other woman replied.

Visitors to Britain also look at our permissive and materialistic society reflected in the media and assume that this is all Christian behaviour. In many countries you must belong to some religion, so they label all Western behaviour as Christian. Because they have a low view of this behaviour they have a low view of Christians, especially any from their own culture. When this happens we need to ask ourselves whether they are rejecting the foreign cultural load which is placed on the message rather than the message itself.

## What's in a Name?

Many new Christians have felt obliged to change their name, sometimes choosing a Biblical name, but often a purely western one. An Indian Christian couple named their son Christopher. When he went to a government school where 99% of his class were Sikhs and said that his name was Christopher Singh he suffered a good deal of abuse from others who felt he was allying himself with the West and trying to deny his Indian nationality.

## Wealth and Lifestyle

People can also be alienated by the apparent wealth of Christians who come to their country. They feel patronised as well as resenting the glaring inequality in their financial positions. A lifestyle well beyond the means of those with whom the expatriate hopes to share the gospel can create a significant barrier to it. In countries where many survive on a bowl of rice a day, to live in a well-constructed house, own a car, dress in imported clothes and enjoy three full meals a day seems like incredible wealth.

This is a delicate subject. A Christian must deal with it not only from the standpoint of his heart attitude but also from the viewpoint of others. We communicate our message as much by our appearance and actions as by what we say. Anything that becomes a barrier to the communication of the gospel must be viewed as a negative fact in the attempt to share Christ with others.

Expatriates may feel justified in maintaining a lifestyle similar to the one they enjoyed in their homeland, even when it is in marked contrast to those around them. Sometimes the physical and emotional health of the family are reasons given for not adapting to a lifestyle which more closely resembles that of the surrounding people. While we do need to preserve our family's health and well-being, it is questionable whether a Christian who maintains a lifestyle which stands out in its affluence will ever achieve identification with the people, which is so essential in communicating the gospel.

We cannot have full control over others' perceptions of us but if the gospel is to be communicated we must address the question of lifestyle. Ideally, we should attempt to adapt as nearly as possible to the economic lifestyle of those to whom we hope to minister.

Of course, we can face this problem in reverse when living in a more affluent culture than our own. How do we adapt there?

# Gospel and cultural environment

Whilst holidaying in a Masai area of Kenya, with friends, I was privileged to be offered hospitality by a Masai farmer. He asked a boy to go and fetch a sheep and slaughter it for us. When we sat down to eat he was very apologetic that in fact we were eating goat, and not sheep. He went on to explain that they are herded together and that it is very difficult to tell them apart. The tails look slightly different and it is only the shepherd who can tell the sheep from the goats.

Later I reflected upon the story Jesus told of the sheep and goats in Matthew 25.31 – 46. I had been brought up with an understanding that sheep were plentiful, white and fluffy and allowed to roam free whereas goats were few and far between, usually brown or black, had horns and were tethered and that anyone could tell which was which.

*Re-read the biblical story and note down the different conclusions you might reach according to your cultural understanding of sheep and goats.*

# Gospel and culture in a changing world

As explained in Unit 1, our worldview, that lies at the heart of our culture, is comprised of both our religious belief and the way that we are shaped by our prevailing culture. Our religious belief gives us a lens with which to view our culture and our culture gives us a lens with which to view our religious belief.

The early church was birthed within Jewish culture; the Acts of the Apostles and the Epistles tell the story of the church beginning to reach out to, and expand into, the Gentile world. In particular the gospel needed to relate to a world influenced by a Greek worldview; by Greek philosophy. Those who have studied Greek philosophy can clearly identify Neoplatonism in the later New Testament writings. As the early church continued to develop beyond the time when the New Testament was written, then the cultural worldview of Greek thought was brought to the task of understanding Christianity and the mission of the church. In his book *Transforming Mission* (Orbis 1991) David Bosch quotes Paul Knitter 'The early Christians did not simply express in Greek what they already knew; rather, they discovered, through Greek religious and philosophical insights, what had been revealed to them. The doctrines of the Trinity and of the divinity of Christ … for example, would not be what they are today if the church had not reassessed itself and its doctrines in the light of the new historical, cultural situations during the third through the sixth centuries'.

Bosch explains that 'That the message about God in human form, about salvific sacrifices, the victory of the resurrection, and new life, fell on ears that did not find it entirely unfamiliar.' Over those early centuries there was increasing divergence between Christian and Jewish worldviews.

In a similar way to the engagement with Greek culture, theologians influenced by post modernity would probably argue that post modern philosophy has helped them not only to express to a post modern world what they already know, but also what has been revealed to them about Christ through a post modern worldview.

In Unit 1 we explored how worldviews change and identified some of the many factors that have changed worldviews in the West, in particular the factors related to a post modern understanding. A modernist understanding would suggest that there is just one true way of understanding any biblical passage; post modernity gives value to different understandings. Let us consider one of the changes of worldview in the West that has come from post modernism. We will explore pluralism more fully in the section on Faith , but the following gives an example of how a changing culture can impact upon one aspect of gospel.

Modernity suggested that there was only one truth and as a consequence other Faiths were either dismissed as having no truth, or viewed as Satanic. One response to pluralism is to say that all narratives are equally valid therefore other Faiths are equally valid and all Faiths lead equally to God. Many Christians in the West hold this view. Another response is to say that all narratives are equally valid therefore, in holding on to my Christian understanding that God is fully revealed only in the person of Jesus Christ, I must respect the validity of the narrative of the other person. Postmodernity means that their narrative is valid, it does not mean that I need to either accept their doctrine or accept a doctrine (that all faiths are equally true) that tries to combine my doctrine and their doctrine.

By accepting their story, and the validity of their experience of God, I need to reflect upon my experience of God revealed in Christ and how I can relate what I believe to be the truth to their experiences. This in turn means that I need to try to understand their worldview and experiences and am more likely to share my faith in a way that they can understand and in a way that might make them respond to my narrative and understanding of God revealed in Jesus Christ.

*Look back at your list, or the list provided, in Unit 3 of changes to your culture in the last 60 years and write down what impact they have made on your understanding of the gospel. Note what the tensions might be between understandings of the gospel between different world cultures.*

If in doing the above exercise you have engaged with the issues of sexual identity and of sexual equality, then you will have reflected on two very big issues that are dividing parts of the Church. Wherever you stand on these issue there are, I think, two key issues to consider:

- **The credibility of mission** - Both sides, on both of these issues, believe that their mission is compromised by the views of Christians who take the other view. In many parts of Africa and Asia, particularly on the issue of sexuality, the churches that relate to churches in the West with different views are being dismissed as irrelevant because of their acceptance of homosexuals. Churches in the West, which have successful work with gay communities, find their ministry is damaged by comments that come from other parts of the world church.

- **The challenge of being a cross-cultural Christian** – All of us, unless we enjoy arguing all of the time, find it easier to relate to those who have the same views as ourselves. Paul argues in Ephesians that Christ not only breaks down the barriers but that it is only together that we can fully see and appreciate the Christ that is revealed to us. Whatever view I hold as a Christian on any issue, I need to do so with an awareness and understanding of the views of those Christians of different cultures who have a different understanding. I need to live with the tension of these different views and allow this tension to enrich my own understanding. Being someone who can understand different perspectives, and explain them to other Christians, is one of the gifts of being a cross-cultural Christian.

# Syncretism and Contextualisation

## Syncretism

As Christianity replaced pagan religions and became established in Europe it needed to work out what to do with existing religious festivals. The term Yule Tide is still sometimes used in England to refer to the Christmas season. Yule, a season that followed on from the time of the year when the days gradually began to become longer again, predated Christmas and was replaced by Christmas.

Bede, an 8th century Northumbrian Church historian, wrote 'Eosturmonath has a name which is now translated 'Paschal month', and which was once called after a goddess of theirs named Eostre, in whose honour feasts were celebrated in that month. Now they designate that Paschal season by her name, calling the joys of the new rite by the time-honoured name of the old observance.' His conclusions have subsequently been debated by scholars, but his suggestion is that the Christian festival of Easter was deliberately used to replace an annual pagan festival in April that celebrated fertility and new life.

In both cases the Church 'baptised' a pagan festival to make it Christian. Both Christmas and Easter are still celebrated within British culture but the nature of their celebration raises the question as to how prominent the remembrance of Christ's birth, death and resurrection are and how much it has to do with celebrating longer days and fertility! The term used for the blending of two or more religious belief systems into a new system is syncretism.

The interesting thing with syncretism is that it is usually easier to be aware of it within another culture than our own! Jesus spoke of being aware of the beam in our own eye, before pointing out the speck in someone's eye.

## Contextualisation

Many churches, in places that were once part of the British Empire, look as if an English church has been uprooted and planted there. The architecture and liturgy are the same although the words of the hymns have been translated into the local language, the hymn tunes played on an organ are the same and the worship is led by people dressed in similar robes to those worn in England. Often there has been such respect for those who originally brought the Christian faith to a country, often sacrificing much and losing their lives to illness at an early age, that the Christian community has wished to remain true to the style of Christianity that they brought with them.

In other places real effort has been made to make the church, its worship and music feel appropriate to the culture. In one place In Hong Kong there used to be a Buddhist monastery; between the two world wars, the whole community there converted to Christianity. There is now a small Christian community living there; the architecture of the chapel reflects Buddhist architecture, the baptismal font is shaped like a water lily, the Buddhist sign for purity. The altar, too, has a distinctly Buddhist feel to it.

I have also heard of a Christian Ashram in India that uses a lot of Hindu symbolism, architecture and styles of worship. Many Christians, both Indian and foreign, can feel uncomfortable with this. Sometimes it is the outsider who is keen to see the church become contextualised while the host community is more aware of the need for conversion and moving on from symbolism that represents another faith.

I visited a Hindu Temple in Birmingham, England with an Indian Christian friend of mine. Whilst observing the Hindu worship I found my eyes focusing upon a candle and reflecting upon my belief in Jesus Christ the Light of the World. Speaking with my Indian Christian friend later, he shared how difficult he finds it to worship in churches that use candles prominently; they remind him of Hindu temples!

**includes some material from *Entering Another's World***

Occasionally a cultural form or symbol from a non-Christian setting has been adapted to Christian expression without those who have done so realising that it has carried with it the meaning attached to it in the former belief system. These old meanings can sometimes distort or obscure the intended Christian meaning.

## Being Foreign

On the other hand, some Christians have been so afraid of syncretism that they have not adopted any local cultural forms for the gospel. So it has remained "foreign". Any attempt to adapt the gospel to a culture must be done very carefully. Some understanding of the religious background from which a convert is coming is essential, as well as some understanding of how and why certain symbols and forms are used in his former religion.

In the traditional religious practices of Taiwan, great reverence is shown to ancestors, a practice that borders upon ancestor worship; as part of this there is festival where you are expected to tend the graves of your ancestors. Many of those who converted to Christianity abandoned this practice and were accused of not showing respect for their ancestors which caused pain, distress and division within their families.

Some Christians got round this by tending their ancestors graves on Holy Saturday, the day between Good Friday and Easter Day when we remember Jesus in the tomb. Not only did they show respect for their ancestors and keep the family graves neat and tidy, but they were able to point to Jesus who died to overcome death and offer the promise of resurrection.

## A Tragic Vacuum

Most cultural forms meet a need and perform an important function which contributes to a culture's existence. When it is scattered or eliminated care must be taken that a vacuum is not left. A cultural substitute must be found otherwise the result may be tragic. In some parts of Africa where polygamy is practised believers are asked to give up all but one wife. Satisfactory arrangements must be made for the others. In some instances this has not been done and without means of support they have been materially deprived. Some have even ended up as prostitutes or slaves.

The question we face is how can we, who have been born and brought up in one culture, take the truth out of the Bible, which is addressed to people in a second culture and communicate it to people who belong to a third culture, without either falsifying the message or rendering it unintelligible?

We may sometimes feel helpless. However hard we have tried to dissociate the Christian message from one particular culture, we must leave the result to God. If not, our tensions and sense of uncertainty about whether we are failing or succeeding will make the message less powerful.

Let us remember that the same Holy Spirit, who guided the original authors of the Bible, can help us to interpret it and show us points of empathy with believers and unbelievers through which we can minister Christ to them. He will do his own work in the hearts of our listeners. We are not responsible for convicting them, that is the Holy Spirit's work. When we have done the best of which we are capable we should leave the results in God's hands.

What things from the list below, do you think would be most likely to lead to syncretism? Which could be used to contextualise the gospel in that particular culture? Explain your answers, in a sentence or two.

Traditional sacrifice of a pig or chicken before a wedding ceremony.

Using national rhythms and melodies for hymns and choruses.

Using local dance within worship

Painting pictures of Christ that look like one's ethnic race

An all night gathering in the home of the deceased nine nights after his death.

*Make a list of the different aspects of your church worship and the life of your church; identify which aspects are biblical and which are cultural. Try to find a Christian from another culture that you can discuss your list with.*

# SECTION 2: LIVING

## PURPOSE

This Unit will help you to understand some of the richness and challenge of living in another culture and enable you to develop strategies to help you grow and blossom through the experience.

## CONTENTS

# Learning Objectives

By the end of this section, the learner will be able to:

- Identify key points from a variety of stories and how they might challenge and enrich pre-existing stereotypes of different cultures

- Understand different symptoms of stress and identify a strategy to help cope with feelings and stress

- Develop a strategy to cope with crisis

- Be aware of some of the challenges faced by single people, couples, families and third-culture kids and be able to reflect on how to face challenges and provide mutual support with others facing their different challenges

- Realise the importance of language learning and develop a strategy to begin to learn a language

- Be aware of some of the ways in which miscommunication can occur and begin to develop a strategy to avoid this

- Realise the importance of avoiding being over dependent upon communication with home and look towards the local community for advice and fellowship

- Understand some of the ways in which the gospel is communicated and the ways in which our lifestyle can be a barrier to good communication

- Be aware of the importance of developing good relationships; identify some of the barriers to this and develop a strategy to develop good relationships.

Unlike Peter, in Acts 10, we can go into our cross-cultural experiences with an understanding of different cultures and what we need to look for and listen out for; but it is one thing to have a theoretical understanding and another to put that understanding into action as we live our life within a different culture.

I find it reassuring that the Peter that we read about in Acts comes over as the same Peter we are familiar with in the gospels. He has the same personality and the same ability to rush into situations that he isn't prepared for, only to discover the real answers as he lives out the experience. Often people believe that they will change in some way when they go into a different culture. We are not miraculously transformed by our mission preparation but we go into the different culture as the same people that we were, with the same baggage and hang ups. It can be tempting to think that we take some superior knowledge or gifts into the different situation that will protect us and give us our sense of identity. The reality is that the experience of the different culture will make us vulnerable and more aware of who we really are and what our weaknesses and fragilities are and what we need to work on. We won't go into the different situation miraculously changed but, with God's grace, we can come out of the situation miraculously changed.

The thing that always surprises me when I re-read the narrative of the encounter between Peter and Cornelius is that Luke repeats himself so often. He tells us what Peter experiences, then he tells us how Peter tells Cornelius what he experiences and then Luke recounts it all again when Peter explains his actions to the Church. Luke is teaching us the need for good communication, and making sure there is no miscommunication. In the narrative, Peter, Cornelius and the Church appear to be speaking the same language, but in a different culture words and phrases can be understood in different ways. The rapid changes in how communication takes place in the current era also raises interesting issues.

Cornelius is actively seeking God, and worships him. For this to happen, it is likely that he experienced something amongst those who believe in the God revealed through Jesus Christ that attracted him to this God. As we shall explore in the next section, often it is the lifestyle of a faith community that encourages someone to take the first step in exploring Christianity. This is exciting and encouraging news, but also reminds us that our lifestyle can be the factor that puts people off Christianity. We need to 'walk the talk'; how we live our life needs to reflect our faith and not be a barrier to others coming to faith in Jesus.

# LIVING IN ANOTHER CULTURE

## SECTION TWO

## CONTENTS

# Carnival

The candombe rhythm echoed proudly in the distance. Eagerly the crowd shuffled forward, everyone wanting to be the first to glimpse the brightly dressed figures marching towards us. A cheerful atmosphere had drawn people out of their houses, away from daily chores and out to the streets to participate in the yearly celebration. The rhythm was becoming louder by the second and people in the crowd had begun to wave flags high above their heads. Younger children giggled happily as they squeezed past adults in their quest to reach the front of the crowd. One more second to wait and they would be here! Yet again the crowd shuffled forward. The excitement was building bit by bit by bit........ An explosion of cheering broke out filling the air with gleeful voices. El Gramillero and La Mama Veija (the man and woman who lead the carnival) burst into dance, twisting and twirling down the street; she dressed in a red skirt covered in sequins which glistened gold like the sun on a hot summer's morning.

The tambor players were marching up the street dressed in red and gold to match La Mama Veija's skirt. Dancers would come next swinging their arms in perfect time with the strong beat that the tambors created. El Gramillero and La Mama Veija had already danced their way to the next street; however they weren't the only dancers! Clattering down the cobbled street came more dancers wearing outrageous costumes decorated in hundreds of feathers and sequins. One of the leading dancers wore a ridiculously large head set towering above her in the shape of a huge bird that seemed to be nodding its head in time to the rhythm. Others dressed in blue and orange masks with pointed beaks and feathered wings followed swooping and swirling after the rest. More dancers wearing extravagant outfits adorned with an unimaginable amount of colours.

Tambor players clothed in traditional carnival costumes and hilarious hats had also dressed their tambors in brightly coloured card and sequins. More and more people paraded behind the carnival as they danced further down the street. Little girls were skipping behind parents who were bobbing their heads to the rhythm without realising; each and every one of them enjoying the experience.

The buzz of the carnival still hung in the air even as the parade faded from sight. Echoing in the distance, the tambors could still be heard loud and clear shouting out their cheerful song to all who would take the time to listen.

**Nicole Gilmore of South American Mission Society (now CMS/SAMS)**

The foregoing article describes a wonderful, memorable experience of the local culture; an exciting assault upon the senses. The scene that is described is full of colours, noise, people and anticipation. The writer doesn't say whether they are there with friends or whether they are by themselves and feeling at one with the crowd, but there is no sense of loneliness, just of joy and excitement. The description uses Spanish words but doesn't indicate whether the writer understands Spanish or understands what is going on. Being in a different culture can be an experience of joy as described, but it can also have the opposite feel. Being bombarded with colour and sounds, and possibly powerful smells, can be a positive experience, it can also be a threatening experience; being by yourself caught up within a large crowd can make you feel at one with the people that surround you, or it can be a very lonely, alienating and threatening experience. Not speaking the language or understanding what is happening can be an enriching and broadening experience, or it can be very confusing.

What factors might make you feel differently about such experiences?

What in you makes the difference in how you feel about a particular experience?

# Ownership and dependency

## Ownership

When working in Zambia I found myself at times advising newly arrived Christian workers from abroad (especially the West) not to lend money to their Zambian counterparts and friends. I had learnt that one of the quickest ways to destroy budding friendships was to muddy the waters with issues of loans of money and, at times, property.

Ubuntu is an African term that describes what it means to be truly human. One of the virtues expected of a person (umuntu) is generosity. One's wealth is in effect held in trust for the whole community and therefore needs to be shared liberally. As a result, African people can be extremely generous even in their poverty. In practice when children from the neighbourhood come to visit (they do not expect an invitation, they will come simply because you have children of your own), they will expect to play with any toys lying around and at times they might even ask you to give them such toys to take away. Similarly when meals are cooked everyone who is present will be automatically invited to share the food. As we say in Bemba, 'Insaka: isaka abalipo' (the rest hut gives shade to all those who are presently under its roof – everybody present is invited and welcome to partake of any food being offered). In addition, loans are not treated as contracts to be repaid promptly but as a sort of wealth distribution mechanism. If you can repay the loans, well and good, but if you cannot it does not really matter - what is a loan between friends or relatives? The relationship already established is far more important than any loan.

Many, if not all, westerners find this philosophy difficult to accept. They find it hard to think that loans and other borrowed property do not have the same currency as they do in the West and therefore many friendships have a short life.

Learn to accept this value in the host cultures for what it is. Observe how the hosts deal with the problems before drawing drastic conclusions about the 'liberties these locals seem to take with one's wealth and property'. My policy is do not lend money or property unless you are prepared never to be repaid.

## Dependency

All of us depend upon others or institutions for survival. John Donne said 'No man is an Island…'. This is true in every part of the world. In October 2008 the world economic system was threatened with collapse because some individuals in the corporate world had been careless, perhaps even greedy, in their quest to make more and more money. Loans irresponsibly given had been packaged as assets and flogged to unsuspecting institutions. And then we all discovered just how dependent we are on each other and the systems we create. One country is in a near state of bankruptcy as a result!

However, in general, dependency is used to describe the relationship between the rich west and the poor third world. Strangely, poor western students studying in western institutions supported by the generosity of a group of local Churches or members are not said to be hopelessly dependent on hand outs, but the term is applied almost all the time to poor third world students! Be that as it may, dependency is widespread across the world. For example, about ninety percent of all the tuition fees we collected from students in a Zambian theological college came from well-wishers in countries in the rich west. Without that support we could not have provided the services we did. Although it is true to say that education everywhere is very costly and it is the rare student (certainly in the United Kingdom and Africa) that pays their way through college without the support of parents, governments or other organisations.

Dependency on the one hand can, and does, develop a certain kind of laziness in the recipients. People often stop developing natural skills and qualities that could enable them to be self supporting. Individuals and local Churches and organisations give up on raising local support and become hopelessly dependent on gifts from abroad. This is sad and to a large extent unacceptable.

On the other hand dependency can and does develop unhealthy attitudes in the giver often leading to power and control, feelings of superiority and tendencies to manipulate others and situations. There is an argument that all wealth held by believers belongs to the Lord and he determines to whom and when it is to be distributed. This argument is often used by those who depend on the charity of others to justify continuing dependency. Another one I heard recently suggested that it is only fair and just to raise money in the west for poor communities in the third world, because after all western institutions have in centuries past pillaged the wealth of third world countries and, through institutions like IMF and the World Bank, still maintain an economic stranglehold on many such countries.

**Joe M Kapolyo**

*Who are you dependent upon?*

*Is your church purely dependent upon 'live giving', or does it depend upon the capital, or the interest on the capital, from those who gave in generations gone by?*

*Have you had experience of others being dependent upon you?*

*How do both experiences feel?*

*How does the above story challenge you, your culture your values and your views?*

# Living in an oppressive regime -Enrique's story

'I believe fervently that when the state does the things that are proper to it, then it commands obedience, but when it exceeds its bounds, when it wants to claim what belongs to God for itself, then it is a religious duty to condemn this abuse of power'- Archbishop Desmond Tutu.

Enrique's life testifies to the consequences of taking Archbishop Tutu's words to heart. It testifies as well to the healing hand of God guiding through and out of the darkest circumstances. This part of Enrique's story begins in 1972 when he was a young man of 25 living in Montevideo, Uruguay, with his parents and an older brother. It was a difficult time in Uruguay.

Since 1967, under the leadership of President Jorge Pacheco Areco, the nation had been in crisis. Out of the political instability emerged Uruguay's National Liberation Movement, known as the Tupamaros. This well-organized urban guerrilla movement mounted a campaign of kidnapping, assassination, and bank robbery while espousing Marxist and nationalist ideals inspired by the Cuban experience. In 1972, Enrique worked in Bao, a unionized soap factory in Montevideo when one day he was rounded up with others simply for belonging to a union. The state deemed him (and an estimated 6,000 other people) to be threats. The next 10 years of Enrique's life consisted of deprivation and torture in a prison and town ironically named Libertad (Liberty).

For the first 10 months of his detention, he was hooded and tortured most days depending on the information he was willing to divulge to the prison guards. To Enrique the extreme violence and brutality of his captors was unanticipated. He suffered prolonged blackouts. He was beaten so brutally that he lost sight in his left eye. Yet, he resolved to hold himself together by concentrating on his responsibility not to "confess" about fellow union members. In his mind, he

reconstructed books, movies, stories, and conversations from the past, and then reinvented them endlessly.

He recalled an ineffable Presence that sustained him and prevented him from hating his captors. The palpable spirit of Jesus as his companion comforted and strengthened him. From May 1973 until the end of 1975, Enrique was in solitary confinement in a tiny cell with only a small window grate. During this time, his life was almost unbearable. A psychologist who specialized in torture applied psychological deprivation to break the prisoners' spirits and will and engineered a wall of hostility and inhumanity between guards and prisoners that was almost complete in its devastation. The guards called the prisoners pichi—scum of the earth. Men were bunked two to a small cell with one bucket of water a day between them for sanitation and to drink. Arbitrary availability of tap water was part of a strategy to psychologically destabilize prisoners.

Cellmates were changed regularly to prevent relationships developing. Family visits (two people per visit) were restricted to every 15 days. Enrique's parents and brother struggled to offer ongoing love and encouragement. Enrique recalled one daily moment of reprieve. At night when the guards drank their maté, a green tea, they would look the other way, while prisoners whispered to each other through their tiny window grates. In the middle of 1982, transitional president, Gregorio Álvarez Armellino offered detainees the option of asylum in Sweden due to pressure from those with economic interests in Uruguay. Many accepted, but others had lost so much by then, including hope, that they committed suicide.

Enrique could not countenance such a move. 'I envisioned myself as a tree with deep roots in Uruguay—family, friends, place. I felt my ideals were the shade or hope I could provide for those on the outside who were continuing the struggle for freedom and justice under great difficulty. I couldn't see myself living in Sweden when everything I needed for life was in Uruguay.' Each time Enrique refused the option of asylum he was reassigned to the prison ward. Meanwhile, pressure from the International Committee of the Red Cross, Amnesty International, and the Organization of American States, as well as the re-emergence of the traditional political parties (Blancos and Colorados), led to a lessening of human rights violations. Conversations with prisoners occurred without the presence of guards.

Some prisoners were released and others experienced improvements in prison conditions. In February 1983, Enrique, now 36, was released from 'Libertad' prison. He weighed a mere 46 kilograms. He was given new trousers and a shirt and directed to walk a kilometre away from the prison entrance to the place where his family awaited. Adjustment to life outside prison was gradual. For months, the noise of traffic overwhelmed him and caused him to walk next to buildings for fear of being run over. But he cherished his freedom daily. Enrique resumed his work for justice and freedom. While putting up human rights posters in Liberty Square in downtown Montevideo, Enrique met Ana who was also involved in the democratic movement. Ana, an English teacher working as a maid, had two young children and Enrique became a 'father of the heart' to them. Ana became the solace Enrique needed to heal and reintegrate back into community life.

He still often wonders what life would have been like without Ana and their sons. Ana too had been in prison. Together, she and Enrique worked to create a home and to embrace the ongoing work to democratize Uruguay. Enrique was, nevertheless, required to report weekly to the military barracks. Today he looks back on his life with equanimity. He acknowledges the deep pain and inhumanity he and his

family and close friends experienced. 'I believe we have all been strengthened by the hard years,' he says. Enrique credits God's presence for his ability to endure the suffering and for his capacity to heal.

The apostle Paul's letter to the Romans comes to mind. "I consider the sufferings of this present time are not worth comparing with the glory about to be revealed to us... But if we hope for what we do not see, we wait for it with patience." (Romans 8:18-25)Today Enrique, 63, and Ana, 60, continue their involvement in bringing about healing and greater democracy in their country. Their sons are grown—one lives in Spain, the other is nearby in Montevideo. Enrique maintains contact with other former detainees, some of whom have entered politics. Enrique and Ana have chosen to focus their energy on advancing women's rights, on working to protect children from violence and on supporting families living with alcoholism. Both find sustenance for their work in the Anglican parish of St. Stephen's in Montevideo where they support people and families living with HIV and AIDS.

Enrique and Ana take to heart the Marks of Mission of the Anglican Church. With Desmond Tutu, they believe 'We must be the Church of the poor and the marginalised ones, who have no power or voice. We must become their voice and strive to empower them, and help them help themselves so that they can enter into their heritage—the heritage of the freedom of the children of God.' (For further theological and Biblical reflection on similar cases of oppression, read Impunity: An Ethical Perspective, edited by Charles Harper. One of the case studies focuses on Uruguay.)

**from the Uruguay Diocesan magazine translated by Carolyn and Mark Gilmore**

What experiences do you have of your faith sustaining you through difficult situations?
The above gives a picture of the reality of living as a Christian in an oppressive society. But what does it mean for the 'expatriate' Christian, who has come from abroad to live and identify with the local Christian community? For biblical reflections on this, read the section Faith and society in chapter 6 of **On Call**.
www.stjohns-nottm.ac.uk/assets/PDFs-FORMS-for-download/EXT-Studies/Book-On-Call.pdf

# Polygamy and the Church in Africa

**Marriage** is often defined as a union between a man and a woman and the child born to them becomes the legitimate offspring of both parents. In Africa this definition may need to be expanded. Marriage in Africa is both a social and religious institution and the means by which life is understood. Marriage in Africa is best understood in the context of the four stages in the life cycle: birth, puberty, [marriage] and death.

**Family** is more difficult to define. This is because no single definition seems to encompass adequately the western nuclear family, the African extended family, the increasing single-parent families and now, other heterosexual families. Not long ago I heard a European gentleman introduce his family as himself, the wife, a son and a dog.

## The Importance of Marriage and Family in African Societies

John Mbiti observes that marriage is the 'meeting-point for the three layers of human life according to African religion'. These are the departed, the living and those to be born. The departed are the root on whom the living stands; whilst the living serve as the link between death and life. Those yet to be born are the buds in the loins of the living, and marriage makes it possible for them to germinate and sprout. For this reason, 'marriage without children cannot constitute a family and if one deliberately refuses to get married it means they are cutting off the vital link between

death and life, and destroying the buds which otherwise would sprout and grow on the human tree of life.' (Mbiti, Introduction, p.104.). Childbearing is therefore seen as a 'medicine' to death. While death continues to demolish life, marriage and child bearing sustain it. Thus, even if individuals die, human life as such does not die.

This understanding explains why marriage and child bearing is so important in African societies and the desire to have more children must not only be seen as merely having a social or economic significance but more importantly, fulfilling a religious obligation.

In this case marriage in Africa is not perceived as an individual affair or the concerns of two people who are in love, but rather a celebration of two families becoming affinal relatives (that is relatives through marriage) with the ultimate purpose of bearing children as kin to sustain their respective lineage or clans.

## Types of Marriages

There are generally three types of marriages and family:

- Monogamous marriage and family – This is a situation of one husband one wife and their children

- Polyandrous marriage and family - one woman with two or more husbands and their children (this is not common in Africa)

- Polygynous marriage and family - one man with two or more wives and their children. Polygamy is a generic term, which refers to multiple marriage partners or spouses.

Polygamy has often been used to mean a man with more than one wife and I have chosen to use it in this way to make easy reading.

# Marriage and Kinship Systems

Marriage in most traditional African societies is determined by kinship systems. The kinship system determines who a person can or cannot marry and the means by which members are recruited into the various clans or kin groups. Kinship refers to social relationships derived from marriage and adoption. Biological and adopted children are fully incorporated into the kin groups of the parents.

The kinship system is governed by specific rules and patterns of behaviour and is one of the most important systems that offers the principles which best explain how traditional societies in Africa are organized and their functions. It is also the basis of institutions such as chieftaincy, mode of inheritance, land administration and political relations. Although kinship ties have weakened over the years as a result of westernization, education and Christianity among others, it still forms an important part in the lives of many African societies.

# Polygamy and the Church: Some Missiological Challenges

Polygamy is one means by which people can quickly increase the members in their kin groups. A man assumes a high social status by virtue of how much contribution he has made. A man who has many children in a matrilineal family does not worry so much about the education of the children except the benefit he could get from the children supporting him on his farm or business.

Matrilineal societies do not require stable marriages to recruit members into their kin groups and fathers tend to be irresponsible towards their children as they are not considered part of their kin group. Some of the social implications of this system are an increasing number of street children who

may not have maternal uncles who are willing to take care of them because their mother had only sisters!

Although nearly all African governments recognize traditional customary marriages and polygamy, most mainline churches do not endorse polygamy (some parts of the African Independent Church do either accept or tolerate polygamists). It follows that polygamists who become Christians cannot have their marriages blessed in the church as in the case of monogamists. Because such marriages are not blessed in the church, they technically remain an 'engagement'. Such families are thought to be living in sin comparable to adultery and therefore cannot receive baptism or participate in the Holy Communion.

The place of polygamists in the Church has remained controversial and a challenge to missionaries and local Christian leaders for the best part of the last century and still remains to be resolved. Here I offer some thoughts.

We first need to note that polygamy in the past was a means to correct social imbalance and provide labour for the family especially in situations where families, particularly men, had died as a result of war and famine and the community faced the threat of extinction.

If a man had a wife who did not bear him a child, the solution was to have a second wife to address the anomaly. Similarly, if a man's wife only bore him girls, and he needed a male heir, it necessitated another wife or wives who were likely to bear him a male child. This situation is particularly strong with those from patrilineal descent who can pass on their inheritance to their children. Polygamous system also facilitates care for widows and was a sure means of sustaining the life of the community.

Various attempts have been made to address the problem of polygamy in the African church. In one instance, a church that took a position against polygamy also ruled that the wives of the man could participate in the Holy Communion but the husband could not. The reason was simple, 'the women have one husband, but the husband has three wives'! In another development, the Church advised that the polygamous husband should leave all the wives except the first one, who was considered as his true wife.

It is assumed that the Holy Communion is the highest level of fellowship with God and it is thought that polygamists have fallen from such grace and the only means of restoration is divorcing the extra wives. It is, however, hard to find a biblical basis for these assumptions. Polygamy has remained an integral part of human society right from the Fall. The Old Testament provides our best examples and the New Testament Church was not devoid of it.

Marriage and child bearing in Africa are inseparable from people's sense of personal identity. In some African countries, a woman or man is called by the name of their children: Kofi's Father; Kwame's Mother. Such a view of life calls for a new understanding of identity in the context of the community.

It is hard to find an injunction in the Bible which stops polygamists from coming to the Lord's Table. The significance of the Eucharist is to affirm the unity we have in Christ and with each other as we partake the bread and the wine. It has no reference to how one is married or how one ought to marry. Baptism on the other hand is an outward sign of an inward, spiritual grace which we have received through Christ by faith alone. Much as the Church should encourage monogamy as the ideal model best representing the union of Christ and the Church, such should be understood as a work of grace rather than judgment.

For this reason, people who got into polygamous marriages before they became Christians should not be judged on the basis of their past. And neither should divorce be a necessary qualification for reformed polygamists to ensure their participation in baptism and the Holy Communion. However, all who come to Christ could be called to account for their faith in matters such as they know best from the teachings of Christ and the Apostles regarding marriage and family.

**Emmanuel Kwesi Anim**
**Dean, Faculty of Theology and Mission,**
**Pentecost University College, Accra,**
**Ghana; Visiting Lecturer All Nations**
**Christian College, Easneye, Ware.**

*How does the understanding of children, marriage and family in the opening paragraphs challenge your worldview?*

*How would you put over an alternative view to someone who had a clear-cut view that polygamy and Christianity were incompatible and wasn't aware of the tensions and complexities?*

# Bribery, Corruption and Nepotism

During 2009 and early 2010, Britain needed to face up to a series of revelations in the media about its politicians. These included:

- Nepotism – Many were employing members of their families to work for them. The jobs had not been publicly advertised but just given to a spouse or other family member. In one particular case a son was being employed part time and it appeared unlikely that he had been available to do any work for the money that he received as a 'research assistant'.

- Corruption – As well as being paid for their work, members of Parliament claim expenses. Because they live in the constituency that they represent as well as having to spend a lot of time in London to attend Parliament, they often have a second home and there were revelations about how the system was being abused by the claims that were made, so that they could make money out of this, or at least increase their standard of living, at the taxpayers' expense.

- Bribery – The third type of revelation was not a new one, but crops up from time to time. Some Members of Parliament were exposed as having received financial payments for lobbying for particular interest groups. Businesses were paying them to influence decisions that would be of financial benefit to those businesses.

The revelations raised two questions for me. The first is how does it affect me personally? The answer to this is not very much. As a taxpayer, some of the money I pay has gone to increase the wealth or lifestyle of MPs, and some decisions will have been made for wrong reasons that have benefited the employees and shareholders of certain companies. Perhaps the bigger impact is that I am embarrassed by the international reputation of my country.

The second question is why does it happen? The first thing to say was that it wasn't a response to poverty; no one was doing this because they couldn't survive financially without being corrupt in some way. Part of the answer is human greed and nepotism is caused by an inbuilt desire to help family members. A big factor is that Parliament obviously didn't have in place appropriate accountability and checks to stop the corruption from happening, and that is currently being tackled.

Probably the biggest factor was that making a profit from expenses and employing family members had become part of the culture of Parliament; it had become the way that things were done, and what was expected. Those joining Parliament would learn about the new culture they would be working in and, while many would feel that it went against their moral code and remain totally honest, many went along with it and no-one really questioned it. That is how an organisational culture works. Efforts are being made to change this, but there is a huge outcry and it looks as if the changes will not be as radical as hoped. Changing an organisational culture can be a long process.

As I write this, we await an appeal by four people against their cases being tried within the courts. They argue that it should be Parliament itself, rather than the Courts of Law, that should consider their case; they believe that they are above the law; the Law of the Land does not apply to them!

If you are going into a different country there may well also be bribery, corruption and nepotism there. Let us return to my two questions. Unlike that found within the British Parliament, it is likely to impact upon you personally and directly and that will make it more obvious to you than the British examples that I have given.

Why does it happen? Let us consider the reasons given above. Unlike Britain, it will often be as a result of poverty. The British MPs, who 'played the system', considered it a legitimate part of their earnings. When your wage is not enough to keep you out of poverty, 'playing the system' is even more likely to happen. Then there is the issue of accountability and checks. In the West we have had a long time to develop systems to make it difficult to 'play the system'; receipts are given when money is paid and are needed before expenses are paid. Auditors will carefully check receipts to make sure that companies are not breaking the rules. In countries where systems have developed more rapidly, such checks will not always be in place, or as well developed.

The issue of nepotism is often greater. Family loyalties are generally far greater in non-Western cultures and there will often be huge pressure on a family member who does have power and position to give jobs to family members. The issue with the British Parliament was that it had become expected, it had become the norm, it had become part of the culture and people didn't question it. As with the British Parliament, it can take a long time to challenge and change such a culture.

Returning to the question of how it impacts upon ordinary people, then the answer is twofold; not only are you more likely to come across such practices, but they are often what stand in the way of a country developing economically. As you work out how to respond and react to situations it can be helpful to try to differentiate between what is a response to poverty, where the extra payment is perceived as part of the going rate and people are paying the extra to get something that they are entitled to get anyway, and where it is a response to greed, and people paying for something that they are not entitled to.

It is also very helpful to remember that, although you are not so directly affected, it happens in your own culture! Bearing that in mind, and with a suitable sense of humility and embarrassment about your own culture, you can ask local Christians how best to respond if you do personally encounter any examples.

*The above five articles give insights into five very different aspects of living in another culture.*

*What do you think the challenges might be that you face in the culture you intend going to live in?*

*How do you think that these articles challenge your own culture?*

# LIVING AS ME

## SECTION TWO

### CONTENTS

# The challenges of being single in another culture

From my experience in Tanzania, it was expected that a man or a woman would be married by the time they were in their early 30s. Therefore the Tanzanians thought it was a bit strange to find somebody who was still single and would often ask me 'when are you going to find a husband?' Also in African culture your identity is very much linked to your family and people would often introduce themselves by saying that they were married and how many children they have. This can make a single person feel quite awkward or even a bit out of the ordinary in such social situations.

Also in African contexts it is not usual for single men and women to spend time with one another alone, so it is an adjustment for a single person from the west to make when they enter an African culture that it is often not appropriate for them to spend time with a person from the opposite sex on their own. The issue of 'touch' can also be a problem for people, but maybe especially for single people. We all need some form of touch, even if we aren't the 'touchy-feely' type, but in other cultures we have to be careful about physical contact with other people, especially those of the opposite sex. Early on in my time in Tanzania, when I was working at a Bible College and there were a lot of male students, I was told that I was being too friendly to the men because I was placing my hand on their arm sometimes and this was inappropriate in a Tanzanian culture and so I had to adapt my behaviour to be more suitable to the culture I was in.

There are also the challenges of loneliness (if you live on your own) and coping on your own with practical things that may need to be done.

I think it is important to begin an article on this subject by looking back at Genesis and the creation story. As we can see from the beginning of Genesis, God created men and women for relationship: relationship with God himself and relationship with each other.

Sect2-2:56

## Relationship with God

Genesis 1:27 'So God created man in his own image, in the image of God he created him; male and female he created them.' God created us in his image so that we could relate to him and respond to him. Jesus said the first and greatest commandment is 'Love the Lord your God with all your heart and with all your soul and with all your mind.' We are created to love God and to know his love for us too.

Many people are looking in the wrong places for their security, self worth and significance. There are three basic needs which human beings require first and foremost in finding a relationship with God through Jesus Christ. Our other relationships need to be built on the foundation and the knowledge of who we are in Christ.

---

*Three questions to ask yourself:*

*1 Are you complete in Christ? Are you a whole person because of your relationship with Jesus? Do you stand complete in him or are you waiting for a man or woman to make you complete?*

*2 Are you secure in Christ? What makes you feel safe and protected? If our security is in houses or people or savings, it is misplaced. Only God can give us true security.*

*3 Are you content with Christ? Are you in love with Jesus? Are you pleased that he is with you in all circumstances? Contentment lies in appreciating who we are in Jesus and not comparing ourselves with other people.*

# Relationship with each other

Whether we are single or married we are all created for relationship. Jesus said the second commandment is 'Love your neighbour as yourself'. We are created to have relationships of love with those around us. It is important for all human beings that we build good, deep friendships. If we are single it is particularly important to build deep friendships. This can take more time and energy when we are in another culture and can take an especially long time when building friendships with those of the culture we are living in. However it is important to persevere and intentionally develop those friendships as they can be so enriching and enjoyable.

# God created us with our sexuality

As a single person it is important to realise that we have been created with sexual desires and longings for physical intimacy. These feelings are not wrong! What is important is what we do with these feelings and desires. If we do not learn to control our sexuality, our sexuality will control us. 1 Thessalonians 4:3-5 says 'It is God's will that you should be sanctified: that you should avoid sexual immorality; that each of you should learn to control his own body in a way that is holy and honourable, not in passionate lust like the heathen, who do not know God.'

# What are some of the ways we can control ourselves in this area?

**Face up to the issues** – sometimes as Christians we pretend we don't have any struggles in this area. We need to acknowledge our feelings and our desires in the first place in order to be able to do something about them.

**Flee temptation** – the Bible tells us in James 4:7 to resist the Devil and he will flee from us.

**Be careful what you fill your mind with** – Philippians 4:8 says 'Finally brothers, whatever is true, whatever is noble, whatever is right, whatever is pure, whatever is lovely, whatever is admirable – if anything is excellent or praiseworthy – think about such things.' We need to be careful about what we read, the films we watch, the internet sites we visit etc.

**Learn to recognize danger** – we all have our weak areas and we need to be aware of them. For example spending too much time alone with somebody, times when your body clock makes you more vulnerable, not having anyone to talk or pray with, being away from home, feeling down, or sad or lonely.

**Discipline your habits** – have some good habits and focus for your life. What are you committed to doing regularly? Who are the people you spend time with? When do you have opportunity to pray and read God's Word during the week? Who can you study the Bible and worship with? Having a pattern to our lives with some regular commitments can have a positive effect on other areas of our lives.

**Develop honest, supportive relationships** – we all need people who we can be accountable to and talk about our struggles in confidence with and who can pray with us and for us.

**Do something physically active** eg some kind of sport. We all need to be involved in physical activity for our physical health but it also helps us let out sexual frustrations as well.

**Pray!** - Acknowledge our feelings and desires before God and ask him to give us the self control that we need and the ability to overcome the temptations.

# Benefits of being single in another culture

There are advantages to being single in another culture, working as a cross-cultural missionary. Sometimes single women are treated differently and included in situations where married women wouldn't be invited or involved. Single people can use their time in a different way and often have more opportunities for immersing themselves in the culture, learning the language and getting to know people. Single people also have more time to give to their work and ministry and can also spend evenings in different ways from married people. The other benefits are that single people can be spontaneous and do what they want when they want because they don't have a spouse or family to think about.

It is important to appreciate and remind ourselves of the benefits of whatever situation we are in, whether single or married and to keep our relationship with God through Jesus at the centre of all that we do.

**Jo Sayer, Means of Mission Team Leader, Crosslinks**

---

*It can be very easy for single people to assume that it is much easier for married couples as they always have each other. Most married couples in the West will be used to having very clear boundaries to which parts of their lives have a degree of separation and which are shared. Usually they will be working for different organisations, or one is out at work and the other at home. Usually they will each have their own friends as well as joint friends. If, as a couple, you find yourself working together in a new culture, then it can feel strange; the marriage relationship can spill over into the work and the work relationships can spill over into the marriage. Going to a new country means not having your personal friends in the same way, but often means only establishing joint friends.*

*Whether you are single or married, note down some of the ways in which married people can be sensitive to the needs of single people and the ways in which single people can be sensitive to the needs of married people.*

# Managing change in mission families

We want our mission families to not just survive but to thrive in their extremely mobile environments. In this article we're looking at how we can assist and empower families to manage that change.

What do we want to do?

- Look at the big picture — the process of going overseas, the dynamics of change, reasonable expectations

- The implications for kids – being a Third Culture Kid (TCK) is a lifetime experience with its own challenges and benefits

- The implications for parents – the impact of the choices they make

- The possibilities – knowledge empowers real choice

- Preparation – of kids, parents, family, sending church and agency

- Long-term planning – assignments may be shorter but the effects of decisions made can be far-reaching

- Maximising the benefits

  'Living overseas was an invaluable experience which I am lucky to have enjoyed'.

## PREPARATION FOR CHANGE:

### 1   Equipping parents

- Understanding what it means to be a TCK

- Relationship skills
  Home for the Mission Kid (MK) is in relationship; the place where they find their security and well being is with their parents so it is of paramount importance that couples prioritise their own relationship.

- Parenting skills
  Many couples have not had good models of parenting. Candidates need to think what skills they may need to develop in this area and what tools and resources are open to them. Increasingly cross-cultural marriages are the norm in missions which can produce extra tension.

- Child Development:
  If parents know the 'normal' stages of child development, when a child is undergoing changes, they can distinguish between normal stress and cultural stress.

### 2   Preparing the child

- Communication — giving information and answering questions

- Expressing emotions — allowing children to say how they feel.

- Having a voice — the older the child gets the more important it is to have a say in decision-making. Careful consideration should be given to moving adolescents for the first time cross-culturally. Moving times and duration of assignments should relate to the needs of the whole family.

### 3   Preparing the extended family

- Educate them on TCKs

- Develop a role for them

- Involve them in the process – grandparents' pastor/day

## CONTINUITY IN CHANGE

Today people come 'home' more often. Everyone has to decide how closely they are going to identify with the local culture — the closer you identify, the harder it is to re-enter. The more rigid the culture, the harder it is.

Areas to consider include:

- Educational considerations – culture and ethos of school, continuity with system back home, time commitment, social interaction of child
- Life-style considerations – acceptability to the nationals, fairness to the children, language acquisition, private or community living
- Faith issues – opportunity to worship, expressions of family life, job and ministry

The next step is to build bridges back into their own culture. The question is much harder for cross-cultural marriages where the couple can't decide where home is.

Bridges ease transition and make effective choices. Consider:

- Communication
- Visits
- Celebrating national festivals
- Link peer family
- Resources on current trends, issues, music etc
- Educational links
- DVDs, tapes etc
- Sacred objects – continuity of environment

Home assignments

- Have clear objectives – personally, professionally, as a family, for the children
- Remember this is not home — think of it positively as an opportunity to connect.
- Have a base — don't live out of a suitcase
- Do the 'national trail' bit
- Forge educational links
- Take advantage of spiritual opportunities
- Minimise travelling
- Participate in secular activities — films, clubs, sports, and drama
- Teach skills not needed in host culture
- Health check-ups/educational testing.

# Integrating for change

- Preparation for re-entry - minimise the stress, have a base prepared, research educational options, talk realistically about what awaits, have peer mentors ready to help.
- Factors affecting re-entry – the age of the child, the reason for leaving, the attitude of the parents, the degree of difference between the two cultures.
- Processing the TCK experience by:

  Permission to feel pain

  Permission to express feelings

  Pathways to saying goodbye

  People to share experiences

And remember, Jesus was a TCK:

*'Every culture in the world is foreign to someone. At first it's scary, then irritating, then maddening. To survive (replace with thrive!) you have to grab it, fall in love with it and make it yours. God understands. He did it too.'*

(Joseph Kim)

**Marion Knell**
**Cross-Cultural Family Consultant with**
**Global Connections**

http://www.globalconnections.co.uk/Shop/resources/familiesonthemove

# Growing up cross-culturally

Arriving at Heathrow airport at 6 o'clock in the morning and being swooped up in a hug by a grandmother I hardly know....Walking in Maasailand scrub and seeing an antelope grazing five metres away from me....Sitting in an aeroplane, waving goodbye to friends I might never see again....rushing home for break time because today we have fried flying ants as a treat...Seeing the sunrise as we climb to the peak of Mount Meru (4500m)....being ill with amoebic dysentery again...seeing brightly coloured fish and corals while snorkeling in Mombasa...flying my Dad's plane ...translating for my parents from German into English...knowing God is in control no matter what happens.

I am a Third Culture Kid (TCK), someone who has grown up in another culture from that of my parents because of my parents' job. Growing up cross-culturally has its' advantages and challenges just as growing up anywhere in the world has. If you ask any person who has grown up abroad, they would always say: 'I would rather grow up cross-culturally than in any other way.'

So what are some of the characteristics of someone who has grown up abroad? Some of the most obvious characteristics are having a multi-lingual ability and good communication skills cross-culturally. With young children there is the possibility of mixing languages, but clear boundaries of language use will help this e.g. mother tongue at home, local language at school.

Educational options are wide and varied, but usually of a high standard. These days everything from boarding school, day schooling, home schooling, internet schooling and even local schooling are available.

Living cross-culturally brings a wide world view, the realization that things can be done in more than one way and with that comes the ability to adapt. TCKs are also good at making relationships.

Some of the challenges of growing up cross-culturally include transience — you or others around you are always moving and as a child you are never quite sure if you will see each other again. As TCKs we don't necessarily know our 'Home' cultures too well and therefore knowing where 'home' is can be more difficult.

## Why talk about Third Culture Kids?

1   TCKs exist: After the first commandment to love the Lord your God with all your heart, with all your soul and with all your mind, there is the commandment to love your neighbour as yourself. The TCK is a neighbour that needs to be loved. Also, Jesus clearly acknowledged the value and position of children; 'Jesus said, "Let the little children come to me, and do not hinder them, for the kingdom of heaven belongs to such as these." ' Matthew 19:14

2   Missionaries: These are the people who are on the frontline of mission as well as being in a foreign country. If their children are unhappy it will be difficult for the parents to complete their assignment. In a study in 1997 of missionary workers, called *Too Valuable to Lose* (Ed. Taylor, W. D.), it was found that amongst the top three reasons for missionary workers returning to their 'passport culture' were children and their educational needs. If we don't support missionaries and their families there will be a high rate of attrition.

3   TCKs have amazing potential: with their cross cultural upbringing they have great advantages in this ever-shrinking world. They are often multilingual; have had multicultural experience, have a broad worldview and often have good leadership skills. All these skills are beneficial to the church, as well as the work place.

# What can you do...?
## ... as an individual?

If you are living with a TCK in the host culture you can help them in many practical ways.

- Being a listening ear outside the TCK's family situation. I remember one of my school teachers inviting me for tea and cake one afternoon and asking me how I felt about a big move that our family was going to make. She spent the afternoon just listening. It is something I have never forgotten.

- Giving them the opportunity to have work experience. Often in host cultures expatriate children are not allowed to work. As I was growing up I had the opportunity to take part in the overhaul of a mission plane. This taught me about working a full day, over several days.

- Spiritual input: TCKs need not only spiritual input from their parents, but also from the people around them. Can you run a youth group or a Bible study? One of the biggest impacts in my spiritual life was a bible study that a missionary set up for the older teens in our town. He showed us how to really study the Bible and understand it for ourselves. And if we didn't understand it...where to find some answers.

- You are a role-model for the TCK whether you like it or not, whether you are single, married or a parent and whatever age you are - especially if you are the same nationality. What do I mean by this? For example, for a while I grew up in an isolated village. There were mainly German missionaries there and my parents and the local people, of course. There were no expat teenagers in the village as there was only primary schooling available. So, all that I knew about the 'Western' lifestyle was from those missionaries. When we moved, to go to secondary school, I realized that I didn't know anything about being a teenager as I hadn't really lived with any. And therefore didn't know how to behave as one!

Also, always be careful with what you say in the presence of children. For example, what you may consider to be harmless joking about the local culture can be remembered and taken seriously by a child. They don't fully understand the context in which you are making your comments and may build up a negative impression of the people around them.

## ...as an organization?

- Send the missionary family as a whole to pre-field orientation seminars/training. Children need preparation as much as their parents, whatever age they are.

- Have one assigned person to keep in regular contact with the TCK and not just the parents while in the host country.

- On return to the 'passport culture' it is good for children to have a debrief, not just the parents.

- Any preparation for re-entry to the 'passport culture' is also helpful.

## Summary

These are just some ideas which can be expanded upon. Be creative. Think outside the box. It is often the little things rather than the big things that make a difference in the end.

There is an African proverb which encapsulates what I am trying to say: *'When it is not your mother who is in danger of being eaten by the wild animal, the matter can wait until tomorrow.'* Until now we have waited until tomorrow for the care of TCKs due to all sorts of factors, whether lack of finances, lack of personnel or lack of experience. TCKs have existed as long as there have been people working overseas. What are you going to do for them?

**Jo Clifford
Director of Xenos
(serving Third Culture kids)**

**Further resources**

You may find it helpful, especially if you are a parent or will be working with children, to visit some of these websites for more information:

**www.tcklife.com** – A resource centre for anything related to TCKs; for TCKs, for their families and for those working with them.

**www.membercareradio.com** – Daily radio programmes and other resources addressing issues of life overseas.

**www.mkplanet.com** – A chat site for missionary children of all ages.

**www.missionarycare.com** – A good resource of all kinds of mission issues. It also has e-Books which can be downloaded free.

**Recommended reading**

Pollock, D. & Van Reken, R. E., *Third Culture Kids: The Experience of Growing Up Among Worlds* (2nd Ed., Nicholas Brealey Publishing, 2001) - Also available in German.

Blomberg, J. & Brooks, D. F., *Fitted Pieces: A Guide for Parents Educating Children Overseas* (SHARE Education Services, 2001)

Freymann, S., & Elffers, J., *How are you Peeling?: Foods with Moods* (Levine Books, 1999)

Dyer, J., *Harold and Stanley say Goodbye* (Torrens Park, SA (Australia), 1998) [A children's story about how Harold and Stanley and their family are going to another country to be missionaries. The preparations and the goodbyes are different for Harold and for Stanley.]

# Coping with crises

Crises can happen anywhere. How will you cope if, while you are serving overseas, a close relative or friend becomes critically ill or dies? Or if you have a serious illness or accident? Depending on the country you go to, you may also be at increased risk of:

- Robbery
- Hostage taking
- Violent attacks
- Natural disasters
- Sexual abuse or rape
- Riots
- Evacuation
- Effects of war
- Persecution
- False accusations / imprisonment
- Seeing extreme poverty, suffering and perhaps death

Simple everyday stresses (such as problems with electricity or water; the frustration of waiting for things; coping with a harsh climate; difficulties with language, communication or relationships; challenging living conditions, or frequent changes in personnel) can all take a toll and leave you feeling unable to cope. Being far from family and friends, over-worked and unable to engage in your usual ways of relaxing and enjoying yourself, can cause you to feel at 'crisis point'. They can also lead to marital breakdowns and psychological disorders (including among children).

## Preparing for difficulties

Preparing for potential difficulties does not cause them to happen. Neither does it signify a lack of faith. Such preparation is both wise, and in keeping with Biblical principles. For example, Proverbs 22:3 states 'a prudent man sees danger and takes refuge, but the simple keep going and suffer for it'. On the other hand, suffering is not an indication that you are outside God's will. There are many Biblical examples of taking precautions to avoid crises, and also many examples of people enduring suffering.

Here are a few suggestions about how to prepare for, and cope with, crises. You will need to select and adapt them for your situation.

1. Build yourself up spiritually. People who are spiritually strong are more able to cope with the difficulties of life. Learn Bible verses and truths which will sustain you in difficult times. Learn to worship God even in difficult situations. Work out a theology of suffering. Read books which will help you and write about them in a journal you can return to. Read how other Christians have grown stronger through difficult times.

2. Take care of your physical and psychological health (ensuring you sleep and eat well and have some exercise). Have a good 'work-life' balance. Build time in your schedule for relaxing, and for 'interruptions'. Work at 80% capacity, not 100%. This will give you time, strength and energy to deal with unexpected demands of life. It will also reduce your risk of accidents and illness.

3. Build up a support network of people you can contact who will listen, offer practical and emotional support, and pray. Look for ways to develop a cohesive, supportive team.

4. Think about the sorts of crises you might encounter. Learn about ways to avoid them if possible, and to handle them if they occur. Be aware of travel, health and security risks. These will depend on where you are, so find out from people who know the context. For example, do you need training in first aid, or changing a car wheel, or reducing risk of HIV infection? Coping with being kidnapped? Avoiding landmines? An excellent book to help you prepare is *The Humanitarian Companion* by John Ehrenreich (2005. Rugby, ITDG).

5. Become familiar with the crisis contingency plans and policies of your organisation. If they don't have any, encourage them to develop them. These should include evacuation plans.

6. Ensure that your insurance will adequately cover the area visited and any possible disasters or evacuation.

7. Consider attending a simulation course (role-playing emergencies). You are likely to be calmer and to cope better if you have practiced handling a crisis before you face it in reality .

8. Make practical preparations for any high risks for your location. For instance, register with a local doctor or clinic; be aware of 'safe places' you can relocate to; maintain an up-to-date list of emergency contact numbers; know how to obtain extra money if you suddenly need it.

9. Keep your passport, visa and health and travel insurance up-to-date. Leave copies of these (and any travel tickets) with someone else.

10. Write your will and keep it up-to-date. This should include your wishes concerning your funeral and guardians for any children. Discuss these with an 'emergency contact person', so that they know your wishes.

11. Ensure that any children also receive appropriate preparation. Don't alarm them with excessive discussion of risks, but talk in factual terms about how they can stay safe (just as you would practice a fire-drill, or teach them about road safety or not going off with strangers).

12. Keep contact details for the people to contact if an incident does occur (including a named person within your organisation).

## After an incident

1. Assess what support and help you need.

2. Be willing to ask for and accept help, and to take a break from work.

3. Remind yourself that it is normal to experience some symptoms of stress (such as tiredness; sleeping problems/ nightmares; intrusive thoughts about the incident or attempts to avoid reminders of it; feeling irritable, angry, anxious or 'jumpy'). These symptoms should fade away over time.

4. Do things which help you relax and feel better, as well as addressing any solvable problems.

5. Don't criticise yourself if you have signs of stress or depression, or if you become ill or need to leave the mission field early. Many people have similar experiences. Consider yourself to be 'honourably wounded'.

6. Find people to talk to about your experiences. If you think it would be helpful, request a critical incident debriefing. Your church or organisation may be able to help you arrange this.

7. Assess how you are about a month after the incident. If you feel unable to function normally, or you are worried that your trauma symptoms appear to be getting worse, seek professional help.

## Remember the positives

Most mission partners cope well with crises. Many say in retrospect that the crisis has had positive consequences. These may include spiritual growth; feeling closer to friends and family; a desire to live each day to the full, and gratitude for being alive

God is glorified when we endure suffering and continue to trust Him. So – prepare with wisdom, and trust that God will be with you and bring you through the storms of life.

**Debbie Hawker - Consultant Clinical Psychologist at InterHealth**

**Useful resources include:**

(i) Roberts, D.L. (1999). *Staying Alive: Safety and security guidelines for humanitarian volunteers in conflict areas*. Geneva: ICRC. (See www.icrc.org).

(ii) *Global Connections* (2006). Guidelines for crisis management and prevention including working in high risk areas. Download from www.globalconnections. co.uk/standards.

(iii) The Peace Corps crisis management handbook - http://www.globaled.us/peacecorps/crisiscontent. html#1.1.See also their rape response handbook and their risk management workbook.

See Foyle, M. (2001). *Honourably Wounded: Stress among Christian Workers*. Second Edition. London: Monarch Books.

See Hawker, D. (2009). *Debriefing aid workers and missionaries: A comprehensive manual*. London: People In Aid.

# COMMUNICATION

## SECTION TWO

**CONTENTS**

# Learn that language!

When Jesus became a man, he did not retreat behind a heavenly palisade every evening so as to appear refreshed next morning. He became one of the people. Today, it is important for a Christian worker overseas, like Christ, to become one of the people; and one of the crucial ways is through learning their language. Without it you will not be able to communicate your own personal needs, let alone communicate the good news that Jesus became a man to save people. Without learning the language of the people you will not be able to serve them with the love and sacrifice of Jesus Christ.

Even if you expect to be serving abroad for only a limited period, it is not a waste of time to try to learn the local language. There are some very good reasons why you should give time to language learning, however short you expect your stay abroad to be. Although many people can speak some English, it remains true that to be really effective in talking about spiritual things we must speak the heart language of our hearers. The English they know may be sufficient for business purposes, but that is not the language they use for intimate matters which affect beliefs and attitudes. We want them to be free to think about the implications of our message, not struggling to understand it.

Learning another person's language says some very important things about your attitude to that person and their culture. It shows appreciation of his value, of her value, as a person. It demonstrates that you are moving toward others, not demanding that they move toward you. It emphasises that the gospel is not just a 'Western' religion, but can be given expression in any language. In a short stay, your attitudes will be of much greater significance than what you say or even what you do. So the fact that you tried to speak the language will count for a great deal. Through your relationships with people outside the strict confines of your job, you will also be able to understand their cultural values much better as you seek to witness.

There are five possible ways to learn:

## 1. Learning by the book

Buy or borrow a book 'Teach Yourself Whatever'. Set aside weeks or months; hang a 'Don't Disturb' notice on your door; wrap a towel round your head (wet or dry according to climate) and work through the book doing all the exercises.

There are certain advantages to this solution, and many people have used it. Books are relatively cheap and you may be able to start tomorrow. You can study independently of other people, and your incompetence in the language will not embarrass anybody – especially you. But there are also disadvantages. You may not be able to find any book on the language you need, perhaps because no one has ever written one. If you do find one it may not be for the dialect that you actually need; Arabic as spoken in Egypt, for example, is quite different from Arabic spoken in Syria or in the north of Sudan, and each of these is different from Arabic spoken in the south of Sudan.

Books, by their very nature, will tend to emphasise the written form of the language rather than the spoken form, and you will not be able to get the right pronunciation from a book alone. Studying independently will encourage you to dissociate language from culture and may prevent you ever speaking the language properly.

## 2. Learning on a course

Enrol for a course designed to teach you the target language, attend it regularly and practise between classes. The course may be in your home country, or in the country where you expect to serve, or in any country where the language is spoken as the main language (e.g. learn French in France).

You will have the discipline of the class schedule to keep you at it, with other students to encourage you. You may have opportunity for oral practice. However, you may not be able to keep up the pace of the rest of the class, or you may become bored because they are too slow. You may be too unsure of yourself or your language ability to participate in the oral class activities. You may be dependent upon the language as known by the teacher, who may be a foreigner to the language, or speak a dialect other than the one you want to learn. Unless it is recommended to you by somebody who knows the course and knows you and your needs, you may have little idea of the scope and quality of the course before you start.

## 3. Learning by immersion

Go out to where you will be working; live with a family who speak only the language you want to learn. Then find somebody outside of that family who will help you with the language. Work with this person one or two hours each day and practise with the family and with anybody else you can find for the rest of the time.

With this approach you will learn the dialect and variety of the language that you actually need; you will focus on oral rather than written language, and you will be using the language to communicate from the very beginning. You will, in fact, learn more than the language – you will learn how people live and think. You are likely to make friends who will remain friends for the rest of your life. You may have great opportunities to share your knowledge of Jesus with the family and great opportunity to learn dependence upon the Lord.

That may sound great, but you will feel lost for words in many situations, although if you do not allow yourself to withdraw you will eventually find the right words. You could also be overwhelmed by the amount of language you are being exposed to. And it may be difficult to find a family willing to take you into their home and put up with your 'stupidity' – even the young children will speak better than you at first.

## 4. Learning by immersion with a life jacket

Attend a course, such as those given by the Summer Institute of Linguistics, to learn how to learn a language; then once you have finished the course, continue with solution 3 above. For many people, this is probably the best method (with a book to help you as well).

At such a course you will learn something of how languages are structured and what to expect in a foreign language – you will then be less likely to sink under the sheer volume of the language as you first encounter it. You will be taught techniques for learning the different aspects of any language. You will learn how to make a whole range of exotic sounds which will prepare you for practically any language. If you do not understand the system used by the people for writing their own language, you will have learned how to write down new words using phonetic symbols; this is especially helpful when the language is not written down at all. You will be working with others in similar situations to yourself, many of whom were not good at languages at school but who will go on to master complex languages all over the world.

On such a course, however, you will probably not learn one word of the language that you want to learn! Rather, you will learn how to learn. To attend the course will take six weeks of your valuable time before going overseas – six weeks which will prepare you for a lifetime of language learning. And it will cost some money. But it is an investment which will pay rich dividends.

# 5. Learning by analysis

For those whose major contribution overseas is going to be in the area of language there is yet one more option to consider: attend courses over a nine-month period at the Summer Institute of Linguistics to learn how to analyse a previously unwritten language. Then devote the next few years to living among the people, learning their language really well and writing it down. You would then be equipped to go to literacy work, Bible translation or other language-related service.

The advantages are the same as for solution 4, but the preparation is more thorough and you will gain skills beyond those learned in the six-week course. Your opportunity to contribute something worthwhile to the people will be greatly increased; you could be giving them the Word of God in their own language. But it takes time. In fact it takes your life – not necessarily your whole life-time, but a total involvement for the years that it takes. It actually takes a specific call of God.

# Problems you will encounter

Language learning is not easily achieved; most of us must expect to face some difficulties. Chief among them may well be slow progress; you feel you will never be able to talk freely! That is just a fact you will have to learn to live with; after all, you did not make much progress with English during your first two years of trying! To keep on trying is the important thing, and to add a little more each day. Therefore you will need to set your priorities carefully and impose a little self-discipline, lest the natural desire to spend time on things which seem to give quick results distracts you.

As all the books and courses will tell you, learning a second language is primarily a question of acquiring a new set of habits and reactions – something like learning to drive a car! Learning things by heart still has a place, but careful listening and a willingness to mimic and be laughed at are as important as memory drills, and much more fun. More than anything else, your progress will be the out-working of your attitudes to the new language and the people who speak it – which is why you need to start to learn even if you are only staying there a month or two.

You must expect to find some unfamiliar sounds which you will master before long, just as every child does — provided that you are willing to keep on being corrected (and can find friends willing to help you). Differences in the sounds will probably include some strange consonants or vowels and perhaps the more subtle differences of tone (syllables being pronounced at different pitch levels to give a different meaning) and of intonation (the tune of the sentence as a whole).

Then there will be differences of grammatical pattern – the way the parts of sentences are put together. You can expect to find a different order of words, such as 'kill man tiger lake by will plural' (the man will kill tigers by the lake). There may be affixes or inflections added to all the words in a phrase (he bought two-a little-a black-a kittens-a) or unexpected ways of saying things (I go come).

You will want to learn a few new words of vocabulary each day, especially at first. Concentrate on words that you will be able to use in your life situation, for using words helps you remember them. You will also want to learn by heart useful phrases such as greetings, questions, imperatives, conversation openers and sustainers (these give the impression you have understood!). So do set yourself up with lists of things to learn and do use the words as you learn them. A few at a time, and put to use straight away, is the way to beat memory fatigue.

Above all, do remember that languages are learned as people try to speak them! So don't give up, all embarrassed, when you make a mistake. In the short term, it is not the progress you make that counts so much as whether or not you make the attempt. The Lord is able to bless your efforts far beyond what they merit in this as in everything else.

**David Bendor-Samuel and John Hollman from *Entering Another's World***

# Miscommunication

The following examples of miscommunication come from very different countries and cultures:

- 'Is it far to the next village?' It is a hot day and you look very tired and weary to the person that you have stopped to ask for directions and distance as you walk to the next village and the chance of rest and refreshment. He knows that the last thing you want to hear is that it is far. Giving you bad news will upset you; it will break the relationship with you, whereas replying "No, it is not far" is the answer that you want to hear; this is the helpful answer, this answer will keep the relationship. Finding out that the village was, indeed, far away I feel that his answer was not 'true'. But my western perspective only sees truth as being 'factual truth'; it has no understanding about being true to a relationship. Vincent Donovan explores this further on pp 28- 29 of Christianity Rediscovered SCM Press 1978

- I am visiting the home of my national friend. More for something to say, than from any real aesthetic understanding, I admire an ornament. 'Do take it.' 'No, I couldn't,' I reply. 'You must. I insist.' I later realise that in admiring the object and commenting upon it, what I have been heard to say is 'please give me that item.' I also learn that when someone is admiring something of mine then they are asking me to give it to them.

- Asking a colleague where he or she lives can be heard as asking if you can visit them – why else would you be interested in where he or she lives?

- At work I am asked to take on a particular responsibility. I am very busy with other work, and also feel I do not have the skills or experience for the task, so I explain this and turn the request down. A few days later the request comes again; again I say no, and so it goes on. Eventually I realise that no one would say a direct 'yes'; that would be very immodest. My 'no' is being heard

as 'I am a modest person, so am saying "no" the first time you ask, but ask me again and the answer will be "yes".' So how do you actually say 'no'? It seems that saying 'maybe' really means 'no'!

- A colleague drops in to see me just before I am going to eat. I ask if he wants to share my meal and he replies no. I expect him to either leave, or be prepared to stay there talking while I eat. I later realise that I should have been persistent in asking him to stay and eat. It would have been rude for him to have said yes the first time, but was ruder for me to take his answer at its face value, rather than continuing to repeat my invitation.

- A friend mentions that I must come round for a meal sometime, but doesn't actually fix a time. I wait patiently, but the definite invitation never comes. Meanwhile, he is offended that I never accepted the invitation and just turned up sometime to eat with him.

- I explain to a national Christian friend that I drink alcohol in my home country. In a culture where there is no 'social drinking' and where those who do drink alcohol will spend much of their pay, on payday, getting blindingly drunk, what am I heard to say? The likely message will not be that I can enjoy an occasional drink, but that I regularly get blindingly drunk.

- As mentioned in the section on Culture, sometimes there is no equivalent word; two examples given were the absence of a word to describe a friend of the opposite gender in Urdu and the lack of the verb 'to have' in Kiswahili. This can mean that the concept that you are trying to explain doesn't exist, and there is likely to be miscommunication.

- I am used to saying 'please' when I ask for something, and 'thank you' when I am given something and naturally find it rude when these words are not used. I needed to learn that the absence of these words doesn't imply rudeness. In fact, if I say please and thank you, but without a smile, and with a voice that gives no hint of gratitude, my words are countered by my expressions. In many cultures the tone of voice and the facial expression say far more than the words do.

*Bearing in mind the above stories, try to find out from someone from the culture you are going to what miscommunication you may come across.*

As the last example shows, non-verbal communication is also important. One study at UCLA University of California, (Los Angeles) indicated that up to 93 percent of communication effectiveness is determined by non-verbal cues. Another study indicated that the impact of a performance was determined seven percent by the words used, 38 percent by voice quality, and 55 percent by the non-verbal communication. You are used to reading non-verbal communication within your own culture but will need to be able to learn to read the signs in a different culture. The issue of 'voice quality' is another factor. We are attuned to hear particular implications in how something is said and need to be able to relearn this.

The other barriers that we can create to effective communication generally lie in our attitudes. We need to be open to others in order to relate and communicate. We go into another culture aware that we can easily make mistakes, but need to be open and vulnerable and show in our attitudes that we know that we don't have all of the answers and that we are prepared to be vulnerable and show that we wish to learn. When we have done that we might find that others are open to learn from us, allowing communication that is of benefit to all that are involved.

# The who and how of communication

When I worked in rural Kenya, in the late nineteen-seventies, it was before the era of computers and mobile phones and the nearest pay phone was ten miles away. To communicate with anyone in my home country I wrote airmail letters and could expect a reply 10 or 14 days later at the earliest. I never used a telephone during my whole time there. I did once think of ringing my parents on my birthday, but decided that a phone call might actually worry them and that trying to have such a conversation after such a long time of writing might prove rather emotional and upsetting. Nowadays, when I travel I communicate with my family most days by conversation or text on mobile phone or email or SKYPE on my laptop.

The wonderful thing about 'the old days' was that the available means of communication meant that I turned to my national colleagues to discuss things. If I wrote to someone in England about a problem I had, then the problem was likely to either be resolved, or much changed, by the time I got a reply. This meant that I found myself looking naturally to my national colleagues as the people that I needed to discuss things with, learn from and find the answers that I needed to the issues that I faced. I found that my point of reference needed to be the views of the local people who understood the local culture and who could explain things to me. Modern communication methods can mean that it is so easy to get back in touch with family, friends, people from your home church and your mission agency that your home culture remains your point of reference.

Not only is communicating with local people and seeking their advice a far better way to be discovering the right answers, but it is also a sign of mutuality. It is through showing that you are a vulnerable person, who depends upon local people to know how to do things, that you actually put yourself in a position where you can make deep and lasting friendships and discover real communication.

# Communicating back home

What are you going to communicate to people when you return from your experience? My work involved me in running a number of re-entry conferences for those recently returned from a period overseas. These often began with individuals sharing their story; it was interesting to note that if one person began by giving a negative spin on their experiences then others could easily follow and try to share their negative experiences. How can we share stories that are life-giving rather than feeding cultural stereotypes?

I used to work in Waterloo, just south of the Thames in London. Within a mile we had Parliament and other centres of government; we had the cultural richness of the Royal Festival Hall, the National Theatre and the National Gallery as well as Westminster Abbey with its history and beautiful choral worship. We had many Christian leaders from other countries visiting our office. I tried to imagine how I would feel if one of them went home and gave talks and showed pictures that ignored all of these but showed:

- How crowded and inefficient the trains were during rush hour

- The vandalism on the local housing estates

- The squalor and despair of 'cardboard city' the home of scores of homeless, in the centre of a roundabout that existed for years, before being cleared to build a cinema

- The beggars on our streets

- The waste that we throw away

- Our empty churches with drab worship

- The sexual immorality suggested by the films advertised on so many of our billboards

- The care homes that we send our elderly to, because we don't want to look after them ourselves

- The huge choice of pet foods, and the other ways in which we indulge animals.

You could probably add to this list and find other things that would be embarrassing about your home country if people photographed them and spoke about them at the expense of the good and life-giving things.

When I worked in Kenya I sometimes saw Masai warriors. They are tall and looked very proud and handsome. It was said that the Masai believed that you stole their soul if you took a photograph of them; silly idea isn't it? Some Masai were prepared to be photographed if you paid them enough. The money would be spent on strong drink and they would get drunk. When drunk they no longer looked proud and handsome. I suppose they were right after all; they had sold their souls! Be careful and sensitive in choosing what to take pictures of.

I have been to a lot of talks about time overseas where people have chosen their pictures and spoken about these. The message is often confusing. Decide what you want to say — something that is life-giving and challenges stereotypes, and then see if you have any pictures that add value to what you want to say.

# Communicating the Gospel

The way in which the gospel can be effectively communicated might differ in different cultures and can impact upon the vocabulary that we use.

- Hindu's believe in a series of lives; the aim is to progress through these so that there is no need to be reborn. It is not very helpful to speak about 'being born again' to someone who doesn't want to be reborn!

- Local understanding of family can impact upon references to family relationships in our understanding of God: if a culture is matriarchal, then it is not that helpful to emphasise the Fatherhood of God; if society is polygamous then the understanding of the Church as the Bride of Christ could be diluted.

- Muslims have come across Jesus through the Qur'an, but will not understand him in the same way as Christians do. Islam and Christianity might share certain words, but have different understandings of those words. Christianity and Judaism have a number of prophets, and often those prophets suffer. Some of these prophets are also considered as prophets in Islam, but others are not. Islam also recognises certain Old Testament characters as prophets that are not considered as prophets in Christianity. In Islam prophets do not suffer. This means that any discussion with a Muslim about the prophets could easily start on common ground before realising that there are some big differences.

Usually we communicate the gospel through our personal relationships, but modern technology has opened up new forms of communication.

## 'Come to Me and I will give you rest'

Throughout the centuries, mass media has proved hugely effective in spreading the Gospel: from early reformers, like Tyndale using tracts, to radio broadcasts reaching behind the former Iron Curtain in the latter half of the twentieth century. The use of media for the spread of the Gospel is currently having a powerful impact in the Arab world. In addition to widespread availability of television and radio, the Arab world also has an estimated 24 million people with access to high-speed internet.

Most countries in the Arab world are not open to receiving traditional missionaries. Mission workers who witness in professional and domestic spheres may wait months, or even years, for an invitation to share what they believe with their colleagues and friends. The ministry of these workers can be greatly supported and enhanced by the proclamation of the Gospel with clarity and conviction over the airwaves and via the internet. A recent survey in one North African country showed that 80% of indigenous believers currently attending church fellowships first heard of Jesus Christ through media.

In another North African country, many tens of thousands have become followers of Jesus Christ despite the anti-conversion laws in that nation. One pastor reports that 'the word of God penetrates more and more in all the corners of our country.'

Recently, an elderly family matriarch sat listening to a Christian radio programme in a North African village. This lady was deeply touched by a Scripture she heard from Matthew's gospel when Jesus said to all who are tired 'come to me and I will give you rest'. Despite having been a Muslim for 62 years, she had never heard a prophet utter such words. She responded to the offer by the Saviour and found peace for her soul.

The intimacy shared by family members in her culture remains strong and this lady was readily able to share her new-found faith with other close relatives. Soon fourteen of her family joined her and received Jesus Christ as Saviour and Lord – and became part of the tremendous growth in the church in that country.

We pray that the watering of the Arab nations by the Gospel through mass media will continue. The harvest is large.

David Innes of Arab World Ministries

What significant role can media play in church planting among unreached people groups?

What valuable relationship could exist between Christian media and mission workers which would enhance the spread of the Gospel?

Given the high value placed on family relationships in certain cultures, how should this inform our approach to evangelism in these nations?

# WALK THE TALK

## SECTION TWO

## CONTENTS

# GOOD WITNESS

Cornelius and his household are attracted to God, and this is likely to be because they have been attracted by the values of those who believe in God. It is our lifestyle, and the values that our lives reflect, that can either attract people to the God revealed in Jesus, or put people off of the God that we say that our values are based upon. It can be easy to think that the values that we share are those that come from our faith, when in fact they are ones that are really rooted in our culture.

Many western values may be respected in different ways, but those of us from the West can be judged because of our colonial history or the neo-colonialism that is reflected in the way that our governments and global companies still try to control financial and political power. The west is also connected with the lack of moral values reflected in films, glossy magazines, celebrity lifestyles and much material that is found on the internet. Sadly, Christianity can be associated with western values, so that western Christians can be perceived to be lacking in morals. This means that those from the West can be assumed guilty, until proved innocent, and it becomes particularly important that what we do and what we say counters the western stereotype, rather than reinforcing it.

Living in the West assumes a high level of privacy that will not be experienced in other parts of the world, so it becomes increasingly important that you live a lifestyle that is consistent with what you say about your faith. A simple example makes the point. If you live in a community where neither the Christians nor the Muslims believe that it is right to drink alcohol, then you need to have a very well worked out strategy, not only about how you buy that bottle of beer or wine and get it home unnoticed, but also about how you dispose of the empty bottle afterwards in a way that no one suspects you! It is not worth it. It is far better to adapt your lifestyle so that you don't drink alcohol.

# DO'S AND DON'TS

All cultures have their do's and don'ts. Make a list of helpful advice that you would give to someone coming to your culture for the first time from a very different culture so that they wouldn't cause offence.

Part of the western worldview that easily spills over into our faith is our individualism. There is an understanding that I know where I stand with God and what is acceptable to God and that is what matters. If other Christians have different views then that is their problem, not mine. We might quote from the Paul's Epistle to the Romans that we are justified by faith, not by our actions. But Paul has other things to say in Romans; read Romans 14.1 – 23. Paul speaks of those who are 'weak in faith' eating only vegetables, but stresses that those who are stronger in faith should not cause offence to them. We must lay aside modern day arguments for or against vegetarianism to understand this passage. Any animal would be dedicated to a pagan god, before it was slaughtered and the meat sold. The question was whether you could eat 'meat offered to idols'. As far as Paul, personally, was concerned there was only one God; the God who is Father of our Lord Jesus Christ. If there is only one God then either the meat has been offered to the true God, or it has not been offered to any god. That means that for Paul, himself, there was no problem.

But for the new Christian, the situation was more complex. If you have been used to worshipping a pagan god and have just come to faith in the True God then the pagan gods might still have some authority and credibility in your life. If you eat meat offered to a god that you still think has some credibility or authority then that is sinful. In that case, it is better that you avoid meat and only eat vegetables.

What Paul goes on to say is that there is a real danger that his actions might cause someone else, who has not yet got it all worked out properly, to do things for the wrong reason. If you still feel that the pagan god has some authority but you conclude that if it is acceptable for Paul to do it so I can do it, then not only have you sinned, but Paul has led you into sin.

What Paul stresses is our responsibility as Christians to others within the Body of Christ; that it is essential that we do not cause other Christians to stumble. If I as a Christian believe that a particular action or practice is acceptable to God, but other Christians believe that it is wrong then, if I carry out that action, my action may cause them to follow my example for the wrong reasons. Yes, we are saved by faith, not by actions, but we need to make certain that our actions do not lead others to sin.

*Thinking of the culture you intend going to, what might be the equivalent of 'meat offered to idols'? Make a list of things you might need to avoid in order not to cause offence. It would be helpful to then discuss your list with someone from that culture, or at least with someone who is familiar with that culture, so that they can advise you about what should really be on your list*

# BUILDING GOOD RELATIONSHIPS

**One of the easiest ways to find that our lifestyle undermines our Christian message is in the area of relationships.**

Christian workers overseas often complain that the amount of energy they expend trying to get on with each other reduces the energy available for the job they came to do. Behind the complaint is the naive expectation that Christians should live together in constant harmony. Yet the disciples quarrelled even when Jesus was physically with them. For example, James and John aroused the anger of the others through their status-seeking behaviour, and they all started arguing about who would be greatest in the coming kingdom. So it is hardly surprising that Christians today quarrel from time to time! What matters, however, is not so much that they quarrel, but what they do to resolve the quarrel and what they learn through the experience.

There are many reasons for poor relationships between people working together. Behind many of the upsets is the fact that everyone is different. This may threaten some people, because we like to slot people neatly into categories. When they do not fit the expected slot, our anxiety is aroused, we become defensive and the group becomes divided.

Then there is the problem of stereotypes — our preconceived ideas about people which are usually based on childhood learning. For example, most of us expect Texans to be boastful, Scots to be mean, the English to be snobbish and the French to be elegant! Before we even meet people, the mental stereotype is raised in our minds and we build defences against them. When we actually meet the people concerned they may not resemble the stereotype at all, which makes us more confused and defensive; they cannot be slotted in.

In overseas work, there are five basic causes of interpersonal relationship problems. Most of them are based on individual or group differences.

## Physical causes

Dr C. B. Dobson points out in his book Stress, The Hidden Adversary that physical differences are responsible for some of our behavioural variations. Some people function best in the mornings, others in the evenings. Nervous people tend to be more anxious on the day after the weekly holiday, and better towards the end of the week. Confident people are the opposite. This is why staff meetings at the start or end of the week can sometimes be difficult – it is wiser to hold them midweek when both groups are at their medium best!

These differences can create tensions in a marriage. If the wife is a morning person, she comes down to breakfast neat and clean, dressed, and possibly made up. Her husband may be an evening person, so he slouches down grumpily to breakfast, and cannot bear her cheerfulness any more than she can stand his slovenliness. Unless they understand the origins of their differences, they may end up quarrelling bitterly.

We all work at different speeds, too; some people are quick and others slow. Difficulties can arise if the quick ones drive slow people to the point of exhaustion, or the slow ones hold back their quicker colleagues to the point of screaming frustration. Of course, physical differences should never become an excuse for unacceptably careless or slovenly behaviour, but understanding them can help us to organise our work and to be tolerant with each other. Those who function best in the evening should plan easy routine work for the mornings, if possible. A similar arrangement can be made for spreading one's workload through the week. Both slow and quick people need to discuss their pattern with each other so that they are free to say, 'Don't hold me back', or 'Don't drive me'. In no circumstances, however, should we use physical differences as excuses for poor work or the inability to handle emergencies.

This is one of the reasons why God gives his children extra strength!

# Causes arising from our work

Friction between old and new workers is highly damaging to interpersonal relationships. Several factors are involved.

## 1. Fatigue and resultant over-rigidity

Older missionaries have often survived long periods of over-work, and they have coped by setting up rigid routines that more or less run themselves. Unfortunately, routines can get out of date, and the older person may be too tired or too out of touch to realise this. New people see what is wrong quickly, and with the best motives in the world may rush in with suggestions for change. Unfortunately the older person often interprets these as criticisms, rather than valid points. The result is that new ideas are brushed aside with the 'it's not the culture' excuse, which makes new people angry and frustrated.

New workers should note that they often (and quite unintentionally) make older staff feel inferior. It is all too easy for the older staff to get out of date, and the tragedy is that they may cover up with the autocratic 'Big Sahib complex'. Sometimes they may even refuse to teach their juniors anything as a result of their deep-seated fear of losing their position. If as a new worker you genuinely appreciate what has been accomplished, it will be possible to present suggestions without hurting anyone, and the genuine desire of the older people to learn new things will at once become apparent.

## 2. Jobs may not be what we expect

Job descriptions are notoriously difficult to write and often emerge heavily weighted towards the positive side without presenting the problems and weaknesses of the local situation. This is no-one's fault, it is just how the mind works. There is no point therefore feeling angry and frustrated at the realities of the situation: the perception by senior staff of well-established work can be just as rigid as the methods they use to accomplish it.

## 3. Conflict between spiritual and secular work

This can become a major cause of stress. Christian workers desire to serve people in the name of Jesus, and also to share in the ministry of the local church as opportunity arises. But they may feel so overloaded with professional work that there is little time or energy for anything else. This leads to resentment against the senior organisers who appear to condone the overload.

The only way to handle this is to avoid the secular/spiritual dichotomy which implies that some work is more spiritual than others. It is wrong to imply that the Holy Spirit is more involved in direct church work than in professional work. However, it is important to try to reduce the professional overload so that the worker can feel fulfilled in all areas of his or her ministry. One solution is to train many people to do small parts of the work, so that senior professionals are released from details to develop other aspects of their lives and ministries.

It is of course essential for you to maintain your personal devotional life, but this may mean changing long established habits. After several disturbed nights on the job, you will find it almost impossible to concentrate on praying and reading the scriptures. There is no need to worry about this – God is compassionate and loving, and well understands the needs of tired people. Jesus himself was tired after travelling. He can communicate with us through one short verse of the Bible, and we can talk to him through short telegram prayers, until we are less fatigued.

# Administrative hassles

In the course of counselling Christian workers overseas I have found a strong link between their anxieties and the administrative structure of the sending organisation. If the organisation has a modern constitution which is reviewed regularly, personnel anxieties can be reduced. Policies which cover the smaller details of expatriate life help to avoid the frustrations which arise if small requests have to be sent back for individual decision by the relevant committee, which wastes everyone's time. It is much easier to have written rules, plus some escape clauses for emergencies!

It is also important to keep channels of communication and decision-making clear. Workers who know they will be consulted about things that are relevant to them, and who are regularly informed about what is going on, feel much more secure.

At the same time, workers overseas should remember that administrators can also have problems. Too often administrators become the targets of other anxieties which in reality are nothing to do with them. They too need to be respected and cherished. They need someone to talk to and periodic administrators' conferences are well worthwhile.

# Cultural Clashes

Our relationships with one another can become strained simply because we come from different cultural backgrounds. Cultural beliefs and habits are usually learnt in childhood, so when we come up against totally different patterns of behaviour, a deep-rooted part of our make-up is attacked. For example, some Scandinavians feel it is wrong to send children to school before the age of seven or eight, whereas other nationalities send them to nursery school when they are three. This difference can become a bone of contention, each person protecting their own way of doing things as a part of protecting their national integrity. Similar differences arise over dress, manners, working patterns and domestic life.

Cultural differences between expatriates and nationals of the host country can obviously strain relationships. Expatriates who stay too long in the same place may hinder the development of local leadership, which is obviously resented. They can offend local customs through sheer ignorance and, while nationals usually understand and forgive, those who do not work so closely with the expatriates may cut off relationships with them. In some countries family demands impinge on working patterns. Expatriates, with their poorly developed tribal sense, may find this incomprehensible and irritating.

The only way to cope with all this is to learn local customs as fast as possible, and then to remain in the humble position of 'having to learn' for the whole of your overseas career. Good humour over mistakes, a readiness to apologise, and increasing freedom in communicating with and relating to each other can result in wonderful friendships with local national colleagues.

Expatriates from different home countries may also experience relationship problems. Language can create major misunderstandings. Even if English is the mother tongue, not everyone speaks the same kind of English. For example, the British and Americans may totally miss each others' meaning despite communicating in English. Where English is the normal language of communication but is a second language for some of the expatriate team, the problem can be even worse.

Social customs differ, too. For some, Christmas Day may be the important festival; for others it is Christmas Eve. Great offence can be caused when we fail to understand each others' different patterns of professional training and the significance of the letters after people's names. Financial disparity may create conflict or embarrassment, especially when team members' children have grossly disparate possessions and lifestyles.

One of the greatest dangers facing expatriates, which can lead to mental ill health and group disruption, is the formation of a subculture. In isolated areas where expatriates live and work together as a separate community, some stress within the group may result in it becoming detached from the outside world. People over-concentrate on the internal problems and levels of stress and tension rise further. In an attempt to cope with this kind of conflict, a subculture develops in which certain patterns of reacting, behaving, and expressing Christian belief become the norm. Conformity to this norm makes individuals acceptable, whereas non-conformity leads to accusations of being unspiritual. The end result may be an epidemic of anxiety, panic, fear of other people's opinions, depression and an increasing inability to cope. As in a physical epidemic, the symptoms are infectious and the mental health of several members of the subculture may be adversely affected.

Two things will help you to avoid this danger. The first is to maintain a healthy balance between the expatriate group (if it has to exist at all) and the outside world by daily social contact and personal integration. The second is to care for every aspect of your personality. Taking holidays away from the job, keeping up an interest in the world as a whole, reading and continuing your hobbies, as well as keeping your professional knowledge and spiritual life fresh, will all help to diminish the subcultural danger. Be careful not to become preoccupied for too long. All Christians are periodically burdened for some special need, but this is not a permanent state of mind; the preoccupation usually gives way to wider interests. If it does not, then you would be wise to see a doctor, or at least to take a short holiday away from the work situation.

# Personality Clashes

We can often have trouble getting on with people because we have different personalities and are at different stages of  maturity. There are many complicated classifications of personality type and I do not intend to use any of them! Usually, we have trouble with other people's personalities because they are either too similar to or too different from ours. For example, two obsessional people who love order and neatness to the extent of becoming over-anxious if things are in a mess, may not be able to get along together at all. In fact they make each other worse. Two people with histrionic natures can rarely work together either. A dramatic outburst from one will often precipitate a similar response from the other! But mix the obsessional and the histrionic together, and the combination may be quite good.

The major difficulty overseas is that people may have to see too much of each other; there is just nowhere to get away from each other for a while. In such circumstances, it helps to remember that the other is the other, and that you are you. Both of you have a right to your own personality, but also a duty to try to curb its abrasive action on others. If it becomes impossible to live and work together, then it is better to split up and work with someone else.

This is just what Paul and Barnabas did after John Mark had caved in under the strain of the work. Barnabas decided it was his duty as John Mark's uncle to stay with his nephew, but Paul refused to take the young man. When they split, the Lord sent Silas to form a new partnership with Paul. It is encouraging to note that after a cooling off and maturing period, Paul and John Mark made it up and became colleagues again.

When we start thinking about our own personality type, it is so easy to feel that God has favourites. He seems to have given other people calm, placid and easy-going natures, whereas we may have to struggle with anxious or thorny personality structures. In fact, the other person may be having just the same struggle but they do not speak about it and it may not be so obvious. It is important to remember that God knew exactly what he was doing when he made us, as Psalm 139 says. Our personalities can get marred during their development but as God works with us to overcome the problems, we end up stronger people because we have had to struggle.

An important aspect of anyone's personality is its maturity. Immaturity can have profound influence on personal relationships. Erik Erikson taught that personality develops in eight stages, with something special being learnt at each stage. Things like basic trust, personal identity, and the importance of being industrious are all related to different stages of personality development.

Some people, due to serious problems at a particular stage of their development, may not complete the necessary learning. For example, they may never have learnt all that is necessary to establish basic trustfulness of others. This usually does them no harm, for they learn enough to manage. However, if several areas of their personality are underdeveloped, immaturity can result which causes trouble not only to the individual personally but also to their capacity to build relationships. This is frequently accompanied by persistent negative emotions such as bitterness, resentment, jealousy and hatred. These cause much unhappiness to the person concerned and to colleagues.

I have found it beneficial to teach people the importance of handling persistent negative emotions. Take jealousy as an example. People can be helped to identify the times in their lives when they experienced severe jealousy. Often, these are related to childhood experiences. To begin to understand why other people provoked such jealousy, to develop compassion for those who hurt them and to be able to forgive them, can be a healing experience, which in turn leads people towards maturity in the damaged areas of their lives.

**Marjory Foyle**
**From *Entering Another's World***

*What have you learnt about yourself from the five different causes illustrated above?*

*What is your strategy for minimising the risk of you being the cause of difficult relationships?*

# SECTION 3: FAITH

## AIMS

To explore how people come to Christian belief and grow in faith and spiritually resource their faith; to explore some of the challenges to our faith and how we can prepare ourselves to counter these; to consider different Christian understandings of, and approaches to, other faiths and spiritual forces.

## CONTENTS

## Learning Objectives

By the end of the module the student will be able to:

- Identify some of the factors that lead to conversion and to growth in faith

- Have a grasp of different ways in which faith can be sustained and nourished and how dry periods can be overcome

- Debate the different Christian approaches to those of other faiths, and an understanding of some key aspects in meeting and discussing faith with a person of another Faith

- Identify key aspects of a particular Faith community

- Have an understanding of spiritual forces and ways of combating these

# CONVERSION AND GROWTH

At the heart of the story of Peter and Cornelius, is the exciting reality that when people who are different come together, listen and share openly with each other, and are open to the Holy Spirit, then they change. Acts 10 tells us not only how Cornelius and his household come to faith as Christians, but also how Peter's faith is profoundly changed. Acts 11. 1 – 18 is the story of how the Church engages with these changes and is changed itself. If you are not open to your faith growing and being changed, then keep well away from those who are different from you! If you are open to the Holy Spirit changing you and growing you in your faith, read on.

The process of Gentiles becoming Christians begins in this passage and is built upon by Paul who sees himself as an apostle to the Gentiles. In Ephesians 2, Paul argues that Christ has made both groups into one and broken down the dividing wall. Another way of understanding what Paul expresses in Ephesians 2 is to consider looking at a distant object through one eye; when we do that we lose our sense of perspective. To gain the full perspective we need to look with two eyes. Because our eyes are a few centimetres apart, they see the object slightly differently and using them both gives us a proper perspective. Another analogy would be listening to stereo music through a single channel; we don't hear the full sound. Or, if we listen to a sound with just one ear, we can't easily identify where that sound comes from.

The truth is that we can never fully see who Jesus is in his true perspective from the single eye of our own culture, or hear who he is by listening to the single channel of our own culture. We need the insights of other cultures to fully appreciate who Jesus is. It is when we can look at Jesus through two or more cultures that we can begin to identify what is truly Jesus and what is shaped and coloured by the lens of our own culture. It is through experiencing Jesus in different cultures and contexts that we can experience growth.

## SECTION THREE

## CONTENTS

How do people come to faith?
How does faith grow and develop?

# How do people come to faith?

*Before reading this unit, write down how you became a Christian.*

Consider how Cornelius came to faith as a Christian:

- Cornelius was a Roman soldier and a Gentile; as such he would have had a very different worldview to that of the Jews and the small, but growing, sect within Judaism that would become Christianity. Your own story may include beginning with a worldview that has been strongly shaped by Christianity or it may, like Cornelius, begin with a very different worldview.

- Cornelius was actively seeking God; he was looking for something outside of himself and his previous experiences and understanding and so would have been open to that which was new and different.

- Sometimes God takes the initiative and finds those who are not seeking him. When this happens it is often as the result of the prayers of others and often such prayers will be sustained prayer over a period of time rather than just a single prayer.

- In order to become a Christian, Cornelius will need to change his worldview. This means that something happens that allows the acceptance of a different worldview. Usually this will be a process, over a period of time.

- For such a process to occur, usually the person will find themselves challenged by the worldview of a different community. Such challenges are unlikely to come from logical argument; logical argument usually only works if you have similar worldviews and assumptions to start off with. The challenge comes from realising that another community has values and a lifestyle, which flows out of their values, that are not found within your own worldview.

- Conversion usually begins in response to what people are **doing** rather than what they are **saying**. It is the values and lifestyles, reflecting these values, that help the potential convert to begin to realise that another worldview makes sense and is more appropriate for them.

- Usually we would assume that repentance is a necessary step in conversion. Repentance literally means a change of direction; a clear indication that the previous direction was the wrong one; an admission of the previous faults and the decision to proceed in a different direction. It must be pointed out that although the text makes no such mention of repentance – in fact no word is spoken by Cornelius and his household between the invitation to Peter to speak and the extolling of God in tongues - the baptism in the Spirit follows immediately after Peter speaks of the forgiveness of sins through Jesus' name. We might assume that the Holy Spirit is aware of an inner repentance that the narrator misses.

- Much is made of sudden conversion, a *Damascus Road* experience such as Saul experiences in Acts 9; the reality is that Saul was probably having his own worldview challenged by witnessing Stephen forgive his killers in Acts 7. Saul's continued persecution of Christians, described in Acts 8 and 9, would have meant that he continued to come across the values he saw in Stephen and he probably found that his head was saying one thing, but his heart another, leaving him ripe for his *Damascus Road* experience.

- Although the first stage is likely to be the response to what people are doing, it is unlikely that people will come to faith without someone, like Peter in the Peter and Cornelius narrative, speaking.

- Peter doesn't start by explaining different Christian doctrines; he doesn't use Christian jargon. Peter tells his story, his experience of Jesus at work in his life and in the world. It is the other person's experience of God at work in their life that can challenge and change our worldview, doctrine will only make sense after the worldview has begun to change.

- Peter doesn't leave Cornelius and his household immediately after they accept the good news and are baptised; he stays on to continue the process.

- In societies where there is a strong sense of community, it is very difficult to hold a worldview that is different from the rest of the community. Often, either the whole community converts and is baptised, or no one converts and is baptised. If an individual from a particular community does convert to Christianity, from a different worldview, they will be cutting themselves off from their community. They may be cutting themselves off from their family and, if single, are likely to be making the likelihood of marriage within their original community impossible. They will need incredible support from the Christian community in order to survive and grow as a Christian. Seeing the decision to convert as being a purely individual decision, rather than a communal one, might be imposing western cultural values onto the situation. To gain a deeper understanding of this read *Christianity Rediscovered – An epistle to the Masai* - Vincent Donovan SPCK.

- Peter doesn't wait until Cornelius and his household have received the additional teaching that he is going to offer. At the Holy Spirit's prompting, he baptises after they have made their initial decision.

- Cornelius and his household are 'baptised in the spirit' before they are baptised with water; they immediately manifest spiritual gifts. Some may disagree and believe that this is an essential sign of conversion, but we don't read of this happening with others who come to faith in the other narratives in Acts, so I believe that the manifestation of spiritual gifts was for the benefit of

Peter and his companions. It was Peter and his companions who needed a sign that this was really of God, rather than Cornelius and his household.

- Peter doesn't try to make Cornelius and his household identical to him and his companions; witnessing the baptism in the spirit convinces him that there is no need to make them adopt the Jewish culture that is part of their Christianity. The Holy Sprit is content for Cornelius and his household to be Christians within their own culture. What we see here is evangelism, where they are exposed to, and respond to, the good news of Christ in an appropriate way within their own culture and context, and not *proselysation* where there is attempt to make the convert replicate your self and take on board all of the manifestations of Christianity found within your own culture and context. Bishop Kenneth Cragg, who has written extensively about the engagement between Christianity and Islam, is quoted as saying 'Mission is not about the claims that we make, but about the discoveries we enable'.

*Note down which of the points on the previous pages reflect your own experience of coming to faith and also the experiences of other people that you know of.*

# How does faith grow and develop?

> *Think of times when your own faith has changed and grown: note down how this happened*

Now let us consider how Peter grows in faith as a Christian:

- Peter is a good biblical Christian, he knows the scriptures well but his scriptures would be what we know as the Old Testament. Culturally he is Jewish and his interpretation of scripture, like yours or mine, is determined by his culture. If we concentrate upon specific biblical texts that fit our cultural views, it is easy to lose sight of the 'big picture' and the deeper biblical principles and truth. The Jews believed that the other nations were outside of the mercy of God. Peter knew the law well enough to be aware of the limitations of social contact that he would be allowed with Gentiles. Gentiles were seen as ritually unclean, and contact with one would make him unclean as well. If he had any concept of Gentiles becoming Christians, his understanding would be that they needed to become Jews first of all.

- The Holy Spirit is going to have to find ways to break down these barriers in Peter. Interestingly, the process has obviously begun. Our narrative begins with Peter staying in the house of Simon, a tanner, in Joppa. A tanner is someone who works with animal skins; this is a job that is ritualistically unclean and anyone staying in the same house would also be seen as unclean in Jewish law.

- The Holy Spirit continues the work on Peter's cultural assumptions through his three-fold dream. For me, the significance is the fact that it is three-fold, rather than that it is a dream. When significant things happen in Peter's life, they happen in triplicate. He denies Jesus three times after the arrest (John 18. 15 – 25), but is commissioned three times by Jesus by the lakeside (John 21. 15 – 19). Often we will find that the Holy Spirit communicates with us in familiar ways to how he has communicated with us in the past.

- The Holy Spirit has been working with Peter at the conceptual level; his beliefs about cleanliness and uncleanliness have been challenged, but will they change his response and his action? The fact that, when Cornelius's men appear Peter invites them in and offers them hospitality, shows that his worldview is changing. Later, when he visits Cornelius, he will receive hospitality and this shows that yet another barrier has been overcome.

- There is yet a bigger barrier to overcome. Peter has been made aware that he should be sharing the good news with Gentiles but will have a dilemma when they accept the Good News. Does he need to now convert them to Judaism? Fortunately the Holy Spirit intervenes and the new believers are baptised in the Spirit; proof that they are acceptable to God, without first becoming Jews and needing to accept Jewish culture.

- A final stage is that Peter's new understanding, that comes from his growth, needs to be shared with the wider Church. This is dealt with in the section on Church, where we see that again the Holy Spirit has made provision.

- For Peter, the stages in his growth appear to be:

  o an action that takes him into a new situation (living in a house that is ritualistically unclean),

  o a revelation from the Holy Spirit that challenges his worldview,

  o being confronted with a situation that forces him to make a choice about actions that flow from a changed worldview (giving and receiving hospitality) and

  o confirmation, from the Holy Spirit, of the rightness of the decisions made (witnessing the baptism in the Spirit).

- In order to grow, Peter needs to let go of some of his previous Christian assumptions. This can be painful and confusing. In fact we read in Acts 11, that initially his new understanding of God's plans and the actions that flow from it are not acceptable to the wider

Church. In my teenage years I suffered from growing pains in my legs. In our faith we also suffer from growing pains but, as with physical growth, the process is worth it.

*Note any similarities between the points made above and your own experiences of growth.*

# SUSTAINING MY FAITH

Imagine how Peter feels during the experiences recounted in Acts 10.9 - 11. 3. He must have experienced a whole roller coaster of emotions. He wakes elated with a vision that includes a conversation with the Lord, but is greatly puzzled about what to make of the vision. Peter finds that his scriptural assumptions are being challenged. Before he can work this out his thought process is interrupted by visitors. Further confusion as to whether he should let them in is answered by the Holy Spirit telling him to invite them in.

When he arrives at Cornelius's household and starts to speak, he finds his audience falling at his feet and worshipping him; a rather embarrassing experience that suggests there is some miscommunication going on. It then seems to be quite straightforward for a while; listening, sharing his story and telling them about Jesus. Then follows the dilemma and confusion of what he should do when they accept Jesus. Then, again, an amazing experience of the Holy Spirit affirming the rightness of baptising them all. This experience is followed by him staying and consolidating their faith.

Peter then has to come to terms with his own growth as a Christian and, having done this, he goes up to Jerusalem full of his wonderful experiences only to be criticised by the church. We know the story doesn't end there and will look at what happens next in the section on the Church, but we have seen Peter experience joy and exhilaration but also confusion, embarrassment, puzzlement and criticism.

When we take our faith into a different culture and engage with Christians who are different from us, who worship differently from us and who have different understandings on certain issues, or when we meet with those of non Christian worldviews, we can also expect to experience different emotions and some of these can be spiritually challenging. To prepare ourselves for this we need to consider our spiritual resources.

## SECTION THREE

## CONTENTS

# Spiritual survival kits

How do you sustain your faith?

What are the resources that you currently have to maintain and grow your faith?

How different do you feel that these resources may be in a different culture?

The resources that you list are likely to include corporate worship, sermons, discussion groups, personal prayer and bible study. It is worth considering some of the different factors within another culture:

- **Language**

  Sometimes when interviewing those considering serving overseas I would ask 'What language do you think the local church worships in?' Given that we weren't usually speaking about a specific location, or even a specific country, it was a question not so much aimed at the knowledge of what language was spoken where, as helping the interviewee to reflect upon the fact that the answer was unlikely to be English. If relationships with God are to be personal and intimate, then faith needs to be shared in the language of the local community, Bibles will be read in that local language, sermons preached in that language and God worshipped and prayed to in that language. The local church in any place, unless it is aimed solely at the expatriate community, should be in the local language and in most parts of the world this will not be English. Until you are familiar with the local language, and this means being familiar with Christian vocabulary rather than the vocabulary necessary for your work, you will not be gaining as much from corporate worship as you do in your own language.

- **Shape and liturgy**

  Some churches will have a specific shape and structure to their worship. If you are familiar with this then you will have a good idea of where you are in the service, what is being said and how your own worship should be focused. I remember being at an Urdu service in Pakistan and trying to identify which part of the service we were likely to be at. One particular prayer, which the congregation joined in, I decided, was the Lord's Prayer so I said it to myself in English; as I said the phrase 'Give us this day our daily bread' I recognised one of the few words I knew in Urdu – the word for bread. I felt such a oneness and fellowship with the congregation; not only had I got to the same prayer

in my worship as they had, but also I was saying the same word in the same prayer at the same time, despite our language barriers.

Some services will not only have a common shape, but will have a written liturgy. Having a copy of this within the local language might mean that you can follow the prayers that are being said and join in saying those said by the congregation; having a copy of the liturgy in your own language will help you to follow what is being said and align your own spiritual focus and prayer with the rest of the congregation. Of course it can also help you learn words and develop your language skills.

- **Sermons**

  Sermons in a language that you hardly speak will not do much for your spiritual growth. I have sat beside kind people who have translated the occasional phrase for me, but my thought processes have sometimes been baffled in wondering how these phrases have been tied together. It is important to try to find out how the Word of God is being reflected upon within the church that you are attending, otherwise how can you understand the local Christian community and what makes it tick. It is probably better to ask someone who speaks your language to give you an overview afterwards. If you are aware what biblical passages have been read, you can actually use the sermon to reflect upon what they say to you within the context and culture that you are in.

- **Sermons from home**

  Many people come from home churches that will either offer their sermons and other teaching material in a written form or as a downloadable audio resource that can be accessed anywhere in the world that has access to the internet. Yes – these can have value in giving you teaching and having a sense of fellowship with your home church, but they need to be kept within the context that they were aimed at, the Body of Christ, the people of God, in that particular place where the sermon was delivered. To be sustained and grow as a Christian in the place that you have gone to it will be important to try to understand which bits of the bible particularly speak to their situation and how their culture and context shapes their understanding of those passages. When did you last hear a sermon preached from the Wisdom literature of the Old Testament or from the Epistle of James? I remember hearing that at one time, in a particular country, a very high proportion of sermons were based on these two books of the bible. The Wisdom literature is often neglected in the West but resonates strongly with certain cultures.

- **Worship songs**
  These can be an important part of our individual worship of God. Again, using those that our home church uses can help remind us of our spiritual roots and prayer support, but might blind us to the local Christian context. I remember going with a group of British Christians to a country where our host Christian community was a persecuted, oppressed minority. Although we were a mixed group of Christians, the girl with the guitar and the songbooks had a very triumphalistic theology and chose worship songs that reflected this. In contrast we found that the favourite worship song of our hosts was called 'Tell my people I love them'. It spoke of a God who might appear to have forgotten his people, but who hadn't; of a God who was actually close although appearing far away; a God who shared in and understood the suffering of his people.

- **Groups**
  It is likely that meeting in some type of regular evening group for study, discussion and prayer has been a significant part of your spiritual support. Unless you live in an urban area, or on a Christian compound, it is unlikely that you will be able to find such groups. It will be important to find other opportunities for discussion of faith issues with other Christians, so that you can allow your faith to engage with the local context and culture. Modern technology makes it possible to have a 'virtual discussion' with those from your own culture, but you need to open up your faith to different understandings of Christianity and allow the Holy Spirit to help you see things from different perspectives. It can be helpful to discuss issues of faith with other Christians from your culture who understand the culture that you are living in, but real challenge and growth occurs when you are listening and discussing with Christians from the host culture; praying with people of different cultures can be part of this.

- **Personal worship**
  How regular are your personal times of worship? Often we are aware of our failings in this area but assume that once we are there, rather than here, it will improve. It doesn't work like that; if you can't establish and maintain regular times of prayer in a familiar culture, it is hardly likely to happen when you move to a new culture. The important thing is to get into good patterns and habits now. It can be helpful to honestly assess what the barriers are now. Is your prayer life better when you are busy or when you have more free time? Is it better when life has routine, or when life is less ordered? Is it better when things are going well or when life is hard? If you can reflect on the answers to these questions, you may be able to try to establish a better discipline of prayer. Do you create time to really listen to God? It is often easier to fill the time with what we want to say to God, but it is essential to create time to really listen, and we need to be open to him speaking to us in different ways.

- **Worship resources**
  It can be helpful to gather some worship resources. Books of prayers can be helpful, and you may also wish to consider some books that provide a short liturgy or office. If you are not familiar with these then you may find that an advantage of these can be that they provide shape and structure that helpfully reminds you of:

  o the need to praise God

  o the importance of thanking God for his many blessings

- o  identifying with the body of Christ by saying prayers that you know that other Christians are using

- o  looking outwards beyond the needs of yourself and those in your immediate circles

- o  confessing your failings

- o  being reassured of God's forgiveness

- o  space to reflect upon God's Word and to listen to God.

- **Intercessions**
I remember reading the minutes of the committee of a Christian society, whilst at university, that read 'the Friday lunchtime prayers for the world have been cancelled as they don't appear to be working'. When asked about this, one of that committee replied that, obviously, they didn't mean that and what was really meant was that not enough people were attending. This of course begged the question as to why more people didn't attend and the likely answer would be because the prayers didn't appear to be working! If we live within a society where those without jobs usually find one and those who are ill usually get well then we can easily have an understanding of how God answers prayer that is different from the one that you have if you live within a society where economies decline, inter-communal tensions increase and problems get worse and people die, rather than recovering, from illness. In such cases we might need to re-evaluate our theology of suffering and how we approach prayer. This can mean both committing more time and energy to prayer, but also being open to the fact that God doesn't always answer prayer in the exact way that we would like, and we need to grow in our understanding of how he works.

- **Expressing your feelings**
Often our experiences of worship will emphasise the need to approach God with respect which can imply saying the right things to him, rather than being totally open and honest. The psalms can be a very helpful resource to enable us to express the whole realm of human feelings and emotions within our worship; the writers of the psalms had no such inhibitions about how they shared their feelings with God. Either using their words, or rewriting psalms to reflect our own feelings, can be a helpful way to bring our inner most feelings to God.

- **Bible study**

As was mentioned in the section on culture, we can come to very different understandings of what the bible means according to our culture and context. Within a different culture and context it will be important that, without losing sight of your original understanding, you try to understand what it might mean within the different culture and context. Does a passage have a different meaning when you are living with poverty, rather than wealth, or living with oppression rather than freedom? Does the imagery of the parables give new insights when you are living in a rural environment, rather than an urban one? It is difficult to do this as an individual and there will be the need to find out how other people understand particular texts.

- **Lectionaries**
All of us can have the tendency to choose the sections, or verses, of the bible that we are familiar with and feel comfortable with. Selective reading of the bible doesn't do justice to God's Word and the 'big picture' or the totality of God's salvation story. A lectionary offers passages from the

Old Testament, Gospels and the rest of the New Testament for each day that encourages you to read the whole bible. Some lectionaries will present linked or related passages so that particular themes are explored from at least two perspectives. Using a lectionary means that you are reading, praying about and reflecting upon biblical verses that other Christians are also studying that day; this can give a deeper sense of being part of the Body of Christ.

- **Prayer support**
  We will also be dependent upon the prayers of others to help us maintain and grow our faith. For this to happen it will be important to enlist prayer support before going into a different culture and also to alert them to your prayer needs. For your prayer supporters to pray effectively it will help to explain situations to them and inform them of the situation that you are in. This will include letting them know about the lessons you have learnt, misunderstanding that you have had and how you have learnt and grown through these.

- **Maintaining and growing faith**
  Different contexts will present different challenges. You may find that at times you are struggling just to retain your faith, in which case you may be dependent upon resources from you home church. To grow you will need to be learning from the different culture and context and from the local community.

# Dry periods or wilderness experiences

Write down any spiritually 'dry' periods or 'wilderness' experiences that you have had.

How did you come out of this time?

How were you changed by the experience?

Assuming that you have had such experiences, and have come through them, then you should be encouraged to realise that, despite the unpleasantness of such experiences, we do come through them. Usually when we come through such an experience we will be aware that we have been changed by the experience; hopefully this means that we have grown in our faith.

In Acts 10, Peter needs to let go of his traditional scriptural understanding of the place of the Gentiles in God's plans and his limited understanding of salvation before he can come to his new scriptural understanding. Peter needs to come to terms with the reality that the God that he used to believe in was too small before he can begin to understand who God really is and who Jesus really is. Growth means letting go of the familiar, which can be an uncomfortable experience. The times for growth of understanding for Israel are the experiences of the 40 years in the wilderness and of the exile. For Jesus the time of growing into an understanding of who he was and what he needed to do was the 40 days in the wilderness. Basically, real growth is likely to occur when we are outside of our comfort zone and not able to look towards familiar support systems.

Looking back at wilderness experiences people often realise that although they didn't always continue to believe in God, God continued to believe in them! It is important during such times to try to continue with regular times of prayer. Often it will be difficult to formulate our own words to speak to God and, again, liturgies and the psalms can be helpful. Liturgies will use prayers that others have developed and used over the years, and will often be verses of scripture, or based upon scripture. The psalms, as mentioned above, will include all sorts of questioning and doubts and a whole range of emotions that others have brought to God.

Often the way out of a dry period will be through changing the pattern and resources of your prayer life. It can be very easy to just continue with 'what works' rather than move on to more appropriate resources or different patterns of prayer; a dry period can be God nudging us to move

on and grow in our prayer life. Obviously it can be healthy to experiment with different prayer resources in our prayer life, rather than wait until we experience a dry period.

If we don't let others know about our spiritual difficulties then they cannot support us in prayer or with suggestions! In fact I am sure that much spiritual damage is done by Christians pretending that all is ok in their spiritual life, and giving the impression that 'proper Christians' don't have difficulties. If we could all be more honest about the realities, rather than how we would like it to be, then those facing difficulties would know that it was natural to have such experiences and be encouraged by how others have come through such times and experienced growth. It would give far more encouragement and support than pretending that such times don't occur!

# OTHER FAITHS

Peter successfully shares the good news of Jesus with Cornelius and his household. But the Peter that we are introduced to at the beginning of this narrative could not have achieved this without the Holy Spirit's intervention. Peter had an understanding of Gentiles that excluded them from God's mercy and salvation. Not only were they beyond God's plans, but they were to be avoided in case they contaminated Peter and made him ritually unclean. Clearly, how we understand those of other faiths will influence not only whether we engage with them, but also how we engage with them.

Does the Holy Spirit need to work upon your views?

## SECTION THREE

### CONTENTS

# Christian understandings of other faiths

## Self assessment test

Choose an answer to the following questions:

**1) Which of the following statements do you agree with?**

a) All religions lead equally to God, and equally share God's truth

b) God can only be fully known in Christianity, but other faiths contain some truth

c) God can only be found in Christianity, there is no truth in other faiths

d) God can only be found in Christianity, other faiths are inspired by the devil and are demonic

**2) Which best describes your understanding of the god of different faiths?**

a) There is only one God, so that all religions worship the same God

b) There is only one God, so those who are not Christians worship a different understanding of the one true God

c) There is only one God, so those of other faiths don't worship anyone

d) There is God and there is the devil, so those of other faiths must worship the devil

**3) When I go to heaven:**

a) Everyone will be there

b) I will be prepared to be surprised as to who is there

c) There will only be Christians there

**4) When those of other faiths worship their god then the one True God, revealed in Jesus Christ:**

a) Appreciates their praise and worship

b) Appreciates the aspects of their worship that reflect his attributes as revealed in Jesus Christ

c) Ignores their worship

d) Is angered by their worship as it is offered to the devil

**5) When I am in discussion with someone from another faith:**

a) I don't feel that I have an understanding of God that they might be excited by and wish to accept

b) I might well find comments that challenge my faith and help me learn more about my Christian understanding of God. If nothing else is achieved then we might both come to a deeper understanding of our own faith

c) I have nothing to learn from the other person

d) I need to be wary of them as their faith is demonic

**6) Other faiths**

a) Are equally salvific (able to save and redeem) as Christianity

b) May have some salvific aspects

c) Have no salvific aspects

d) Are of the devil

One paradigm, that some find helpful, that has been used in recent decades to understand attitudes to other faiths, is to use the terms pluralist, inclusive and exclusivist.

## How did you score?

Mainly a's – Pluralism

Mainly b's – Inclusivism

Mainly c's – Exclusivism

Mainly d's and some c's – Exclusivism with a tendency to demonise other faiths.

John Taylor, the then General Secretary of the Church Missionary Society, writing in 1977 pulled together two contrasting stories from the Franciscans. One was about a meeting that was meant to have occurred during the Crusades between St Francis and Sala'din. It ended with Sala'din saying 'If I ever meet another Christian like you I would be prepared to be baptised. But that will never happen.' The second story, less than 300 years later, was the response of the King of Peru to a Franciscan Monk. The Incas were being offered the choice between conversion to Christianity and death. After having his hands cut off the King was offered a final choice 'Be baptised and you will go to heaven'. The King replied 'No, for if I went to heaven I might meet a second Christian like you.'

I remember interviewing a young lady who told me proudly how she had been told off at school for telling another girl that she would go to hell unless she became a Christian. At the time I had just read the account of a Roman Catholic priest living and working in a Muslim village in North Africa. One day he noticed that a young boy that he had befriended was in tears. He asked him why and was told 'My family say that as you are not a Muslim you will go to hell.' There was a deep contrast between how the same message was conveyed on the two occasions. If you are going to say, or imply, that someone is destined for Hell then, however sensitively you may do this, you can only really do this with tears in your eyes.

Theologically, it is easy to select texts to back up our existing views; examples might be:

- John 14.6 - Jesus said to him 'I am the way, and the truth and the life. No one comes to the Father except through me.'

- Matthew 25.31 – 46 – The judgement of the nations according to who responded to hunger, thirst, material and pastoral need.

- John 14:2 - In my Father's house there are many dwelling-places. If it were not so, would I have told you that I go to prepare a place for you?

It is worth considering the other factors that may influence how we interpret scripture and use passages to back up our opinions.

### Exclusivist

Exclusivists are those who believe that salvation can only be found through Jesus Christ. Although many would respect the goodness and wisdom found in other faiths, some would deny that there is any good to be found in any other faith.

Thirty or forty years ago in Britain it was easy to find that you did not ever meet someone of another faith and weren't really aware of the questions that such encounters might raise, and certainly didn't need to try to engage deeply with these questions. Although the British Empire was ending, there was still a colonial understanding that shaped views and assumed that Western values, civilisation and understanding of issues was superior to those found elsewhere. Therefore, if you were a person of faith, Christianity was right and other faiths misinformed. Other faiths weren't so much viewed as evil, but would be seen as products of culture, filling a god-shaped space and misinformed.

Although there have always been some who view other faiths as demonic, the rise of Islamic fundamentalism, and the terror and violence that are connected to some manifestations of this, has led to an increased perception of Islam, or some manifestations of Islam, as demonic. Interestingly, those from these sections of Islam will often use similar language about the West and Christianity.

## Pluralist

It is a lot easier not to take another person's views seriously if you never meet the person or need to hear first hand about their beliefs and their understanding of their experiences of God. Increased contact with those of other faiths in the West meant that Christianity, as the only way to God, was one of the meta-narratives that post modernity challenged. It became popular to suggest that all religions lead equally to God and that all paths are equally valid. Any form of evangelism came to be seen as a hangover of a colonial mentality. Post modernity would suggest that all narratives were equally valid and suggest that ultimate truth could not be known and would deny the concept that God could reveal himself. Terms like spiritual imperialism or, more emotionally, spiritual rape, were used by many about attempts at evangelism.

A classic narrative, to emphasise this understanding, is the Indian story of the king who invites five blind beggars into his palace and asks them to identify what the elephant in his large hall is. The first touches its side and says it is a wall; the second touches a leg and says that it is a tree; the third touches an ear and says it is a fan; the fourth touches its trunk and says it is a hosepipe and the fifth touches its tail and says it is a rope. In the story God is the elephant and we, the adherents of the different religions, are the blind beggars with our partial perceptions of God.

As someone who does not buy into this view, I am left wondering who the king is in the story. He appears able to not only see God (the elephant), but also control both God and the adherents of the different faiths (the blind beggars)!

## Inclusive

Although there was polarisation between the above two views, an increasing strand of thought has endeavoured to take seriously both the claims of Christianity and the encounter with those of other faiths. There are four questions that might be taken seriously:

- If I can love the person of another faith that I meet, and believe that God is a God of love with a far greater capacity for love than I have, then can that person really be outside of God's mercy?

- As I encounter the spirituality of the person of another faith, how do I respond to the aspects of their spirituality that challenge my own spirituality? The commitment to regular prayer of my Muslim friend, the respect for human life of my Buddhist friend? The emphasis upon simplicity, rather than worldly goods of my Hindu friend? The understanding of God being in there within suffering of my Jewish friend? I can recognise these as all being biblical and there in Christianity, but need to cope with the fact that they have been watered down within my own tradition, but are still important within a different spirituality.

- What about those who have never heard about Jesus and have had no opportunity to respond to the God revealed through him?

- What about those who are genuinely searching within their own traditions?

There are different ways of trying to remain loyal to the uniqueness of the Christian revelation as well as engaging seriously with these questions.

If it is only those of other faiths who have heard about Jesus, but rejected him that are not saved, then it begs the question of whether it would be better not to try to share the good news of Jesus in the first place. The counter to this question is whether eternal life only begins when we die, or whether we believe that it begins as soon as the person moves into a new relationship with God through Jesus in this life. If the latter we will wish this to begin as soon as possible.

Some, in trying to refer to those who show Christian attributes without belief in Jesus, have spoken of 'anonymous Christians'. It is a nice theory, but could be considered rather patronising to 'sign someone up' to a belief without their knowledge!

Others have developed models to make sense of the situation. One is a series of concentric circles with the Cross at the centre and your own brand of Christianity nearest to it, followed by other expressions of Christianity, followed by the other monotheistic Faiths, followed by the other major Faiths etc.

Another model has the Cross at the top of a set of steps.

We are all on a journey through life that takes us up the steps to Christ but we have reached different positions on the steps.

Matthew's account of the wise men from the East visiting Jesus in Bethlehem provides a narrative of those of another worldview being led through their own worldview, to an encounter with Jesus.

I find an interesting significance in the fact that they return via a different route. We are introduced to the wise men as star-gazers; their worldview is that what will happen has already been pre-ordained and is revealed by the position and movement of stars in the heavens.

But the warning in their dream suggests that their worldview has changed. No longer is the future pre-ordained; their own actions will change outcomes. If they return via Herod, Jesus will be killed; if they return by another road, Jesus will be saved.

We don't know exactly what changes occurred to their views, nor how they fitted in with God's plans for salvation, but we do know that part of their worldview changed in response to the encounter with the baby Jesus.

# Meeting at the foot of the Cross

The late Lesslie Newbigin took this model and inverted it; not to give a model that positions the different faiths, but in order to suggest an approach to those of other faiths.

He reminds us that our own encounter with Jesus was at the foot of the Cross; in that encounter with Jesus we needed to be aware of our sins, repent and allow him to take our sins upon his Cross. We then move, as Christians, on our journey up the steps and away from the foot of the Cross. In order to meet with the person of another faith we need to move back to the place where Jesus first met us, at the foot of the Cross. In doing so we need to meet with the other person not full of what we have done as Christians, but with humility; aware of our own sinfulness and of our own dependence on Jesus to redeem us.

By meeting with the other, in humility at the foot of the Cross, each is changed. We and the person of the other faith will move on, up our own ladder of life, but both are changed by the encounter at the foot of the Cross. We may not know how the other person has been changed but we must trust that if we have met them with openness and humility, at the foot of the Cross, then Jesus will have been in the encounter in some way.

We are also aware that it is God, through his Holy Spirit, who converts, not us.

# Paul in Athens

A helpful biblical model for engaging with
another faith is found in the narrative about
Paul in Athens (Acts 17:16 – 34).

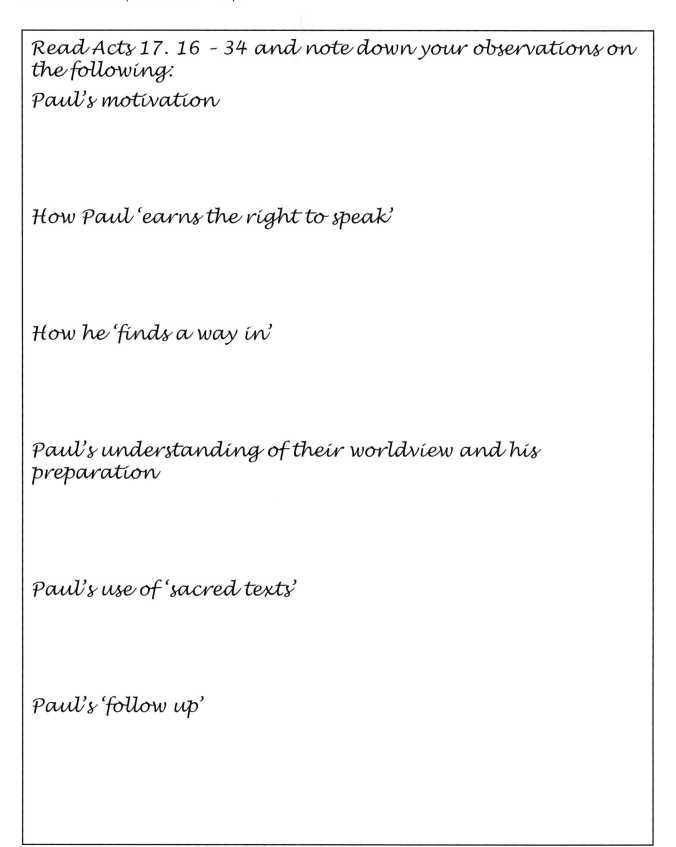

Read Acts 17. 16 - 34 and note down your observations on
the following:

Paul's motivation

How Paul 'earns the right to speak'

How he 'finds a way in'

Paul's understanding of their worldview and his
preparation

Paul's use of 'sacred texts'

Paul's 'follow up'

## Motivation

The Athenians were into new ideas and arguing and discussion for the sake of it. We get the impression that philosophy and debate were an intellectual exercise and whatever the conclusions, it was all in the head and not in the heart. Sometimes we can want others to accept our point of view because we like winning an argument. It boosts our sense of self-worth if we can prove that what we believe is right and what the other person believes is wrong. If we feel like this, we are guilty of wanting the other person to accept our view for the sake of our credibility rather than the credibility of the God whom we worship. These are not good reasons for being involved in dialogue. Paul, as we are told in verse 16, was motivated by his great distress at seeing the idols and engaged in dialogue out of compassion caused by this distress. In this passage we find the Greek word dialegomai, from which the English word dialogue is derived. We need to be clear what our motives are before we engage in dialogue and be sure that they are selfless.

## Earning the right to speak

Paul starts off (verse 17) talking to those who do believe in the God of the Old Testament, to the Jews and the God-fearing Greeks. It is through these discussions that he engages with the Epicurean and Stoic philosophers. Through this encounter he is invited (verse 19) to go and speak at the meeting of the Areopagus (the Greek for Mars Hill - where a court of no more than 30 people met, who, as well as considering cases of homicide, had an oversight of public morals and religious issues). Paul will get an audience there because he has been invited to speak. If we are to be heard we will need to earn the right to speak, which will often take time. We do not know how Paul earned the right to speak this time. It might have been because of his eloquence at speaking and arguing a point, but it may well have been because he showed interest in what the philosophers were saying. As we shall shortly see, Paul had certainly understood and engaged with their thinking.

Often it will be through our actions that we will earn the right to speak. It will be because we can be seen to care for the whole person and live out God's love in our actions; or it might be because there is respect for our values. It is no good speaking too soon. If we have not earned the right to speak, it is likely that nobody will listen to us. Equally, it is pointless to put off speaking indefinitely, just in case the time is not yet right. In finding the right moment, as in so many other things, we need to be sensitive to the leading of the Spirit.

## Finding a way in

So how does Paul begin his talk? Does he blast them for their idolatry and sinful nature? No. He starts by praising them for their religious zeal (verse 22). The huge number of idols says something about their enthusiasm for religion, and Paul begins by affirming this. It is a successful method, whatever your message. If you wish to make a point to someone, but begin by being critical, they are likely to become defensive. If you start off praising them, they are likely to listen!

Vincent Donovan, a Roman Catholic

missionary who worked with the Masai in Tanzania, paraphrased the words of Paul in his excellent book on cross-cultural mission *Christianity Rediscovered*. (SCM press 1982) 'Everyone knows how devout you Masai are, the faith you have, your beautiful worship of God and he has loved you. But .......'

This praise, rather than condemnation, must not just be a glib exercise, however. It must be built upon an understanding of what we are praising, otherwise it will sound insincere.

# Understanding and preparation

Paul has come across a shrine to an unknown god. Six hundred years previously there had been a severe plague and to try to halt it the poet Epimenides had released a flock of black and white sheep from the Areopagus into the streets. Wherever one stopped and lay down, it was sacrificed to the god of the nearest shrine. Where there was no shrine, it was sacrificed to 'an unknown god'. Paul proclaims that this unknown god, who has been worshipped for the previous 600 years, was knowable.

There is a danger in thinking that we have to take God with us into new situations. God has created this world and is already there in his creation. Our task is not to take God with us but to discover where he is already and proclaim him as the God who is the father of Jesus Christ. Paul explains that this 'unknown god' is knowable, and that he is the God of creation who is not housed within temples and idols. Vincent Donovan again adopts Paul's methodology and uses the imagery of a national god of the Masai really being the High God of all creation. In *Peace Child* (Regal Books Division, G/L Publications 1973), Don Richardson describes his work with the Sawi people of Netherlands New Guinea. This culture appears to be one with no obvious starting point to share Jesus until they discover that reconciliation can only come about between warring factions by each party giving a child to the other party. From this they are able to show that God gave Jesus, the ultimate Peace child, to reconcile himself with his creation. Dialogue is not a matter of bringing in an opposing God, bigger and better than the existing one. It is showing that the existing God is bigger and better than has previously been assumed, and can be experienced more fully through Jesus Christ.

# Using sacred texts

Paul wishes to make the point that we are all God's offspring. Rather than using his own Scriptures to do this, Paul quotes from the poem Phainomena by Aratus. His hearers do not know or accept his Scriptures and will not be impressed

or influenced by them. If we are to engage with another faith, we should try to use pointers from their sacred texts or holy books to point to our Christian understanding of God. There is, however, a danger in 'using' their scriptures. We cannot just take quotes out of context to make our point because this is patronising, insulting and, ultimately, damaging to our cause. It is important to know the context of the quotation and how it is traditionally understood. To do this we should try to see and understand things the way the other person does. It is essential to take their beliefs and experiences seriously and empathise with their understanding. The late Jeremy Hinds was a CMS mission partner engaging with Islam in West Africa and then in Lancashire. I have heard people ask him what was the hardest thing about his work. He replied, somewhat tongue in cheek, that the hardest thing was not becoming a Muslim! That showed how deeply he empathised.

He was so well known and accepted by different families and communities that he was often asked to pray at weddings and funerals and with sick people. Although he spoke Arabic he would pray in the local language of Hausa and this surprised his hearers, as many Muslims believe that Allah can only hear prayers in Arabic. Jeremy's empathy with Islam highlighted the risks involved in such encounters. Sharing with those of another faith, if we take their experiences seriously, can be very challenging to our own faith and raise some questions for which we will not necessarily find easy answers. If this is to be our calling, we need to be prepared for it.

The more we look into what Paul was doing in Athens, and Jeremy in West Africa, the more we realise that they were well prepared for their encounters. Of course we should wait upon the prompting of the Holy Spirit but we should also work as Paul did, using his knowledge of the shrine to the "unknown god". He understood the local culture and history and was able to find the right starting point. He also knew their literature well enough to find an appropriate quotation to use. Paul was in dialogue with both the Epicureans and Stoics who each had totally different understanding of the meaning of life. In looking at Paul's speech (verses 22 – 31), it is obvious that he knew their beliefs thoroughly, and also where they would particularly disagree with each other. And his earlier discussions, before his invitation to speak to them, had been an important part of his preparation.

## Follow up

Paul's speech did not produce amazing results. When he finished some sneered, some wanted to hear more and some became followers. If some do want to hear more, like Paul we have opportunities for more prayerful research and another chance to share our beliefs.

In Athens Paul had to find the right starting point within the other faith for his dialogue. And we need to do the same in our encounters. The Qur'an does have a bit to say about Jesus, although we Christians will disagree with much of it. It does mean, however, that Muslims have their own understanding of Jesus. One aspect of this understanding is of Jesus the healer (The Holy Qur'an, Surah V 110). Mohammed made no such claims about himself. There are many stories of Muslims coming to Christian hospitals, because they recognised Jesus as a healer and looked to the healing ministry of the hospital. There are also stories of those who have been healed and have been sure, perhaps through a vision, that it was Jesus who healed them.

# Exploring another faith

You may well be thinking of going to a particular country, or going to work with a particular people group. If not, just choose a particular faith group in a particular country. Research it and note:

How that faith came into being

How it became established in that country

What the relationship is like between that faith group and Christianity

What life is like for those who convert from that faith group to Christianity, or vice versa if it is a missionary faith that seeks converts

What the sacred texts of that faith are

What followers of that faith actually believe

How does their faith actually influence their lives and are
there specific religious practices

What the positive aspects are that you can identify in that
faith, perhaps beliefs or practices that might challenge
your faith

What questions you would like to ask a follower of that
faith

# SPIRITUAL WARFARE

## SECTION THREE

# SPIRITUAL WARFARE

Two groups of Christian workers in Africa disagreed over a plan of action. They became critical of each other and harsh words were spoken. A visiting leader was told about this by one group, and as he prayed he felt sure this was a spiritual attack. So he called the group to pray that God would defeat Satan and expose his lies and blindness. Within three days an apology came from the other group. 'We can see things clearly now and don't know why we were so negative,' they said.

Right through the Bible we read of spiritual warfare. Satan continually opposes God and tries to block his plans to give eternal life to all people. This battle reaches its climax in the gospels as Satan repeatedly tries to destroy Christ. He seems to win a great victory when Christ is crucified, but the willing, physical death of the eternal Son of God is not defeat. It is in fact the greatest victory because as his sinless life-blood is shed, atonement is made for our sin, God's law is satisfied, and forgiveness for sin is freely offered to all humanity (Leviticus 17:11, Ephesians 1:7). So the sin and death sequence is smashed and Satan's power over us is broken. Satan goes on trying to deceive the world, and he has his helpers, but his efforts are doomed. The fact is, Christ has conquered Satan: 'Having disarmed the powers and authorities, he made a public spectacle of them, triumphing over them by the cross' (Colossians 2:15).

So there is nothing new or unusual about spiritual warfare. The Christian is part of a very big campaign; the crucial battle has been won already, victory is secure and there are adequate instructions and resources for our protection and advance. But because of Satan's tactics, Christians are constantly in warfare against him and his allies. 'Our struggle is… against the authorities, against the powers of this dark world and against the spiritual forces of evil in the heavenly realms. Therefore put on the full armour of God… stand your ground… and pray in the Spirit on all occasions' (Ephesians 6:10-18).

No one goes into a major warfare on his own. He is always part of a big campaign, although sometimes he may feel alone or face a single opponent. In warfare each person has a vital part to play for which he is given orders and equipment. He also needs to know who the enemy is and what the battle is about. That is as true for us as we embark on any form of Christian service as it is for a military person.

## Recognise the signs of attack

In the physical germ warfare waged by our bodies, we are constantly being attacked and surrounded by germs, yet we are not often aware of them. But if our defences are weakened, we show signs of illness.

Similarly, in spiritual warfare we have our normal God-given protection (which I outline later), but if this is weakened for any reason, or if we are in a place of strong spiritual attack, we will become more aware of the warfare and will need to know how to resist and combat these forms of attack. We also need each other's help, care and prayer.

There are two kinds of 'symptoms' of spiritual attack:

### 1. Personal and within ourselves.

In our Christian life we may find we start doubting God's presence or the power of the Christian message. We may neglect listening to God, praying, and having fellowship with others. We may fall into lower standards of Christian living, or into negativity which leads to discouragement and despair. Finally, we may forget that the Holy Spirit is our constant companion and help.

### 2. Corporate and from outside.

In our Christian service we may discover resistance to the message which makes us discouraged. Rejection by local people may produce dismay, and their misunderstanding of our motives may produce anger. There could also be misunderstandings within the team which break down fellowship. Opposition by those of other faiths can make us fearful. We may become conscious of spiritual oppression and wonder if it is worth going on. We may also be subject to direct spiritual attack, even including curses or the use of occult powers against us.

All these signs may be 'the flaming arrows of the evil one' (Ephesians 6:16), and we need to remember how Jesus recognised Satan in the wilderness temptations and how he dealt with them.

# Recognise the enemy

Before studying anything to do with Satan, we should always focus on our Lord Jesus Christ who came 'to destroy the devil's work' (1 John 3:8). Over every activity of Satan we can write: 'Jesus has power and authority to destroy this work.' Praise Jesus, worship him and ask him specifically to destroy Satan's work whenever you encounter it. A good example of this is in Acts 4:23-31.

Satan has many names in scripture, and these reflect his activities. He is 'the god of this age/world.' He stops people coming to faith in Jesus by 'blinding the minds of unbelievers' (2 Corinthians 4:4). They literally cannot take in what we say. He is also the ruler of the kingdom of the air, and as such is 'the spirit who is now at work in those who are disobedient' (Ephesians 2:2). He actively prevents them from turning to Christ.

The name Satan means adversary, accuser. He accuses Christians to God, as he did Job (Job 1:9). He was wrong! He accuses Christians to themselves, making them feel unworthy and rejected, not righteous (Revelation 12:10). He accuses Christians to one another, especially in the church. His lies and deceptions can divide us and cause us to exaggerate faults and differences. Satan accuses Christians to the world by distorting their teaching, causing caricatures to be drawn of them, drawing people's attention to our failures, and so on (Matthew 5:11).

Satan can cause physical illness and harm too, as with Job (Job 2:7) and the woman who was bent over (Luke 13:16). For example, a Christian worker was cursed by evil, antagonistic men and before long his son was found to have cancer. This particular cancer was completely removed by specific prayer to break the curse and free the whole family from its effects.

Satan also destroys life. Violence, murder and suicide are often the results of his deception as people are drawn into drugs, alcohol and occult practices (John 8:44).

The term 'the devil' means tempter, slanderer. He tempts Christians to sin and diverts them from believing God's Word, as he did with Eve and with Jesus.

He also leads Christians into extreme doctrine and heresy (2 Timothy 2:26), and inspires false teaching. This can include cults and ideologies which may look good to people, such as the Spiritualist Church, but the power in them is satanic (1 Timothy 4:1; Revelation 3:9). He hinders the work of the church, even stirring up opposition and persecution (Revelation 2:9ff).

As Beelzebub, the prince of demons (Luke 11:14-26), Satan causes demonic oppression and possession. There are many examples of this in scripture, notably the Gadarene man (Luke 8:29), an incident which also demonstrates the complete authority of Jesus over demons.

# The hidden power of the occult

In Saudi Arabia I was once the guest for dinner of a Christian couple and their two small children. They had lived in Riyadh, the capital, for several years and had all kept fit and well. A few months before my visit they had moved to their present house and had all been sick off and on. The little girl was especially unwell. My host and hostess asked me what I thought about the situation. I replied that the sickness could be due to natural causes like a contaminated water supply or that it might have a satanic origin due to evil powers inhabiting the house. At this, one of the other guests laughed and I knew that I could not proceed to explain more. I promised to pray for the family.

I shared the problem with the couple with whom I was staying and we specifically prayed for healing and for the Lord's victory to be evident. Unexpectedly I visited the home the next day. The scoffer was not present. The little girl was still ill. I suggested to the parents and the three other visitors that we should join together as a team and pray for cleansing in each room of the house. Accordingly we went from room to room and prayed for the casting out of evil and for cleansing through the blood of Christ. We then praised God and prayed for those who used the particular room and for its special uses. For example, in the kitchen we prayed for the one who cooked, and for those who ate the food.

A Muslim neighbour visited the house a few hours after this service had taken place. She exclaimed in astonishment: 'Your little girl is now well and your home has a different atmosphere. What has happened?' The lady of the house told her of the power of Jesus Christ and how a group of believers had prayed in his name and that all evil had been expelled. This proved an effective and convincing way to share with her the good news of Jesus' victory over sin and evil.

God is constantly warning his people of Satan's power and activities and telling us not to get involved with supernatural power which is not his power but Satan's. Deuteronomy 18:9-12 lists occult practices forbidden to God's people. These are common today under a wide range of names and it is important that we know what they are and teach young Christians to renounce them.

**Divination** is discovering hidden knowledge by using satanic power such as clairvoyance, astrology, horoscopes and ouija boards (Acts 16:16-19).

**Sorcery** is fortune-telling by interpreting dreams, visions, reading palms and head bumps.

**Interpreting omens** means foretelling events by reading signs such as the flight of birds, entrails of animals and tea-leaves in cups.

**Witchcraft** is the use of magic, manipulating spirits to control people, casting spells, and using drugs and potions to induce certain actions or conditions of mind. Any form of bewitching, enchanting, spells, curses and incantations invoking the power of evil spirits over people or animals falls into this category.

Sect3-4:116

**Mediums** are controlled by evil spirits and become a channel for communicating with demons who impersonate the dead and give false information (Leviticus 20:3-25).

In addition to the normal beliefs and practices in most religions, there are also superstitions and occult activities. These are most obvious at times of crisis, particularly illness or disaster, when people go to mediums, shamans, witch-doctors, etc. In Hinduism, transcendental meditation and Yoga are stated ways of contacting the power of Hindu gods and applying this to yourself. In Islam there is fear and belief in Djinn (spirits), 'evil eye', 'hand of Fatima', etc. The Zikkas and the practices of Dervishes directly invoke occult power, inducing trances and supernatural phenomena. In much traditional religion there is open demonstration of demonic possession and the manipulating of spirits. Many ceremonies performed in other faiths fascinate Christian workers. It is important to realise that sometimes demonic powers are being invoked and to be near them can make us vulnerable to spiritual oppression.

# How to win the battles

There are six steps which we should take in order to experience the Lord's victory in our lives and service.

## 1. Know your weaknesses

If you have un-confessed sin, this will weaken you and your witness, and invite Satan's accusations. Share the problem with someone and claim God's forgiveness and victory. If we refuse to forgive others, we will cause broken relationships. Paul speaks of this in 2 Corinthians 2:5-11: 'I have forgiven in the sight of Christ for your sake, in order that Satan might not outwit us. For we are not unaware of his schemes.' If you have been involved with any cult, heresy or occult practice, renounce it, receive God's cleansing and forgiveness, and ask someone to pray that the power of it may be broken in Jesus' name. It is possible that parents' actions in drug taking, immorality, and occult practices (particularly Spiritism) can harm the next generations (Numbers 14:18; Leviticus 26:39-42), and if we are oppressed spiritually we may need to seek release from this hold which other people's past actions has over us.

Being close to a ceremony or activity where spirits are being invoked may be dangerous (1 Corinthians 10:19-20). It is vital for Christian workers to pray for one another often, particularly in times of stress, fear and political unrest. Openness with one another, forgiveness and love will strengthen and protect us against Satan's attacks.

## 2. Follow Jesus' example

Matthew 4 describes how Jesus handled Satan's temptations. He recognised where the thoughts and suggestions were coming from, and so did not even consider them, although they perfectly fitted his situation (physical desire, recognition, ambition). He knew the scriptures, chose statements from them and applied them right into the temptation, so silencing each one. Then he commanded, 'Away from me, Satan!' And Satan left! Jesus submitted himself to his Father's will whom he had just obeyed (in baptism), and he was filled with the Holy Spirit. Remember that Jesus is now praying for you, and each of these steps is possible for you in facing your temptations.

## 3. Put on your armour

First of all, remember the truth that you are 'in Christ Jesus', chosen, accepted, loved, and even in a sense seated with him in the heavenly realms (Ephesians 1:1-2:10). Scripture gives us many promises of protection. Read often Psalms 18, 46, 121. 'The Lord is my rock, my fortress and my deliverer.' 'God is our refuge and strength.' 'He who watches over you will not slumber; The Lord watches over you.' Notice too Proverbs 18:10: 'The name of the Lord is a strong tower; the righteous run to it and are safe.' God has given us ample protective 'armour' (Ephesians 6:13-17). Paul's list includes a helmet to keep our minds at peace; a breastplate to protect us from accusations; a belt of truth to hold us when lies and deception try to disrupt us; shoes to keep us steady and ready for action even in rough situations; a shield to keep Satan's fiery darts from getting into us; and a sword, the word of God to use accurately, with the Holy Spirit's power behind it. This armour is God's gift to us. Live in it at all times.

## 4. Pick up your weapons

We have three types of weapon. One is the Bible, God's Word, and a second is prayer. Both of these 'have divine power to demolish strongholds' (2 Corinthians 10:4). They are to be used for people, in building faith and encouragement, and against the enemy of souls wherever he is at work. The Holy Spirit is our teacher and he empowers us as we speak and pray. It will be right sometimes to fast and pray to bring us more into line with God's purposes and authority.

The third type of weapon is the gifts God has given to the church for our equipment and spiritual warfare. We can ask God for them. Particularly relevant to spiritual battles are 'distinguishing between spirits', and 'speaking in different kinds of tongues' so that the Holy Spirit can pray through us in effective power (1 Corinthians 12:10).

## 5. Take Jesus' authority

Christ's authority, never our own, is effective. He said: 'All authority in heaven and on earth has been given to me. Therefore go...' (Matthew 28:18). It is at the name of Jesus that every knee shall bow (Philippians 2:9-11; Mark 16:17). Jesus gives us the right to use his authority as we submit to him. It is given, not just assumed (Luke 9:1; 10:19). Jesus told his disciples that they would receive his empowering (Luke 24:49; Acts 1:8). They obeyed and acted on it right through the book of Acts. It is important that we know we have authority to meet situations of spiritual warfare, and we prepare for this by spending time with the Lord. For example, a police cadet has to submit to discipline and study, and gradually moves up the ranks gaining more authority. He can act with authority, arrest wrong-doers and know that the law will ratify his actions. So we are given authority to 'bind on earth' (i.e. to rebuke and stop evil) and to 'loose on earth' (i.e. to set people free from wrong bondages). This authority is ratified in heaven because it originates with Christ and is part of his work on earth (Matthew 16:17-19; Luke 4:18).

## 6. Get into the battle

As you get into your work, always praise God. Declare his power and greatness, sing to each other and to the Lord using 'psalms, hymns and spiritual songs'. Our faith is strengthened as we worship and praise (Ephesians 5:19; Colossians 3:15-17).

Build each other up in faith and expectation; let God's love and grace flow to one another (Jude 20, 21). Forgive and pray for one another, asking for the full equipment of God including the gifts of the Spirit, and the anointing of the Spirit for authority.

Declare over all you do and are that Jesus is Lord. Recognise and deal with sin and hindrances in your own life. Keep alert to the Holy Spirit's promptings and obey them. Keep being filled with the Spirit. Claim the promises, protection, forgiveness, cleansing and authority of Christ. Claim his power as you pray that he will break the power of the enemy, and claim protection for your health and safety.

Pray for the place where you live, for its leaders and authorities. Pray against evil practices around you, violence, pornography, drugs, abuse, and occult practices including films and literature. Ask the Lord Jesus Christ to break their power, and always pray as a group for this. Pray too for the cleansing of your house and other buildings you use, especially when you first move in. Claim the power of Christ to destroy any evil power which may have been there. Destroy any signs of occult practice and dedicate buildings to the service of God and declare over them all that 'Jesus is Lord.'

Pray for deliverance for one another and especially when anyone is spiritually oppressed. The deliverance ministry is outside the scope of this chapter, but read the incidents in the ministry of Jesus and the disciples.

Always look for what God is doing and give him thanks. A grateful, appreciative heart will keep you positive and praising. Remember that the 'one who is in you is greater than the one who is in the world' (1 John 4:4). Finally, 'be strong in the Lord'. Satan is strong but the Lord is stronger. Keep your thoughts focused on the Lord and not on Satan or his work. Satan is not the cause of everything that happens; he is not that powerful. God is the one who is ultimately in control and he is steadily at work all the time. 'Magnify' the Lord to one another so that all can see how great he is.

Take courage; you are 'in Christ', in a living relationship with him, united to him. You are raised up with Christ and seated with him in the heavenly realms, that is in the place of victory and supremacy, far above all rule and authority. You have been made complete in Christ who is the head over every power and authority. You know his incomparably great power for us who believe. Christ is Lord over the principalities and powers; he created them, conquered them, is exalted over them and has rescued us from them (Ephesians 1, 2; Colossians 1, 2). So recognise your position in Christ, rely on him and ask for fresh supplies of his power through the Holy Spirit, to wage a good warfare, and having done everything to still be able to stand your ground.

**Ruth Giesner**
**from *Entering Another's World***

Although we read right through the bible about spiritual warfare, we also read about fallen humanity; people who are difficult to get on with, stubborn, unpleasant and argumentative. How do we discern whether it is people, perhaps me, that are the root cause of a problem rather than spiritual forces, as such? The sections on Culture and on Living can give us some clues as to how we can naturally expect certain behaviour to be different in a different culture and how anyone can expect to act strangely when in another culture.

# SECTION 4: CHURCH

## AIM

To develop an awareness and appreciation of some aspects of what it means to be 'church'; the main forms of church around the world and how they came into being and models of relationship between churches.

## CONTENTS

## Learning Objectives

By the end of the module the student will be able to describe:

- some aspects of what it means to be church in some different parts of the world
- the differences between partnership and paternalism and some of the barriers to true partnership
- how the different churches and denominations evolved
- how they have determined their own denominational identity
- the ecumenical movement, United and post denominational Churches

Even before the story of Peter and Cornelius in Acts, the Church had survived a possible split. Although the Church was only comprised of those who were Jewish, these formed two distinct groups: Hebrews and Hellenists. The Hellenists were those who were from part of the Greek speaking Diaspora but were now living in Jerusalem; they would be Greek speaking and have taken on some of Greek culture. We read in Acts 6 that the early Church was responding to the physical need of its members but the Hellenists complained against their widows being neglected in the daily distribution of food. The Church remained one by dealing with the problem by asking the Hellenists to choose seven deacons from amongst their numbers who were then appointed by the apostles to take on this task. We know that two of the seven, Stephen and Philip, rapidly found themselves involved in sharing their faith rather than just 'serving at table'.

In the story of Peter and Cornelius there is again the potential for the Church to split. It could easily become divided between a Jewish Church and a Gentile Church or between a Church that is open to Gentiles and one that isn't. When Peter returns from his time with Cornelius and his household, we read in Acts 11 that he was called to account by the circumcised believers in Jerusalem. Basically he had been converting the wrong sort of people! If he was going to baptise Gentiles then shouldn't he convert them to become Jews first?

Reading his response, it looks as if he convinced them quite easily. As mentioned in Section 3, it is easy to miss the significance of Acts 11.12, where Peter refers to the six brothers who accompanied him. The narrative that he gives is affirmed by him and six others; by seven males. In the local legal system of the day, an event is deemed as proven if witnessed by seven males. I am sure that it was the Holy Spirit, rather than Peter himself, that made sure that there were seven witnesses present! The Church avoids a split over this issue but we know from Paul's Epistles that the matter is far from over and Paul has to reprimand Peter himself on the issue. One lesson from the Acts of the Apostles is that God wants his Church to remain as one and not split, and the Holy Spirit is active in guiding the Church to prevent splits. In John 17 we read of Jesus praying for the oneness of his disciples.

When Peter shares his faith with Cornelius and his household, and is aware that they are taking on board what he is saying and coming to a belief in Jesus, he is approaching a dilemma. As all Christians at this point are originally Jews, will he have to convert these people to Judaism before they can become Christians and join the Church? Fortunately, the Holy Spirit anticipates the dilemma and responds before Peter finishes speaking; the listeners receive the gift of Holy Spirit and speak in tongues praising God. If God can baptise Gentiles in the Spirit, then Peter has no problem with baptising them with water and admitting them to the Church.

Until just over a hundred years ago, spiritual gifts were not something experienced in the Church, they were felt to be something that belonged solely in the age of the first apostles and early church. Nowadays some would feel that spiritual gifts still belong solely within that period and modern expressions of them are an emotional rather than a spiritual response; some others would say that if you don't have spiritual gifts then you are not a proper Christian. This is just one example of what shapes particular churches.

Another example is the issue of baptism. I feel that it is a shame that Luke didn't use a few more words to explain exactly what happened at the end of Acts 10; if he had done so we may have avoided one of the biggest splits to the Church in our own age. When Peter baptised Cornelius's entire household, all who heard the word and who the Holy Spirit fell upon, did it include children? As it is, different Christians will interpret this in different ways, and have strong views on the issue of whether it is right to baptise infants or only those who are old enough to make a mature decision that they personally accept Jesus.

The beginning of Acts 11 helps us to understand that Peter and his companions, as part of the Body of Christ, are accountable to others for their action. Being part of the Church means that you cannot just act as you wish; it brings mutual responsibility and accountability.

Read Jesus' prayer for his disciples, found in John 17, offering it as a prayer

# WHAT DOES IT MEAN TO BE CHURCH?

Peter is not just a solitary person of faith; he is part of the Body of Christ, the Church. In Acts 10.42, Peter states that 'He commanded us to preach to the people and to testify that he is the one ordained by God as judge of the living and the dead.' Peter didn't see this as a command to him, personally, but to Christ's followers, the Church. He goes on to say '… everyone who believes in him receives forgiveness of sins through his name.' The Church is also part of the process of allowing people to receive forgiveness, through Christ's name.

Peter and his companions baptise Cornelius and his household and stay for several days. We can assume that this was to begin the process of building up discipleship.

As we move into chapter 11, we realise that Peter and his companions are not free agents who can act on their own or act as they individually feel guided to by the Holy Spirit; they are accountable to the Church.

## SECTION FOUR

## CONTENTS

# What elements comprise a Church?

From the Peter and Cornelius narrative, we have seen that being Church includes preaching and testifying to Jesus; allowing people to receive forgiveness in Christ's name. What else does it mean to be Church? List the aspects that you feel are part of being Church

We understand in Acts 11 that Peter and his companions are accountable to the church. If you are sent by your church to work in another culture, then who are you accountable to?

What are the mutual expectations of that accountability?

# The Church and the Great Commission

For many Christians, the starting point in considering mission is the Great Commission, found in Matthew 28:16 – 20.

> *Now the eleven disciples went to Galilee, to the mountain to which Jesus had directed them. When they saw him, they worshipped him; but some doubted. And Jesus came and said to them, 'All authority in heaven and on earth has been given to me. Go therefore and make disciples of all nations, baptizing them in the name of the Father and of the Son and of the Holy Spirit, and teaching them to obey everything that I have commanded you. And remember, I am with you always, to the end of the age.'*

Jesus commissions his remaining eleven followers to go and make disciples of all nations. We need to ask ourselves about the relevance of that commission to us today. Who is Jesus really commissioning? Just those eleven men or are you and I included, nearly two thousand years later, commissioned to take and preach the gospel throughout the world?

Before offering my answer, consider Luke's version in Acts 1:6 – 8.

> *So when they had come together, they asked him, 'Lord, is this the time when you will restore the kingdom to Israel?' He replied: 'It is not for you to know the times or periods that the Father has set by his own authority. But you will receive power when the Holy Spirit has come upon you; and you will be my witnesses in Jerusalem, in all Judea and Samaria, and to the ends of the earth.'*

Here they were instructed to wait until after the Holy Spirit came upon them. The events of Pentecost, described in Acts 2, brought about a great sharing of the gospel around Jerusalem. We read in Acts 8 that the Holy Spirit needed to disperse the early Christians through the persecution that followed Stephen's martyrdom in order to get the gospel out of Jerusalem and a lot of work was needed to convince those early Jewish believers that the gospel was for the Gentiles as well as the Jews. Eventually it was taken into the wider world. It certainly sounds as if the first disciples obeyed the Great Commission in response to the promptings of the Holy Spirit, rather than as the result of any human strategy!

Jesus' words, in Acts 1.8, are a promise rather than a command; a promise which would be fulfilled with the gift of the Holy Spirit. But before the Holy Spirit is given, a twelfth apostle must be appointed to replace Judas. The fact that it is Matthias who is chosen, in verse 26, rather than Joseph called Barsabbas, seems immaterial; neither of them is ever heard of again. What is important is that the apostles are twelve again — within Hebrew tradition this is the number of completeness. There were twelve tribes of Israel and Jesus deliberately chose twelve disciples to show that he represented the fulfilment of Israel. The completion of Christ's mission is symbolised by the advent of the New Jerusalem, described in Revelation 21. 12 – 14, complete with twelve gates, twelve walls and twelve angels.

The fact that the Spirit does not come until the disciples are twelve again indicates that it is the whole Body of Christ, the Church, that is being commissioned and not just a group of individuals.

There is a danger that we, with our individualistic western culture, will interpret the passage to suit our circumstances, and assume that it is addressed to each of us personally, and not to the Church as a whole. All of us, not just those who feel that they have a special calling, are part of that commissioning. The Great Commission is given not to individuals, but to the whole Church.

When we go abroad to share in another country's work of mission, if there is a church there the initiative and the invitation should come from the church of the receiving country. If there is no such invitation, there should be very good reasons for going there uninvited. If we think that the church in another part of the world can gain from our contribution, can we also look at how we might benefit from their contribution to mission in our locality? Often those who return from being involved in mission overseas are aware of how much their own culture could gain from the different Christian insights that they have heard elsewhere. Through the invitation of one church and the mission programme of another church, God still calls individuals to go and be involved in the work of the receiving church. What is important is that they see their role as being within the context of the whole Body of Christ.

# Self-governance, self-supporting and self-propagating

Henry Venn, General Secretary of the Church Missionary Society in the middle of the 19th century, proposed that churches should follow the three principles of self-governance (making their own decisions rather than policy and practice being decided by those of another church in another country), self-supporting (financial independence from foreigners) and self-propagating (indigenous missionary work)

The reality is that often missionaries found it difficult to hand over responsibility and authority to national Christians and it took a long time before these three principles became a reality. Often churches in poorer parts of the world are still financially dependent upon the churches in richer countries. Many churches in the wealthier parts of the world are realising that they are not really self-supporting themselves but are living on the wealth and generosity of earlier generations, who built up capital and established trust funds!

---

*A Prayer*

*CHRIST AND THE CHURCH*

*Oh Church, [Christian people,] submit to Christ, as to the Lord.*
*Christ is the head of the church, his body, and is himself its Saviour.*
*The church should submit to Christ in everything.*
*Christ loved the church and gave himself up for her,*
*that he might sanctify her,*
*cleansing her by the washing of water with the word,*
*so that he might present the church to himself in splendour,*
*without spot or wrinkle or any such thing,*
*that she might be holy and without blemish.*
*He loves the church as his own body.*
*He nourishes and cherishes the church,*
*because we are members of his body...*
*the two [Christ and the church] have become one flesh.*
*This mystery is profound, and refers to Christ and the church.*

*(Reflection on Ephesians 5:22-33 by Bill Godfrey, Bishop of Peru)*

# Understanding an African church

Paul set out from Antioch on his missionary travels, to spread the good news of Christ, and to make as many converts as possible and establish a local church. This was in line with the Great Commission as recorded for us in the last Chapter of the Gospel of St. Matthew.

> And Jesus came and spoke to them, saying, 'All authority has been given to Me in heaven and on earth. 19 'Go therefore and make disciples of all the nations, baptizing them in the name of the Father and of the Son and of the Holy Spirit, 20 'teaching them to observe all things that I have commanded you; and lo, I am with you always, even to the end of the age.' Amen. Matt 28:18-20 (NKJV)

He made no attempt to turn that local church into a homogeneous part of the one from which he started out – nor indeed of the one at Jerusalem where the original converts and apostles met in fellowship. He simply led people to Christ from their former ways. Prayer, worship and whatever other things were relevant to their meeting together were uniquely based on their particular cultural setting.

When Jewish believers from Jerusalem attempted to confuse the church in Antioch with the idea that true Christians must practise Jewish customs, the matter was thrashed out at the council of Jerusalem (Acts 15). It pleased the 'church' and the Holy Spirit that they should not burden other people with an unnecessary load. The Christians in Antioch were free to express their faith within their own cultural setting, so long as they were not idolatrous or immoral.

That principle should be followed in every age, and it forms the foundation for understanding any national church. By 'national church' I mean a church that exists within a national boundary, not necessarily a church of that nation in the sense of the Church of England or Church

of Ireland. Many Third World countries were 'mission areas' and therefore received missionaries of different and at times divergent callings. The result was that within many countries several different churches were planted, each claiming dominance of truth and practice. No one church (except perhaps in India in recent times) can claim to be 'the church' of that country. The church is the body of believers who all over the world accept Jesus as Lord and Saviour and worship God through him as the only mediator and advocate. Any local assembly, be it in a city or a village, Western or Third World country, becomes the local expression of that universal church.

## How churches were started

I come from West Africa and it will be helpful to describe the past and present situation of the church there; it is probably typical of many other areas of the world to which the gospel was taken from the West.

Before the coming of Christianity to West Africa, there had existed some form of religion. It can be rightly said that the African peoples were and still are very religious. Religion, however, is not synonymous with Christianity. The only advantage to the early missionaries in their work of evangelisation was that they met people who were seeking God in very vague and ignorant terms but who did have definite beliefs in gods. Their task, therefore, was something like that of Paul on Mars Hill.

The Church Missionary Society – now Church Mission Society (CMS) – began work in Sierra Leone in 1804, but before then there had been a Methodist as well as a Baptist congregation there, started perhaps through the activities of freed slaves. Other missions followed, such as the Baptist Missionary Society and the Wesleyan Methodist Missionary Society in Badagry,

Nigeria in 1842. They preached forgiveness of sins and had converts. They were later joined by the Sudan Interior Mission, the Sudan United Mission, the Qua Iboe Mission and probably some others. All came with the liberating message of Jesus Christ as Lord and Saviour – the Messiah not just for the Jews but for the whole of mankind. Now that made sense and the Africans 'bought it.'

What resulted from these ventures was a mixed bag of blessings. Whereas it was good for Africans to break with the past and embrace this new way, the baby was thrown out with the bath water. The early missionaries were handicapped in that they confronted people whose different cultures and habits they did not fully understand. In many cases they had no time or patience to understand. Something had to be established and something therefore was established.

The church was born and God was praised and worshipped, not in the way Africans would have done but in the way missionaries did. Both hymn and tune were as foreign as the accordion, the 'wonder' instrument that made lovely sounds as the missionary squeezed and stretched the colourful contraption from side to side across his chest. The local instruments were not considered fit for worship. For one thing they produced no music recognisable to the missionary, and for another they did not look refined – and of course 'God would not have been happy with unrefined things!' Indigenous names were abandoned and Biblical or European names were chosen at baptism. All these may have had their uses and values then to the Missionaries, but the weakness was in assuming that every indigenous instrument or vernacular name had to do with paganism. This trend however has now been reversed.

Not only were names foreign, but church buildings took on the architectural shapes of the church buildings found in the missionaries' 'home' countries. Anything that did not look like that was not truly considered to be a church building. This trend has also now stopped as modern architectural shapes have emerged, in some cases replacing the old ones.

In those early times, the whole concept of Christianity became encapsulated in the Western culture. To worsen matters, colonialism in many places followed hotly behind evangelisation and at times arrived with it. In many cases this caused mission and government to become inseparable.

## Illusions

Three illusions grew out of the advent of Christianity from the West. One was that Western culture is the only possible form that Christianity can take anywhere because the Western culture is a Christianised culture. The second was that high development of certain art-forms in the West was necessarily a part of the good news of Jesus Christ. And the third was that since the Western culture developed in part from Christianity it is a full and perfect expression of Christianity in society.

The mission stations were often too closely associated with trading factories and government. Christianity was therefore in danger of – and in fact fell prey to – being associated with exploitation instead of liberation. This mistake was to be costly for the mission and the church in the West. Furthermore, sectarianism was imposed on the countries. Baptists would not have anything to do with Methodists, and Anglicans regarded all the other Protestant churches as non-conformists, while the Roman Catholics regarded all of them as pseudo-Christian, people who must be converted and re-baptised. The Third World was left with a divided church and no cultural identity.

The early missionaries also brought education, but this very blessing was to spark off an explosion which brought about more divergence, religious dissidence and organised syncretism. It is common knowledge that all the independence struggles within the then colonised Third World countries were spearheaded by nationalist figures who were products of mission education. They had been educated and had travelled to the West. They returned and began to question the 'establishment'.

# The changes that are taking place

National churches are now reversing the trends. Hymns and liturgy generally are being translated, and at times written, in the local language. Some of the hymns, though translated in the local language still retain recognizable Western tunes. Serious attempts are being made to write songs and choruses in purely African fashion and rhythm, and this practice is becoming more and more widespread among the mainline Anglican, Methodist, Presbyterian and Baptist churches.

Apart from the mainline Churches that grew from missionary endeavours from the West, a lot of Pentecostal Movements came as a second wave of missionary activities in Africa. They tended to import some of their ways but not quite as intensive as the former. They made more allowances for local expression. As time went on many indigenous churches began to emerge - and there are different types.

One is the kind of indigenous church begun by African Christians mostly influenced by the Evangelical and Pentecostal church planting associated with the USA. Most churches of this type have some acceptable theology and lean towards the Pentecostal or charismatic. The founders are often educated; and this is an advantage in church organisation. Another type is often charismatic and founded by men 'full of the Holy Spirit' who in themselves have little or no education. As the churches grew, mistakes crept in which led to problems. Nevertheless they provide some Christian answers for the ordinary Africans who cannot go along with the Europeanised churches. These two types of indigenous church can be called 'Evango-Pentecostal Indigenous.'

A third type of church can be classified as Spiritualist using the term in a different sense from the Western occult group. Having begun from scratch or by breaking away from some other church, many of these tend to possess a shaky and dubious theological base. Syncretistic ritual practices, and prophecies, dreams and visions, all play important roles; authority for some doctrines is often misinterpreted portions of the Bible taken out of context. It is pertinent to note that some clever rogues and con-men and women have begun such churches as a way of making an easy living.

Members of such groups are controlled by indoctrination and in extreme cases by fear. One may argue that these Spiritualist churches do help turn people away from their idols. But in fact this turning away from idols to 'God' is often not essentially different from the common practice in African religion in which one god is abandoned in favour of another believed to be more effective. Thus most adherents pursue a result-oriented follower-ship where blessings are earned by the efficacy of rites, sacrifices and ceremonies – just as they would normally do in tribal religion. The catchment area for these churches is wide and elastic, cutting across social and educational barriers. But they remain by and large very pseudo – at times a façade for paganism.

So we now have within the countries, the Mainline (Western-origin) churches, the Pentecostal churches, both foreign and home-grown, the Evango-Pentecostal churches and the Spiritualist churches all claiming to be the right type. Apart from the Mainline churches and some of the big Pentecostal churches emanating from the West – mostly U S A – the others are all reactions against an 'over-Westernised' church. There are hundreds up and down Africa. They may have their uses and their strengths but they also have their weaknesses.

Their strengths lie in the fact that they approach Christianity from an African perspective. They adopt a less formal, livelier form of worship using indigenous music and instruments or a mixture of African and Western instruments like the guitar and drums. On the whole they identify more closely with the African culture. The best of them, mainly from the Pentecostals and some of the Evango-Pentecostal group, seek to express their Christian faith through indigenous and familiar forms of worship while maintaining a sound theology and doctrine. Their growth rate is phenomenal.

The weakness often identified with the Spiritualistic churches is in the area of Christian scholarship. Many times biblical interpretations and usage are mixed up. There is a neglect of theology, and the training that church workers receive is rudimentary in the extreme. The result is that sermons are noted more for 'heat' than 'light'. Equal weight is given to the Old and New Testaments and the idea that Jesus Christ is a fulfilment of the Old Testament is not clearly understood. It is thus no wonder that sacrifices, polygamy and other rituals are practised. This is very disturbing.

Within the mainline churches, particularly the Anglican Church in the Anglophone West Africa and East Africa, things have begun to change; and in some cases have changed already. For some, the liturgy may still be European-influenced but many have now written their own liturgies. The services may bear some resemblances to what obtains in the West but, by and large, they are a lot warmer and participatory. This is African and there is a reason for this change.  I take Nigeria as a case in point

The church in Nigeria began to grow due to the three-self principles of CMS. From the onset the CMS laid down these principles as the governing ethos for their missionary work. The churches formed in Nigeria from their work must be helped to be: self-governing, self-financing and self-propagating. It was slow at first but currently this has become a huge success, to the Glory of God.

There was an encounter in Samaria between Our Lord Jesus Christ and the woman by the well as recorded in the gospel of John 4: 1-43. When the woman recognised Jesus as the Messiah, she left her water pot, went into the city and told the men of the city that she has seen the Messiah, and wondered whether He could be the Christ. Many of the Samaritans believed in Him because of the word of the woman who testified, 'He told me all that I ever did'. But when they came out to Him they constrained on Him to stay for two extra days teaching them. Many more believed in Him; and then they said to the woman:  'Now we believe, not because of what you said, for we ourselves have heard Him and we know that this indeed is the Christ, the Saviour of the world.'

This is, in a way, what the 'Church' in Nigeria seems to be saying to our brothers and sisters from the United Kingdom who brought us the Gospel. The church is now moving on with the gaze squarely on Jesus Christ. Like the early Church, the Bible remains the authentic word of God to the Churches in Africa and the Anglican Church in Nigeria in particular. Now we know that to be Christian means to surrender to the Lordship of Jesus Christ. It means to accept the Lord Jesus Christ as Lord and Saviour. To us Anglican Nigerian Christians, the Bible is the final authority for life. Culture is viewed and interpreted in the light of the Scripture. Where there is a conflict, culture and tradition give way to the supremacy of the Scripture. It is as a result of this growth, since the advent of the 'Missions', that the Anglican Church in Nigeria has added another 'self' principle: 'Self –Theologising'.  I choose Nigeria as a case in point but I believe that experiences in Nigeria can be noticed in parts of East Africa.

We now have our own scholars who have studied the original languages of the Scripture and who are able to translate the same into meaningful local languages. They are also able to interpret the Scriptures from our stand-point. And with this and other ways of moving the church forward, we are able to develop our own contextualised liturgy and a Biblical theology. Self-propagation has brought in a phenomenal growth in the last two decades and the Church, at least in Nigeria, is also self-financing.

## Pressures

The early church faced the same type of pressures that the church is facing today from the society around it. These early Christians did not give in to the threats and persecutions. Peter and his companions boldly withstood the authorities in those days:  But Peter and John answered and said to them, 'Whether it is right in the sight of God to listen to you more than to God, you judge. 20 'For we cannot but speak the things which we have seen and heard.' 21 So when they had further threatened them, they let them go, finding no way of punishing them, because of the people, since they all glorified God for what had been done.  Acts 4:19-21 (NKJV)

In contrast we perceive that the Church in the West has given in to some of the pressures of the society around it and it seems now that the church's agenda is 'driven' from without. This, no doubt, has begun to affect the Church spiritually and otherwise. If care is not taken, that church may be in danger of being overrun by other faiths. This is what frightens the church in Africa and what drives their determination to stay faithful to the Scripture and the scriptural requirements.

The Church in many parts of Africa is resisting that pressure and trying very much to remain the conscience of the society. We know this is not easy, but the Church is doing its best. John the Baptist played such a role as far as Herod was concerned and it cost him his head. The Church in Africa is prepared to pay the persecution cost, if need be.

# Come alongside us – and learn as well as teach

Any Christian who is going to work in a cross-cultural setting in Africa has to be prepared to take his or her task seriously, and not look on it as an adventure. It is true that Paul and his entourage met some 'adventures' during their journeys, but his letters show that he took his work very seriously and prayerfully.

The churches in these nations of Africa have their problems already. In West Africa, many of the mainline churches are struggling with how to shed off the European 'skin' and emerge as truly African. The younger people are very eager to see the church become African, not only by having African ministers but also by using African-style worship and expression. Some of the older people resist this and there is a mild tension. This, however, is being slowly overcome in places. The problem is that many of the older educated people want to maintain their background, which means their Europeanised education. Some of these people take their churchmanship very seriously, but the danger is that often real Christian commitment is lost in 'efficient' churchmanship. To them the wish to be

seen as different from the indigenous Evango-Pentecostal or Spiritualist churches involves a further embracing of 'Western' style church. This group is getting less and less as many are starting to accept the inevitable.  The change is sweeping fast in many parts of Africa. We must stress here that the influence of the fast-growing Pentecostal churches have assisted this rethink within the Anglican and other mainline churches.

The dilemma for anyone from the West working with the mainline national church is that you cannot but comply with its wishes and desires. One may be tempted to assist this change by encouraging the church to move on to what happens now in some of the Evangelical churches in the West whose liturgy and hymns have been modernised. But that will be to start the vicious circle again. The ideal is for the mainline church to contextualise its worship, but that has to be done very carefully and prayerfully. The cultural patterns must be tested very deeply with the pure gospel of Jesus Christ, for all cultures are earthly expressions of 'being' from people within an environment. And since all peoples are 'fallen', cultures have to be tested to find out which parts oppose scripture, which parts agree and which parts are neutral. This will help churches not to absorb those aspects of culture that originate from a sinful base. At present the mainline churches are grappling with this situation and we are seeing a lot of changes already.

The best stance to take towards the national mainline churches today is to come alongside them as partners. Then you can advise, lovingly criticise and encourage. The national church needs help to assume a purely national character under Christ without any literal copy-work. Unfortunately some Western Christians equate affluent society with Christian ethics and therefore tend to assume a paternalistic attitude to the national church. Many have discovered through bitter experience that this does not work any more. Even at their own level, and within their impoverished circumstances, the faith of these Christians rises above that of many in the established Western churches.

In the other national churches apart from the mainline churches, growth is an accepted norm and many people are turning to the Christian faith from various backgrounds as a result of evangelistic activities. There is also 'biological growth' as populations steadily increase. In the mainline churches, the growth used to be mainly biological, but quite a lot of people are finding faith due to evangelistic activities of these churches, more so since the declaration of the 'Decade of Evangelism'. Something at last has stirred and new churches are being planted from fresh converts. This move is mainly from the younger members as a result of the awakening that took (and is still taking place) within the mainline churches. The growth rate is now beginning to match that of the 'Evango-Pentecostal' and in places has surpassed them.

We readily agree here that the churches do need more in-depth teaching and discipleship. More workers are needed to train, prepare and equip the vast numbers coming to the Christian faith. This is probably the task that needs the most attention from the well-meaning Christians coming from the West since evangelising is best done by the local people. The teaching, preparing and equipping must however be contextualised.

On the whole, the African is religious and willing to be shown the Way which is Jesus Christ. He is willing to be taught and he is willing, like Andrew, to go and tell his brother about his new faith in Christ. Generally, Christianity within the Third World countries, whether mainline or otherwise, is coming to a level where one is beginning to wonder whether the West will not become the mission field. Perhaps the West can, through interactions with the national churches, re-learn and re-capture this lost quality of excitement in telling the good news. When new life and zeal sweep through the flagging churches of the West once more, and children of God are moved around from west to north, south to east, Western to national and vice-versa, the world may yet again begin to hear it loud and clear that Jesus saves!

**Ken Okeke**
**Bishop on the Niger, Nigeria**

*What are the lessons that you learn from this article that would help any church that is considering planting a church in a region that has not yet received the gospel?*

*What are the lessons for any church considering planting a new church in a region that already has existing churches of other denominations?*

*What are the lessons for someone from the West going to work with a well established church such as the Anglican Church in Nigeria?*

# You are the Body of Christ

'Church' is not necessarily a word that we readily associate with the Arab world. Yet, in some parts of the Middle East, a minority Christian community has lived and worshipped together for thousands of years. In several North African countries, a strong vibrant church has started to emerge. While in other Arab countries, believers from a Muslim background are fellowshipping together in small discreet groups. Arab believers are increasingly experiencing the Body of Christ – but that experience comes in a wide variety of forms and situations.

Many Arab Christians are now fully engaged in local and cross-cultural ministry to their cousins across the whole Arab world. Recently, a conference in the Middle East attracted 550 local young people who came to hear God's call to the work of missions in their lives. God is raising up a new generation of committed Arab believers who are willing to go to the nations with the Gospel. For other Arab Christians, the commitment to fellowship and the ministry of the Gospel comes at a great price. Just recently, seven Christians paid the ultimate cost when gunmen opened fire on churchgoers exiting a Christmas Eve midnight mass service in Egypt.

In another incident, a growing church in North Africa opened a new building to accommodate their 350 regular worshippers. A mob tried to prevent believers from gathering and later came to the service threatening worshippers, and manhandling the pastor. The building was vandalised until police arrived and restored order. But perhaps it is the story of the courage of individual believers and their commitment to the Body of Christ which is the most encouraging – and the most challenging for UK Christians who perhaps take freedom to worship together for granted.

Abdul* is a Believer from a Muslim Background (BMB) serving the Lord in the Middle East. He has been persecuted, interrogated, questioned, and kicked out of his apartment because of his commitment to his faith in Christ. The authorities have threatened to cause him more trouble unless he stops holding church meetings at his house. Due to the strength of persecution, Abdul had to suspend regular group meetings with other believers - however, he arranged to meet each member of the group individually to disciple them.

Farid* recently visited a house church in a very isolated village in the mountains of Kabylia. As believers filled the various rooms and corridors, Farid had to pick his way between people to the front to preach. Afterwards there was a time when people were invited forward for prayer. One elderly lady came with her face covered in bruises. She explained that her whole family (including grandchildren) had beaten her to try to deter her from attending church. She told Farid that even if the beating continued, she will not stop coming to church! Whereas persecution is rare in that congregation, many believers are under pressure from their families.

Nina* first heard of Christ from an American friend at university. Initially she rejected the Gospel but after thinking deeply about what she had heard, she decided to give her life to Jesus. As a result she stopped wearing the hijab (head covering) much to her family's displeasure. They refused to go anywhere with her for a whole year although they still didn't know about her change in faith. Nina began to meet with a Christian for Bible study and much needed times of prayer.

When her sister in law found out about her faith and told her family, Nina found herself in a very difficult situation. As she is still in her late twenties the culture demands that she remains under the head of the family. Nina has a strong and living faith but is no longer allowed to visit her Christian friend. Some families feel obliged to kill members who leave Islam - although this doesn't always happen. Nina has been put under great pressure from her family to 'return to Islam'. She often mentions how much she longs for the rest of her family to experience her faith, and she has already led her younger sister to faith in Christ.

**David Innes – Arab World Ministries**

*Names have been changed

What various expressions of the Body of Christ do you imagine are necessary under the circumstances faced by our brothers and sisters in the Arab world?

How do you think discipleship models would be required to vary in form and substance in the Arab world?

# A contextualised church building

Trinity Sunday, 30th May 2010, marked the 120th Anniversary of the creation of Holy Trinity parish, which is one of the oldest parish churches for the gathering of Chinese Anglicans in Hong Kong; Praise the Lord! On that same day, Holy Trinity Church was dedicated and consecrated as a cathedral church of the recently formed Diocese of Eastern Kowloon.

If you have the opportunity to walk around the Kowloon City area trying to find Holy Trinity Cathedral, you may find it difficult. The cathedral church has a special feature; it was constructed in the architectural style of a Chinese temple rather than style of western cathedrals or churches. Such a Chinese style of architecture has a long story behind it.

Bishop Hall, who was consecrated in 1932 as the 7th Diocesan bishop of the Diocese of Victoria (also known as the Diocese of Hong Kong and Guangdong), was renowned for his devotion and dedication to preach the gospel of God both in Hong Kong and China. In 1933 Bishop Hall had the innovative idea of constructing new Chinese church buildings in a special contextualized manner. His proposal was that the external appearance would be built in a Chinese architectural style whereas the internal layout of the church would be finished in a western design.

When the old church building of Holy Trinity Church needed to be relocated in 1933, Bishop Hall suggested constructing the new church building in a Chinese style. Under the leadership of Mr. Kin Chung NG, Holy Trinity Church became one of the most successful examples of the Christian indigenization movement in Hong Kong.

The Cathedral Church of Holy Trinity is typically a combination of traditional Chinese architecture and Christian faith. There are three elements included in traditional Chinese architecture; the foundation, the building and the roof. The three steps in front of the main entrance of the Holy Trinity Cathedral symbolize the Trinity. The church building is supported by four rows of tall pillars, with paintings of Chinese style clouds and patterns. The whole roof is covered with black or dark green tiles, replicating the design of most Ch'ing Dynasty Buddhist temples.  A cross is erected in the middle of the roof top where three pigeons are found as gargoyles on each side of the four directions. This perfectly substitutes the traditional dragon, phoenix and lion heads found on most roofs of Chinese buildings.

Within the church, itself, there is evidence of the Chinese building style. On both the northern and southern sides of the wall some paintings of lightning and cloud in a Chinese style can be found; these symbolise the universe and the nature of God's creation. For all the frames of the windows, as well as the Chinese design, a cross is inlaid in the middle. This is, indeed, an ingenious merging and blending of Chinese traditions and Christian faith.

The building was finished in 1937. This style of architecture, though still a minority in the history of Christianity in China, reflects the concern for the contextualization and indigenization of the Christian faith in both Hong Kong and China.

**Revd Kwok Keung Chan**
**Diocese of Eastern Kowloon, Hong Kong**
**Sheng Kung Hui**

*Looking through these articles from Nigeria, the Arab World and Hong Kong, note down some of the points that surprise you or excite you. Look again at your list of the aspects that you feel are part of being Church; what do you need to add to the list?*

*Which points that you identified from the stories and which aspects on your own list are cultural, and which ones should be essential to any church?*

# PARTNERSHIP AND PATERNALISM

SECTION FOUR

# Partnership

The term partnership has been used increasingly, in the last 40 years, to describe the relationship between churches. That doesn't mean that it is a recent concept; it is a biblical word. Depending upon which translation of the bible you use, the word appears in the Epistles and Paul, Barnabas, James, Peter, John, Titus, Philemon the readers of the letter to the Hebrews and Christ himself are all referred to as partners. As someone who was involved in testing calling to mission service, I was excited to realise that Jesus uses a partnership test to choose his first disciples in Luke 5. 1 – 11.

Simon, later to be known as Peter, and Andrew, James and John had fished all night in their two boats and caught nothing. Jesus comes and uses Simon's boat to teach from and then tells them where to fish. The first test that they pass is recognising and responding to Jesus' authority, but there is a second test to follow. Simon and Andrew catch more fish than they can land by themselves and call to their partners to help them. They would have been equal partners used to responding to each others' needs. They would have been used to working together as a pair of boats so their partnership would have been based on equality and a mutually enriching relationship.

So what happens when you work in partnership? They nearly get into deep water as both boats begin to sink! Why did this happen? Perhaps because they were tired from being up all night, perhaps because of the enormity of the task, perhaps there was confusion as to who was in charge and meant to be saying what should be done, perhaps there was miscommunication going on; if two boats face in different directions then left and right, fore and aft, port and starboard are different for the two boats, perhaps there were 'forces'; strong winds, high waves or strong currents.

But they do manage to land the huge catch, to show how effective partnership can be. But what is Simon's response to the difficulties? We know that Peter is never one to hide his feelings; who will he blame for the fact that they struggled with the task and both boats nearly sank? Peter kneels before Jesus and admits his sins. To pass the partnership test, you need to be able to admit where you got it wrong and confess your failings to Jesus, in front of your partners.

> *The comments above suggest reasons why the two boats 'nearly got into deep water'; what might the factors be in the situation that you are thinking of going to?*

*What are the strengths and gifts that you take into any partnership, and what do you think are the strengths and gifts of the other partners?*

*What attitudes and assumptions might you need to confess to that could get in the way of true partnership?*

In the nineteen-seventies, the Anglican Churches around the world started a series of consultations called Partners in Mission. Each independent province held a consultation to look at its own mission needs, but brought in partners from other parts of the world to help them identify what they were getting right and what their needs were, and how those needs could be met. By 1980, only two provinces hadn't had such a consultation. One was Myanmar (Burma) a country that was quite isolated politically from the rest of the world at the time. Can you guess the other province? Yes it was England! There was a sense of thinking that partnership was about helping others, rather than allowing others to help you identify your needs and meet your needs.

The partnership between the two pairs of fishermen was between equal partners, who were used to helping each other. It is interesting to note that the early church managed to get this balance. The first deliberate sending of personnel was Jerusalem to Antioch (Acts 11.22) but the first sending of financial aid, in response to a prophesised famine, is from Antioch to Jerusalem (Acts 11.27 – 30). Also Antioch soon starts sending mission personnel itself (Acts 13.1 – 3). Sadly, much so called, partnership today is based upon inequality and has hints of paternalism in it. Christians who have the financial, academic and professional gifts, so easily ignore the spiritual gifts that they could receive from other churches. Many now feel uncomfortable with the word partnership and we are moving into an era that is post partnership as we try to rediscover the true biblical understanding of the word.

**The Anglican Principles of Partnership**

These were drawn up by the Anglican Consultative Council at a meeting in Dublin in 1973

- There is one mission in all the world

- It is shared by the world-wide Christian community

- It involves a process of giving and receiving in which all have gifts to offer and needs to be met

- The local church in each place is primarily responsible for mission in that place, although as part of the universal Church it also has gifts to offer and advice and resources to receive

# Genuine partnership

In church relations between the West and the Third World countries, genuine partnership is generally illusive if not impossible. Genuine partnership, in my view, can only happen when the two parties involved are in some way equal. They share a similar level of understanding of the issues involved, the power issues are balanced not weighed heavily in favour of one or other, and there is mutual respect and perhaps also mutual benefit of the rewards of the partnership.

In the matter of dealing with sin, Christians cannot be said to be in partnership with the Lord Jesus Christ. What we bring to the table is that from which we desperately wish to be delivered. Power, love, ideas, commitment, indeed everything needed to get rid of sin or deliver us from sin are heavily stacked in favour of the Lord. Even after we have been saved by grace, everything we do in his name is done out of gratitude.

Perhaps this is stretching the analogy too far but at times the so called partnership between the Western Churches and the rest of the world seems very much like the relationship we have with the Lord Jesus Christ. We bring to the table the poverty we desire to be rid off and all the attributes of agency, power, money, philanthropy, love, knowledge and ideas are greatly stacked in favour of the West. The disparities between the parties are simply too great for true partnership to thrive.

Under these circumstances it is easier for people of good will to be paternalistic. After all, in history over the past five hundred years, during the transatlantic slave trade, colonial period, even the post-colonial era, people of good will in the west driven by all the best motives have found it easier to be paternalistic than equal partners in their relations with people of the southern continents.

But perhaps the situation can be redeemed if the agencies and their agents consider themselves as debtors to the objects of their good will. There are a number of ways by which anyone of us can fall into debt. First, and the one that is used in everyday economics, we fall into debt when we engage in a transaction involving the transfer of money, goods or services from a creditor. The resulting contract from such a deal compels the debtor morally and legally to pay back to the creditor what is owed. This is the normal logic of the use of the terms debtor and creditor. Paul uses the word in this sense in Romans 15:27 where the churches of Macedonia and Achaia had given money for the materially deprived Church in Jerusalem in exchange for the benefit of receiving the Gospel from the saints in Jerusalem. Quite clearly, this meaning would not apply to our situation today. One day soon the African Church will acknowledge its debt to the Western Church and hopefully give back something in recognition and appreciation of the powerful impact of the Gospel on Africa brought to us by the Western Church.

A second use of the word debtor is to be found in the Lord's Prayer (Matthew 6:12); 'forgive us our debts as we forgive our debtors'. Accordingly, a person incurs a moral debt on account of some wrong doing. That is why the NIV and other more modern translations use the word trespass instead. By using trespass the translators wish to get rid of the economic connotation that the original word debt carries. This second meaning forms a kind of a bridge to the meaning I am proposing. It has the sense of wrong doing towards the creditor and therefore a debt has accrued. Paul persecuted the Church but even he found forgiveness in God. He considered himself to be indebted to God. Christians in development can quite legitimately consider their work to be acts of gratitude on account of what the Lord has done in our lives.

A third way by which people enter into debt happens when one is entrusted by one party to deliver money or goods or services to a third party. We find this sense in Paul's use of debtor in Romans 1:14.

Paul describes himself as a debtor to the Gentiles. But the Gentiles hadn't done any wrong thing to Paul. And yet Paul has this strong sense of obligation to them! In this verse Paul uses the economic analogy but changes its normal logic. He did not incur a debt from the Gentiles; he owed them nothing. Instead he incurred the debt from God. But what kind of debt is this? In his commission (Acts 9:15, 26:15-18) Paul was given instructions to be the apostle to the Gentiles. He was entrusted with the Gospel. He considered this trust as a debt and he would not rest until he had discharged his debt completely.

Similarly, do not people in the West, to whom God has entrusted the Gospel, tremendous deposits of learning and material wealth, have a debt to discharge in relation to the underprivileged of the world? Most, if not all, the resources available to the development enterprise come from benefactors and are entrusted to the development agencies for the purpose of alleviating poverty and other problems of underdevelopment in Africa, Latin America and Asia. Surely then there is a double sense in which western Christian development agencies and their agents have a debt to discharge.

**Joe M Kapolyo**

*In what way do you have a debt to discharge?*

*In Unit 1 you considered who you were accountable to and the mutual responsibilities of that accountability. In the light of the material that you have considered since answering those questions, would you answer those questions in different ways?*

# DIFFERENT CHURCHES AND DENOMINATIONS

## SECTION FOUR

**CONTENTS**

# Why do I belong to the church I belong to?

*Before reading this unit, write down:*

*Why do I belong to the church/denomination that I belong to?*

My grandparents were all born in Scotland and brought up within the Church of Scotland; this is the national Church in Scotland and is Presbyterian in its governance and doctrine. It wasn't surprising that, when they moved to London, they joined the English Presbyterian Church and my parents and myself were brought up in that tradition. In England most Presbyterian Churches combined with the Congregationalist Churches in 1972. It was at university that I found myself mixing with Christians of different denominations and particularly with Methodists and I started to go to Methodist churches; there seemed to be a friendly welcome in their churches and I found that an outworking of their faith was a real concern for the social welfare of the poor and marginalised.

My concern for the poor and marginalised led me on to explore the whole issue of violence and war and realising that I had strong pacifist sympathies, I started to attend the Quakers. I was attracted not only to worshipping with others who agreed with me on various moral issues, but learnt to appreciate the Quaker form of worship; the silence took away the clutter and busy-ness of worship and provided a real opportunity to listen to God, rather than spend all of our time speaking to him. I would find that when people did feel moved to speak their words would, usually, really connect with where my own thoughts had reached. I had a real sense of the Holy Spirit being active in our worship in a way I had not previously experienced.

Some years later, I found myself working for an Anglican organisation and also, through friends, living in a Christian Community House that was attached to the local Anglican Church. Becoming familiar with Anglican worship at work I sometimes found myself attending the local Anglican Church instead of the Quakers. Again, it was through friends that I made the move, but I found that some Anglican worship can provide the space to listen to God. I began to appreciate the shape and flow of Anglican liturgy the importance of confessing our failings early within the worship and being reminded of God's forgiveness and receiving Communion became important to me. The Anglican use of the lectionary, so that readings and sermons came from the whole of the bible, rather than the preacher's favourite passages, was challenging to me. I missed being only with those who agreed with me on certain moral issues, but realised that it was more healthy to worship with those who disagreed with me as well. In fact I concluded that the diversity found with Anglicans is good for me, it helps me to work out why I believe what I believe and to be able to respect and listen to those who come to different conclusions from me.

I find myself agreeing with Anglican doctrines and appreciate connections that the structures provide with Anglicans in other parts of the world. In Scotland my grandparents were part of the national church and, as an Anglican in England, I too am part of the national church and can appreciate the opportunities that this gives for mission.

The writer identifies the following factors that influence his denominational journey:

- family;
- friends and community;
- the outworking of faith in the local community;
- friendliness of the welcome;
- agreement with others on moral issues;
- listening to and experiencing God in worship;
- order and shape within worship;
- including different elements of worship, such as confessing;
- the use of the whole bible, rather than favourite passages;
- receiving Holy Communion;
- holding together a diversity of views;
- Church structures, including those that help relate to churches in other parts of the world;
- doctrinal beliefs;
- the potential to be involved in mission.

Which of these factors influence your choices?

The factors change at different points in the writer's life. Are you influenced by the same factors throughout your life to date, or do you feel that they will change for you?

# How did the different denominations and churches come into being?

Although we have seen that the model during the Acts of the Apostles was for the Holy Spirit to help the Church overcome its differences and keep it united, this didn't continue as the early Church evolved and there have been a succession of splits. If any church or denomination believes that it can claim to be the descendents of the early church it is the Eastern Orthodox. They are the Church that has never broken away from any other churches, whereas other churches have tended to come into being as the result of splits. What follows is a brief overview of some key events; although it doesn't do justice to Church History, it hopefully provides the reader with some understanding of how different churches and denominations have come into being and gives them the basis to explore further on the internet.

## 1 Christendom Churches

From the 4th century until quite recently, many countries were predominantly Christian and Church and State were deeply linked; within such countries, this era was known as Christendom. The denomination that you belonged to was likely to be determined by the country that you lived in. Part 1 considers the Christendom churches, those churches that had this privileged relationship with the state, and how they came into being.

Jesus was born, executed and resurrected within a province of the Roman Empire; a century later the Empire stretched from Britain in the west to the Iraq border in the east; from the German border in the north to include North Africa in the south. The early Christians started as a persecuted minority. With the great fire of Rome in AD 64, Emperor Nero tried to put the blame on the Christians and Emperor Domitian AD 81 – 96, continued the practice of killing off Christians. Various other Emperors continued the practice of persecuting Christians but, as Tertullian said, 'the blood of the martyrs is the seed of the church' and the church continued to grow. The other positive about this persecution is that when you are persecuted you are less likely to split from your fellow Christians over your disagreements! By 301 AD Armenia had become the first Christian country but elsewhere Christians continued to suffer persecution for a while.

The Roman Empire was so large that it split in the 3rd century into two parts with different rulers for the Latin speaking west and the Greek speaking east. In the fourth century Constantine had a vision that he would win control of both parts by fighting under the sign of the Cross, the symbol of the Christians. He did so and won; immediately Christians were tolerated and Christianity soon became the state religion; the Imperial Religion of the Roman Empire. This connection between Church and State marked the beginning of Christendom. It gave Christians great security, power and influence but, as we shall see later, many have subsequently argued that there was a cost in being so closely connected with the status quo and this took away the cutting edge of the Christian message.

As the early church developed and spread in the Roman Empire it became focused around four centres – Rome, Jerusalem, Antioch and Alexandria. After Constantine's death and the birth of Christendom, Constantinople was also viewed as such a centre. As Jesus had given St Peter responsibility for the Church, and as Peter had gone to Rome, Rome became seen as the 'first amongst equals' of these centres; it had a certain primacy.

As was mentioned in the section on Culture, David Bosch quotes Paul Knitter

'The early Christians did not simply express in Greek what they already knew; rather, they discovered, through Greek religious and philosophical insights, what had been revealed to them. The doctrines of the trinity and of the divinity of Christ … for example, would not be what they are today if the church had not reassessed itself and its doctrines in the light of the new historical, cultural situations during the third through the sixth centuries.' Now that the Empire was Christian, Christian leaders were free to travel and meet to formulate their understandings of the faith and to establish doctrines. The key topic of debate was 'who was Jesus Christ?'. Such meetings took place at Ecumenical Councils. No longer being persecuted gave freedom to disagree with each other and differences were often increased by language differences, with different Christians speaking Latin, Greek, Syriac, Coptic or Armenian, as well as the political tensions that developed between different parts of the Empire.

> *How would you describe who Jesus is, in terms of being human and divine to:*
>
> *A Christian?*
>
> *A person of another faith?*
>
> *A person of no faith?*

# The Arian heresy

Arius (250 – 336) was an Egyptian teacher who said that Christ was not fully God but someone created by God with a special status, who helped God in the task of creation. This heresy didn't create any new denominations, but took the Arians, followers of Arius, out of the Body of the Church. This heresy did bubble up at later times in Church History and, to be honest, you may well know those who call themselves Christians who share the views of Arius!

# The Nestorian and Monophysite splits

Both Syria and Egypt, with their Christian centres in Antioch and Alexandria were part of the Empire but were economically poor and marginalised politically within the Empire. Ethiopia, Armenia and Persia were not part of the Empire and Christians there spoke their own languages rather than Latin or Greek. With political and language differences two different splits evolved; each, to a certain extent, was a reaction to the opposite view.

The Ecumenical Councils concluded that Jesus was both fully God and fully man at the same time. This truth is affirmed in the words of the Nicene Creed. The Nestorians or, Assyrian Church of the East, argued that Jesus was two distinct natures – human and divine – but these were separate; almost two distinct persons occupying one body. Mary only gave birth to the human part of Jesus and it was the human part that suffered on the Cross, so Mary would not be described as 'Mother of God' and it would be impossible to speak of the crucifixion as God suffering. This split meant that the Assyrian Church of the East became separate from the rest of the Church.

Given that they were mainly based in modern day Persia, to the east of the Roman Empire, their break with the Empire was to their advantage politically as they were no longer seen by other Persians as agents of the nearby Roman Empire. The churches that they had broken from lay to their west so they expanded to the east and took Christianity as far as China

Professor Diarmaid MacCulloch, in his programme on *The History of Christianity* produced for the BBC, illustrated these two perspectives by pouring oil and water into one wine glass and wine and water into another; the oil and water separate completely, illustrating the Nestorian viewpoint of two distinct and totally separate natures, and the wine and water mix into a single liquid illustrating the Monophysite perspective of a single nature.

and established a church there that lasted several centuries before persecution wiped it out. Adherents of the Assyrian Church of the East mainly live in Syria, Iraq, Iran and Southern India as well as those who have emigrated to the United States and Australia. They would argue that their understanding of the nature of Jesus was not quite as described and is much closer to orthodox understanding. The reality is that politics and language probably had as much to do with the split as doctrine.

The Monophysites, or Oriental Orthodox Churches, include the Copts based in Alexandria as well as the Syrians based in Antioch, Armenians and Ethiopians. The Syrians and Armenians argued that Jesus was one nature that was both human and divine. Although the Copts and Ethiopians did not take this theological view, the Council of Chalcedon thought that they did. This misunderstanding has been addressed in our own day with these Oriental Orthodox Churches.

However, this divide meant that the Coptic, Ethiopian, Syrian and Armenian Churches all became separate from the rest of the Church. Armenia and Ethiopia have remained predominantly Christian countries. Syrian Christians are not just found in Syria, but widely around the Middle East. Although Christians have been in the minority in that area since the rise of Islam, it was Syrians who first took the gospel to India and many Christians there, particularly in Kerala, are still part of this tradition and have a Christian heritage that dates back to the early centuries. The Coptic Church in Egypt became a minority after the rise of Islam and currently makes up about 10% of the population. Given the positions of Egypt and the Middle East as marginalised within the Roman Empire and of Ethiopia

and Armenia being outside of the Empire, these splits didn't make things any worse politically for these churches. These Churches are referred to collectively as the Oriental Orthodox Churches.

# British Christianity and the Council of Whitby

The Irish had never been under Roman occupation and the Christianity established there had a monastic rather than structural emphasis, with an abbot responsible for the community and monks going out to evangelise, rather than the close parallel between church and state hierarchy found in Christendom. Without state resources, monastic communities tended to be a collection of cells, rather than huge monasteries. The western part of the Empire declined politically and the Romans left Britain in 410 leaving Britain isolated from European influences. What Christian influences that had come through the Romans to Britain were lost as Britain was invaded by pagans from what is now Germany. Britain was re-evangelised through two different strands of Christianity; Celtic missionaries, originally from Ireland bringing their monastic emphasis and through Pope Gregory sending Augustus, to be the first Archbishop of Canterbury, in 597. The two strands had differences, including the date of Easter; the Council of Whitby was called to resolve these in 664. Although the Roman tradition won, there was a sense of trying to be 'both and' rather than 'either or'. (We will return to this attitude when we reach the Reformation.) So the British Church became part of the 'one true Church'.

# The split between East and West in 1054

After 476 AD the Latin and Greek speaking parts of the Roman Empire were never ruled by the same Emperor; one Eastern Emperor briefly ruled most of the original Empire, but was unable to rule it all. Both East and West had their political ups and downs with different invasions and the West suffered more during this time. Later, the rise of Islam led to many areas, including most of North Africa becoming Muslim and pagan tribes often invaded part of the Latin speaking Empire; the pagan tribes of the West were very powerful during this time. Politically, the two parts of the Empire became more distant from each other and there was a tension caused by Rome seeing itself as having a primacy over the rest of Christendom.

In the 9th century there was a resurgence of the Arian heresy in Spain and the western Church, centred in Rome, responded by changing some words within the Nicene Creed. The original phrase saying that the Holy Spirit 'proceeds from the Father' was replaced by the phrase 'proceeds from the Father and the Son'. This meant that the Western Church no longer agreed with the original Nicene Creed and so was seen by the Eastern Church to have broken away from the One, True Church. In 1054 both East and West excommunicated each other.

# The Crusades

Although Islam conquered the Holy Land, most of the population remained Christian, loyal to Constantinople. At various times from the end of the 11th to the end of the 13th centuries the West sent armies to try to re-conquer Jerusalem; often the western crusaders massacred the eastern Christians, as well as the Muslims, furthering the divide and suspicion between the two halves of Christendom. In 1204 the West destroyed the Eastern, Byzantine Empire. Although this was recaptured in 1261, Constantinople was seriously weakened and fell to the Muslim Ottoman Empire in 1453.

This may all seem like ancient history to you but, if you are a western Christian, you are seen as a spiritual descendent of those that did so much damage to Eastern Christianity and there is still much suspicion.

# The Eastern Orthodox

The Eastern Church is generally referred to as the Eastern Orthodox, or the Orthodox. The Eastern Orthodox expanded north through the Balkans and eventually became established in Russia in the late 10th century. Unlike the Western Church that did everything in Latin, even though most people were unable to speak Latin, the Orthodox Church used the language of the peoples. When Russia was evangelised the liturgies were written in the Russian of the 10th century. In many places they have continued to use the original liturgies, so many congregations use language that is a thousand years old and difficult to understand.

With the capture of Constantinople in 1453 by the Ottoman Empire, the Eastern Orthodox were reduced to a very small Christian minority in the area ruled by Muslims that was previously covered by the Eastern part of the Roman Empire and the Balkans. The Ottoman Empire ended with the end of the First World War in 1918. The Eastern Orthodox have been able grow again in this area since then. Interestingly, as the Eastern Orthodox regained its freedom in this area, it lost its freedom in Russia following the Communist revolution in 1917; the Balkans then becoming Communist after the Second World War.

With the fall of the Iron Curtain, at the end of the nineteen-eighties, there has been a growth again of the Eastern Orthodox in these countries. As the Eastern Orthodox have often lived as persecuted minorities their evangelism has been through their presence amongst a different worldview, rather than through evangelistic campaigns. They pride themselves upon the beauty of their worship, seeing it as giving a foretaste of heaven, and see the liturgy as being a powerful way of bringing people to faith. Due to emigration, there are many Orthodox in western countries. Although Christianity is in decline in such western countries, the Orthodox are seeing growth that is not just from immigration.

# The Western Church

Until the Reformation, the Western Church, following the split between East and West in 1054, consisted solely of the Roman Catholic Church. East and West had grown apart before the divide of 1054, but the change of words by the Western Church to the Nicene Creed, had an impact on doctrine. Because of the threat from the Arian heresy, the Holy Spirit was seen to proceed from both the Father and the son implying that the Holy Spirit was not an equal partner. Although the 6th century Athanasian Creed, which is still affirmed in the West, stresses the equality of the Father, Son and Holy Spirit within the Trinity, there was a sense in which the Holy Spirit was demoted within the Trinity.

This has had an impact upon doctrines and in the West there has traditionally, until quite recently, been quite a 'low' view of the Holy Spirit. It is only within the last century, with the Pentecostal and Charismatic movements and a rediscovery of the Holy Spirit through an interest in Celtic Christianity and through certain recent theologians across the denominations, that the Holy Spirit has been seen as an important part of the Trinity again in parts of the Western Church.

In the western Church the medieval period gave rise to some deeply spiritual people as diverse as Julian of Norwich and St Francis of Assisi. It saw missionary endeavours bringing the gospel to pagan areas of Europe, St Francis sharing his faith with the Saracens in the Middle East, the religious order that took its name from him, the Franciscans, taking the gospel into parts of Asia including China. There was also corruption in the hierarchy of the Church. During the 14th century some people began to challenge both the teaching of the Roman Catholic Church and the corruption that had invaded much of its hierarchy.

# The Reformation

People like Wycliffe (Oxford), Hus (Bohemia) and Erasmus (Rotterdam) all tried to change things from within and so began a process that would come to a head in 1517 when an Augustinian monk and professor in theology called Martin Luther nailed his 95 theses, or proposals, to the door of a church of his home town of Wittenberg in Germany. Having studied the book of Romans in detail, his underlying emphasis was on justification by faith rather than by deeds or donations and on God's word revealed in Scripture rather than the traditions of the Church. Again, his aim was to change things from the inside but not only was he excommunicated by the Church but he was also made a political outlaw. Politically Europe had changed and Western Christendom had lost its power

and its authority and nation states and cities were shaking off their allegiance to Rome and exerting their own authority. The 'outlaw' Luther was able to find sanctuary in Saxony where he translated the bible into German. Other autonomous areas agreed with his proposals and Rome ceased to have control of all of the Christians in the West.

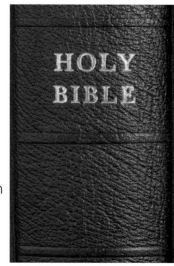

Two key aspects of the Reformation were that people could access the bible in their own language, rather than Latin, and that God could be approached directly, rather than just through the priest. Luther was seeking spiritual liberty at a time when many were seeking political liberty but he rejected this believing that although secular rulers had no right to interfere in the Church, Christians were obliged to give civil obedience to the state. John Calvin was persuaded by Luther's views and found that he needed to flee his native France for French speaking Switzerland where he developed his own theological views based upon Scripture; these including the rediscovery of St Paul's understanding of predestination. Calvin's theology is at the heart of Presbyterianism and there was a real zeal for evangelism amongst his followers. In England the theological mood for reform coincided with King Henry VIII wanting freedom from Rome so that he could divorce and remarry. The English monasteries were 'dissolved'; they were closed and the land and buildings given to the followers of the King. The theology of the English Church, that would be known as the Church of England, would be developed by Thomas Cranmer. What had begun as attempts to reform the Church from within led to the great split in the Western Church that gave birth to a movement known as Protestantism.

In England, as previously experienced at the Council of Whitby in 664, the spirit of the 'both and', rather than 'either or', prevailed and the Church of England declared itself to be 'Reformed Catholic' rather than 'Protestant'. The Eastern and Oriental Orthodox and the Roman Catholic Churches would claim to be part of the 'Apostolic Succession', that is they claim that their bishops are successors of the original apostles. St Peter would have laid hands upon the first generation of new bishops to consecrate them and they would have laid hands upon the next generation of bishops and so on so that there would be an unbroken line between St Peter and any current bishop. The Church of England, and any Church within the Anglican Communion which includes those who describe themselves as Episcopal as well as Anglican, would claim that their bishops are part of the apostolic succession, but some would also question how important this is. Some parts of the Lutheran Church could also make a similar claim and other parts would say that the apostolic succession comes through the Church's continuing to hold the Apostle's faith, rather than the physical laying on of hands.

In England, Henry VIII was followed as king, briefly by his young son Edward VI. He, or his advisers, instigated a period of extreme Protestantism with severe persecution of Roman Catholics. After his early death, Edward VI was followed by Mary who reintroduced Roman Catholicism with a vengeance, persecuting the Protestants. Her five year reign gave way to the 45 year reign of Elizabeth I that allowed the Church of England and Protestantism to become established in England. Scotland had periods of being Roman Catholic, Episcopal (based upon Church of England) and Presbyterian; the Church of Scotland, the national Church there, is now Presbyterian. For a long time Europe was racked with religious wars that were driven both by personal beliefs and political power mongering. There were many who were deeply committed to both causes and many martyrs on both sides in what followed.

# The Roman Catholic Church

The original reformers tried to reform the Church, rather than split away from it, and their ideas did eventually lead to reform within the Roman Catholic Church. There was a Roman Catholic – Lutheran meeting in 1541, but this failed to reconcile differences. The Council of Trent met between 1545 and 1563; it considered and rejected Luther's propositions as heresy but change introduced various reforms. Ignatius of Loyola was given permission to found the Jesuits in 1540. These practiced deeply Christ-centred spiritual exercises with a military-style devotion to spiritual discipline and were deeply committed to mission, leading to many Protestant martyrs as well as expansion of the Roman Catholic Church outside of Europe. In the 16th century Francis Xavier, a Jesuit, took Christianity to India and Japan.

# Religious tolerance

All the churches mentioned above are Christendom Churches; that is they were closely tied in with the state and the official church of the state and all would affirm and practice the baptism of infants as a rite of passage into the Christian community. Initially, after the Reformation, if you belonged to the state, you were expected to belong to the church associated with that state. In the years following the Reformation, the European Nation States that belonged to different denominations often fought, and dissent from the national denomination could often be seen as treason. Religious wars were fought in Europe between different alliances of Nation States, that affirmed different religious traditions, and the Peace of Westphalia brought an end to the Thirty Years War in 1648. Religious tolerance within the different countries of Europe followed at different speeds. In 1689 Britain allowed religious freedom to all Protestants.

# Colonial and missionary expansion

European colonial endeavours meant there was the need for chaplains to the colonial powers; this in turn led to missionary work in the colonies. Often there was deliberate missionary work to other countries as well. The Protestant denominations spent many decades in debating what the truth was, so that Protestant mission didn't really start until the 18th century.

# 2 Non-conformists and other Christian groupings

This part considers churches that are not the majority denominations within any particular country and have often come into being in reaction to what has been going on within the denomination that is the majority.

## Uniate Churches and similar movements

In some countries where the dominant church was Eastern or Oriental Orthodox, as a result of intentional mission by Roman Catholics, significant groups of congregations have decided, often for socio-political reasons rather than doctrinal reasons, to look to the Roman Catholic Church and the Pope for authority, rather than their original church. In such cases the church would continue with its original liturgy and practice but go into 'Communion with the Roman Catholic Church'. This has resulted in Greek Catholic, Coptic Catholic, Armenian Catholic, Assyrian Catholic Churches etc.

Although within the Roman Catholic Church a priest cannot be married, in most of the Orthodox Churches a married man can become a priest, but not a bishop, but once ordained priest, marriage is not allowed. This means that since Eastern Catholic Churches follow this practice, there are a number of Eastern Catholic priests who are married.

There have been similar movements where groups of Churches have decided to go 'into Communion with Canterbury', keeping their original liturgy but identifying with the Churches of the Anglican Communion instead of their original Church family. In Kerala, India in the 19th Century, Anglican missionaries came across Syrian Orthodox Christians, who looked to St Thomas as their founder and who still worshipped and read the bible in Syriac (a language from Syria very similar to the Aramaic that Jesus spoke). The missionaries didn't try to convert them to Anglicanism but translated liturgy and Scriptures into Malayalam, the language of Kerala. This led to a 'reformation', and

part of the Syrian Orthodox Church formed the Mar Thoma Church, which is Reformed Syrian Orthodox and 'in Communion with Canterbury'. In parts of Europe, there are also 'Old Catholics' and in the Philippines the Philippine Independent Church; both were originally Roman Catholic, but now 'in Communion with Canterbury'.

## Effect of the Reformation

Being able to read the bible in your own language rather than in Latin and no longer being dependent upon the Church to explain the meaning of every passage, meant that the momentum to question and reconsider faith and church continued. Once splits had begun in the Western Church with the Reformation it was easy for them continue. The churches that had come into being through the Reformation were also closely aligned with the state and they, too, opposed the challenges of new denominations. Many fled from Europe to America to seek spiritual freedom and it was not until 1689 that the British Parliament passed the Toleration Act allowing religious freedom to all Protestants. Although America was seen as a place of religious freedom this was not always the case; some states only tolerated a particular denomination and some of those who fled persecution in Europe oppressed others when they arrived in America. Many Christians sought a split between Church and State.

## Anabaptists

The word means re-baptisers. The baptism of infants implies that the whole community, or the whole nation, is Christian. Anabaptists feel that only those who declare themselves as believers should be baptised, and will not accept infant baptism as valid and those who join them will need to be re-baptised as believers. This movement developed in 16th century Europe and they strongly opposed the making of oaths and involvement in civil government, and were pacifist. Direct descendents of this movement would include the Mennonites and the Amish. A British movement related to the ethos of the Anabaptists is the Quakers or Religious Society of Friends. Quakers do not have structured worship and the worship is directed by the Holy Spirit rather than by a human leader. The name Quaker was given to them as many 'quaked in the Spirit'. Although the Quakers are generally seen as believing strongly in pacifism and campaigning for social rather than spiritual causes, in some parts of the world, such as Mid-West America and East Africa, they are evangelistic and have structured services led by a pastor.

# Baptists

Like the Anabaptists, and for the same reasons, they believe that baptism should only be for believers, not for infants. Much of their theological roots and their evangelistic zeal stem from Calvin and they developed initially in both England and Germany but many fled to America to escape persecution. In America there are several distinct forms of Baptist.

# Congregationalists

All of the Christendom Churches had strong forms of hierarchy; all but Presbyterians having bishops who were responsible for the churches in their diocese. Congregationalists believed that each congregation was responsible for its own governance. Many derived from the Non-Conformist movement at the time of the Puritans and moved to America to seek freedom from state religion. Many Congregationalist churches in Britain united with Presbyterians in 1972 to form the United Reformed Church.

# Moravians

The Moravians actually came into being 100 years before Martin Luther, through followers of Jan Hus, mentioned as a reformer in part 1. Although this movement was allowed some freedom in Moravia, it was driven underground during the counter Reformation and then revived by Zinzendorf in the 18th century and experienced renewal through a strong movement of the Holy Spirit. There was a strong emphasis upon social concern and missionary work.

# Brethren

There are different groups that use the term Brethren. The original started in Germany at the beginning of the 18th century and was in the Anabaptist tradition. Various other groups use brethren in their name. The Plymouth Brethren started in both Plymouth and Dublin in 1820. The only creed is the New Testament; there are no clergy or hierarchy and quite a strong anti-charismatic emphasis. In 1848 a split led to the formation of Open Brethren and Exclusive Brethren.

# Methodism

The founders, John and Charles Wesley, both lived and died as Anglicans. Both had deeply spiritual experiences through encounters with Moravians. John spoke of being 'strangely warmed' on hearing Luther's book on St Paul read aloud and a deep sense of God's salvation. Unlike those who followed Calvin, the Wesleys believed that all could be saved and John's itinerant preaching and Charles' hymns brought many converts. Methodism started as the 'society' within the Church of England that provided a home for these converts. The enthusiasm of this movement proved too much for the Church of England and in 1795 the inevitable split occurred. In America, a further renewal within Methodism in the mid 19th century, emphasising purity and sanctification, rather than just conversion, gave rise to the Methodist Holiness movement.

# African Instituted Churches

Apart from in Egypt and Ethiopia, where Christianity had been since the Ethiopian Official and St Mark, the gospel arrived in Africa with the European missionaries. Sometimes their churches were seen to be too closely tied up with the colonial power and they were too reluctant to inculturate the church and hand over to African leadership. In such cases new churches evolved with African leadership. Often these churches would be Pentecostal in ethos (see Understanding an African Church in Unit 1 for more about the development of such churches in Nigeria).

# Pentecostalism

In Acts, we read of spiritual gifts: speaking in supernatural tongues, interpreting tongues, discernment, healing and prophecy.

This phenomenon appeared to vanish after New Testament times. The Orthodox Churches kept a high view of the Holy Spirit in its doctrines but the Holy Spirit appeared to become a minor player in the Trinity in the Roman Catholic and Protestant Churches. Pentecostalism claims to rediscover the importance of the Holy Spirit for the individual and the Church. It came into being at the beginning of the 20th century gathering momentum through a series of meetings in a church with a mainly African American congregation, within the Methodist Holiness tradition, in Azusa Street in Los Angeles, California in 1906.

There was no deliberate intention to form a new denomination but those who received and practiced these spiritual gifts could not be contained by churches that felt uncomfortable with them and different Pentecostal Churches came into being. The largest is the Assemblies of God. The worldview of many Western Christians had rejected an understanding of a spirit world and preached a Christianity that 'rationalised' good and evil spirits. Pentecostalism has spread rapidly amongst those that include a spirit world within their worldview. Given the growth of Pentecostal churches and rapid expansion it is difficult to try to estimate the number of adherents, but globally it is the fastest growing Christian movement.

Traditionally Pentecostalism has focused upon individual conversion and not concerned itself with politics and has been criticised in many countries of the Global South as supporting the status quo and a force for conservatism. Evidence suggests that this is changing particularly in Latin America and Asia.

# The Charismatic movement

Many who have received the gifts of the spirit have remained within their own denominations and worked to renew these. There have been Charismatic renewal movements within many of the Protestant churches, the Anglican Church and Roman Catholic Church.

**Size of denominations (figures taken from Wikipedia and based upon claims by the denominations themselves and not verified)**

**Catholicism - 1.2 billion, including:**
  Roman Catholic Church (Latin Rite) - 1,129.9 million
  Eastern Catholic Churches (Eastern Rite) - 17.1 million

**Protestantism - 670 million, including:**
  Baptist churches - 105 million
  Methodism - 75 million
  Lutheranism - 87 million

**Reformed churches - 75 million, including:**
  Presbyterianism - 40 million
  Continental Reformed churches - 30 million
  Congregationalism - 5 million

**Anabaptist and Free churches - 5 million, including**
  Mennonites - 1.5 million
  Plymouth Brethren - 1 million
  Moravians - 0.7 million
  Amish - 0.2 million

**Pentecostalism - 130 million, including:**
  Assemblies of God - 60 million

**Non-denominational evangelicalism - 80 million**

**African initiated churches - 40 million, including:**
  Zion Christian Church - 15 million
  Eternal Sacred Order of Cherubim and Seraphim - 10 million
  Kimbanguist Church - 5.5 million

**Eastern Orthodoxy - 210 million, including:**
  Russian Orthodox Church - 125 million
  Romanian Orthodox Church - 18 million
  Serbian Orthodox Church - 15 million
  Church of Greece - 11 million
  Bulgarian Orthodox Church - 10 million
  Georgian Orthodox Church - 5 million
  Other Greek Orthodox Churches - 7.5 million

**Oriental Orthodoxy - 82 million, including:**
  Ethiopian Orthodox Tewahedo Church - 45 million
  Coptic Orthodox Church of Alexandria - 15.5 million
  Syriac Orthodox Church - 10 million
  Armenian Orthodox Church - 8 million

**Anglicanism - 82 million**

**Assyrian Church of the East and Ancient Church of the East - 0.8 million**

# 3 The Ecumenical Movement

If it has been considering belief and doctrine that has split the Church into Churches and denominations, it has been concern for God's mission that has brought it together again. Traditionally there has been much competition between churches to bring new converts into their church and to win over adherents from another denomination, but the last 100 years has seen a new emphasis.

# 1910 Edinburgh Missionary Conference

The major Protestant missionary agencies of North America and Europe sent 1200 delegates to this conference on mission. Although designed as a mission conference, Edinburgh 1910 excited the churches about what could be done by working together and gave birth to the Protestant ecumenical movement. The centenary of this conference was celebrated with Edinburgh 2010; this conference included those excluded from 1910 such as Roman Catholics, Orthodox, Pentecostals and those from the whole Christian world, rather than just North America and Europe.

# World Council of Churches (WCC)

In 1920 the Orthodox Synod of Constantinople suggested a fellowship similar to the 'League of Nations'. The idea of the WCC was agreed before World War 2, but only implemented in 1948. In 2009 there were 349 member churches from 110 countries. On the WCC website http://www.oikoumene.org/ you can find full information about different churches and denominations mentioned in parts 1 and 2. As a result of the Ecumenical movement there is local co-operation between churches with national organisations such as CCTBI (Churches Together in Britain and Ireland) and local towns having a 'Churches Together' group to encourage ecumenical co-operation.

The ethos of being ecumenical is not to diminish everything to 'the lowest common denominator' but, secure in what you believe and where you stand on issues to be able to co-operate with others. In the true spirit of ecumenism, churches are encouraged to consider what they can do together and only do apart what they cannot do together. Generally we are still a long way away from this being put into practice.

# The United Churches of the Indian Subcontinent

As India prepared to become independent Christian leaders in South India reflected upon the church. Many saw denominations as a consequence of European history and not only irrelevant to India, but also a barrier to mission. The Church of South India (CSI) is the result of the union of churches of four different traditions: Anglican, Methodist, Congregational and Presbyterian. It was inaugurated in September 1947 and caused much difficulty for some of the European 'mother' churches. The church has bishops and a common liturgy but the actual practice will often follow that of the denomination that the local church was originally part of.

The Church of North India was founded in 1970 and as well as those who formed the CSI includes some Baptists as well as some other smaller denominations. The Church of Pakistan founded in 1970 includes Anglicans, Methodists, Presbyterians and Lutherans; the Church of Bangladesh comprises Anglicans and Presbyterians.

# The Post Denominational Church of China

The officially approved Three-Self Protestant Church in China is known as the Patriotic Church. After the Communist Revolution, to survive the churches needed to break their links with denominations that founded them and the church that came into being describes itself as 'post denominational'. Some will say that the church is controlled by the State; in some places this is obviously true but in other places it has freedom and has seen considerable growth. (As

China does not allow other expressions of Christianity, there is also a very large 'underground' church in China made up of those who are not comfortable with the official church or where open expressions of church are not tolerated. Because of the underground nature of these churches, it is impossible to estimate numbers.)

## Purity or co-operation?

The spirit of co-operation that has grown in the last century reflects the post modern trait of engaging seriously with other people's narrative. Some churches have been concerned that working with others takes away the cutting edge of their own identity and waters down belief. Recent decades have raised questions about biblical interpretation, the uniqueness of Christ, women in leadership and human sexuality that have made it harder for some Christians to work with others who have different views. In many cases it can be easier to work with those of other denominations who share your views on these issues than those within your own denomination who differ from you.

The Edinburgh 1910 Mission Conference gave birth to the Ecumenical movement. Edinburgh 2010, celebrating the centenary of that Conference by trying to represent the global and denominational diversity of the World Church, reflected a wonderful experience of co-operation and fellowship and showed that differences do not need to be barriers when the focus is on God's mission.

Choose one church/denomination from part 1 that you know little about and that is different from your own tradition and another from part 2:

Using the internet, or other resources, research each of these.

Imagine that you are inviting an adherent of each to meet together, write paragraphs to each of them introducing each of them to the church of the other one.

Write down what questions you think that they may wish to ask of each other and, if possible, research answers to these.

If you were working ecumenically with these two churches/denominations what do you think you might be able to share from your tradition and practice with them?

What do you think you could learn from their traditions and practices?

# SECTION 5: MISSIOLOGY

## AIM

To understand that God is a missionary God and to understand the bible as an account of God's missionary initiative; to explore how the Church in every age has sought to fulfil its part in God's mission purposes and identify the mission challenges of the 21st century.

## CONTENTS

Unit 1 Biblical basis of mission
Unit 2 Holistic mission
Unit 3 Mission: Where to? Where from?
Unit 4 Mission paradigms I: What is a paradigm and the early paradigms
Unit 5 Mission paradigms II: The later paradigms and an emerging paradigm for the
21st century

## Learning Objectives

- Understand how God has instigated mission throughout history and summarize the bible as an account of God's missionary initiative.

- Explain the breadth of mission and give examples of holistic mission and current mission issues.

- Identify where mission needs are greatest and identify where some of the new energy for mission is coming from.

- Understand the factors that have impacted upon how mission has been understood and implemented globally from the time of the first apostles until the present day and understand the current trends that are emerging in mission.

The word 'mission' comes from the same Latin root as the word 'Mass' and means 'to send'. 'The Mass' was 'the sending out' of the congregation back into the world. 'Missiology' is the theology, or study, of mission – of sending.

Who takes the initiative for the good news to be taken to Cornelius and his household? The fact that it is God, through his Holy Spirit, is a reminder that it is God's mission, not ours. The Latin term Mission Dei means sending of God and is a reminder that God is, by nature, a sending God; that the sending is initiated by God. We have been reminded, in considering Acts 11, that we are accountable to the Church, the Body of Christ, for the mission that we are involved in.

Looking at the story of Peter and Cornelius we realise that the way that the Church understands mission changes. Acts 10 begins with a understanding that the Good News is just for the Hebrew people and ends with Peter realising that it is for all people; by Acts 11.18 the believers in Jerusalem, the Church, have accepted this truth. Our understanding of mission is not fixed. Mission is God's initiative and needs to be reinterpreted afresh in different contexts in different generations.

It was impossible to assemble:

- Section 2 on Living, without considering how lives impact upon Christian witness and how we communicate faith

- Section 3, on Faith, without considering both conversion and other faiths

- Section 4, on the Church, without considering the missionary nature of the Church

So Section 5 is written with the assumption that Sections 2, 3 and 4 have already been covered.

# WHAT IS MISSION? – A BIBLICAL BASIS FOR MISSION

## CONTENTS

## SECTION FIVE

# A Biblical basis for mission

To understand mission in the bible, we need to understand the overall story of the bible. In Luke 24:27, when the risen Jesus met the two disciples on the road to Emmaus, he went through *Moses* and *the prophets*. The original readers of these words would recognise the term *Moses* as meaning the first five books of the Old Testament, and *the prophets* as meaning both the history books and the books that we would consider as being the prophets. It is a shame that Luke did not give us more detail about Jesus' overview of the Old Testament. If he had, I could refer you to it. Instead I need to take you through my own lightning tour of the Bible. I want you to imagine that you are reading the Bible for the very first time. I want you to ask yourself the type of questions that you would ask as you begin to read any lengthy book.

## Who is the bible about?

> *Who is the bible about? I imagine that you are beginning to read from Genesis 1 for the first time and write down who the bible is about.*

As I read the first few pages I see that it is about God and about the whole of his creation. I then come across Adam and Eve and then their descendants. As I progress through Genesis chapters 1 to 11, I read about a God who is relating to all of the families of the earth. By the end of chapter 11 I find that the Bible is referring to all of the nations of the earth. I begin to conclude that this book is about God and his creation and about all of the nations of the earth and then I move on to chapter 12 and the emphasis changes. It now appears to be about an individual called Abram, later known as Abraham, and then about his descendants who become a nation known as Israel. Before trying to make sense of what this book is about and what its message and relevance are for me, today, I want to know who it is really about. Is it about God and the nations or God and Abraham or God and Israel?

I don't know what you do, when you have this dilemma of not knowing who a book is about, but I cheat. I look at the back page, or at least the last few pages. By doing this I can find out who the story is really about and I can concentrate on those characters as I read the book. If we jump ahead to Revelation 21 and 22 we see that the Bible ends with God's relationship with his new creation, all the families of the earth; with all of the nations. The Bible starts and ends with the relationship between God and his whole creation, all of the families of the earth, all of the nations. God is concerned about his whole creation and about all of the people on the earth.

Those first eleven chapters of Genesis tell us about God creating the heavens and the earth and about something going wrong between God and his creation. It is at that point that this wonderful, loving God takes the initiative and sends Abraham to be a blessing to the nations (Gen 12. 1 – 3). Abraham is given the task of putting things right again between God and his whole creation. As we read through the Old Testament, looking for how the stories relate to this bigger theme of God and his whole creation, we see that Abraham eventually fathers Isaac and, as the chapters and the centuries go by, his descendants become the nation of Israel.

More centuries and chapters pass and Israel becomes established in Palestine. What a choice of location! God has not only called Israel to be a blessing to the nations but strategically placed them where the surrounding nations cannot help but trip over them or bump into them. Situated at one end of the Fertile Crescent, with the sea to one side and deserts in other directions, many of the known trade routes came right through the land. Through the experiences of the Exodus and the wilderness God tries to shape Israel into being a model nation. Israel is called to be an example and a witness to the nations. In this way they should become a blessing to the nations, bringing the nations back to God. A thousand years before Christ, Israel reaches its pinnacle during the reigns of King David and King Solomon. The surrounding nations take notice of Israel and its monotheistic faith. After that, with a few reversals, it is downhill all the way. There is the split into two different, and often rival, kingdoms of Israel and Judah.

As I read further, through 2 Kings and 2 Chronicles, I begin to lose sight of Israel's role as a blessing to the nations. Israel, the northern kingdom is attacked by Assyria and many of its people taken into exile. The occupiers move other peoples onto the land instead. Those who are left intermarry and lose their identity as a Hebrew nation. Their descendants become known as the Samaritans. The southern kingdom of Judah is also defeated by Assyria, but not exiled. As Assyria loses its power it loses its hold over Judah. Judah has learnt some lessons from the experiences of Israel but, a hundred years later, these lessons have faded and the behaviour of the nation is just as bad as ever. By now Babylon is the powerful nation and Judah succumbs to her power. Most of the people are taken into exile in Babylon and the temple and most of Jerusalem is destroyed.

Israel is elect. It has been chosen for a task, for responsibility. Instead, Israel falls into the trap that exists for all those who are elect. Israel thinks that it has been chosen

for privilege and protection instead of responsibility. Through much of the Old Testament there is an emphasis upon Israel keeping itself separate from the nations so that it should not be contaminated by them. During the period of exile in Babylon the people begin to reflect on the nature of this election. A deeper understanding develops, of Israel having a special purpose rather than special privileges. Isaiah sees Israel as a suffering servant, called to suffer on behalf of the nations in order to be a blessing to the nations. Isaiah's thinking is summed up in the beautiful language of the four servant songs: Isaiah: 42.1 -- 9; 49:1 -- 6; 50:4 -- 9 and 52:13—53:12.

As Isaiah helps the exiled people to understand their calling, of being a blessing to the nations, he also sees how God will act to bring about their liberation. Babylon is on the wane and Persia is on the ascent. The Persian ruler King Cyrus releases the exiles and encourages them to return and also to rebuild their temple. Some return and the Temple is eventually restored but the emphasis returns of trying to remain pure and separate from the nations.

The book of Jonah can be read at different levels, one of its messages being the imagery of Jonah, like Israel being the reluctant missionary who runs away rather than taking God's message to another nation. The writer tells us that God wants the other nations to repent and turn to him. He also shows that, with God's help, the task is not difficult. A reluctant Jonah witnesses successfully not only to Ninevah, but also to sailors on the boat that he takes flight upon.

The return to Judah and the rebuilding of the Temple in Jerusalem are followed by invasion by the Greeks. Whilst the Babylonians had allowed freedom of worship and Cyrus had encouraged the rebuilding of the Temple, the Greeks tried to force their culture and religion upon those whom they conquered.

By the time that Jesus is born, Greek rule (which is the background to the two books of Maccabees - these two books are in what is known as the Apocrypha; they were in the Greek version of Old Testament Scriptures, but not the Hebrew version and are not included within most

Protestant versions of the bible) had given way to Roman rule and the golden age of King David is a distant memory from a thousand years before. The emphasis is upon survival and, as for many who struggle to survive, there are deep differences in understanding how this should happen. Some compromise or collaborate with the ruling power and others keep their distance. Some are looking forward to the Day of the Lord, as predicted in the book of Joel. This would be a time when God's reign would be a direct reign upon earth. Many expected that God would send a Messiah, probably a military leader, to throw out the Romans. Some went about their everyday lives as they waited and others retreated to form uncontaminated communities in the desert. The idea of being a blessing to the nations has been lost completely.

As we move into the New Testament the change is as sudden as it was when we moved from Chapter 11 to chapter 12 of Genesis. Then we moved from the nations to an individual and this time we move from the story of one nation to a new individual, Jesus. The gospels are an account of his life, ministry and death, resurrection and post resurrection appearances. As we read through Matthew, we experience déjà vu. We read about the flight into Egypt and, later, a baptism in the Jordan seems to replace a crossing of the Red Sea as a prelude to a period in the wilderness. It comes as no surprise, as we read the events of the passion, that those four servant songs, in Isaiah, seem to be describing Jesus.

John structures his gospel differently. Jesus becomes the fulfilment of the different Jewish feasts. The Old Testament is rich with imagery and that imagery is echoed in the gospels. Particularly in John's gospel we see Jesus as the bread of life, as the water of life, as the vine, as the shepherd.

The relevance of Jesus to the nations can, at a first glance, seem as hidden as this blessing was in the Old Testament. Some of his words, such as those given to a Canaanite woman in Matthew 15. 24 – 26, seem to deny this role, but the representatives of the nations are there at two key events. In Matthew 2.1 – 12, we read of wise men, arriving from the east, to go and pay homage to the newly born

Jesus. In John 12.20 – 26 the arrival of some Greeks, who wish to speak to Jesus, is the sign to Jesus that the events of his Passion are about to begin.

One of the promises that God had made to Abraham was about the Land. A Messianic expectation was God would return the Land, and political and military control of the Land, to Israel. Jesus does not refer once to the Land during his ministry. Instead, the theme that he develops is the Kingdom of God. The final discussion between Jesus and his disciples, according to Acts 1. 6 – 8, is immediately prior to his ascension. They ask him about the restoration of the kingdom to Israel. In response to this question about the Land, Jesus talks once again about a broader understanding of the Kingdom - a kingdom that is for all of the nations. All of the gospels end with Jesus commissioning his disciples to go and witness to the nations.

God's plan for redeeming the nations starts off concentrated in one person, in Abraham. That calling is passed on to Abraham's descendants and the whole nation of Israel then takes on this calling to be a blessing to the nations. After the reign of King Solomon, the nation splits into two kingdoms, then Israel is destroyed and the focus remains with Judah. Judah is taken into exile and only some of them eventually return to the land, the remnant referred to in 2 Kings 19. 30 and 31. God's purpose is focused on an ever decreasing number of people until we find it centred entirely on one person, Jesus. Jesus is the one who has taken on the mantle of Israel and who will bring a blessing to the nations. He is the one who fulfils the prophecies, made by Isaiah, about a suffering servant who suffers on behalf of the nations.

But the Bible does not end with the gospels. As we move into Acts we find that the story is no longer about Jesus, but about his followers. If parts of the gospels seem to echo themes from parts of the Old Testament, then the Acts of the Apostles has parallels with the book of Joshua. As Joshua consolidated the land, so the early Christians consolidate their numbers. It looks at first as if the gospel of Jesus will only be shared with the Jewish people and the rest of the nations will, again, be forgotten.

At last, however, the gospel is taken to the nations. The Acts of the Apostles tells particularly of Paul and Barnabas within this task. According to tradition, Mark took the gospel south to Egypt and Thomas took it East, possibly as far as India. Acts ends with Paul having arrived in Rome. Although he is in prison he is at the centre of the economic and political power that controls the known world. The rest of the New Testament consists of the letters sent by some of the leaders of the early Church. These address the issues faced as the Church grew and developed and expanded into the nations and engaged with issues found within both Jewish and Gentile cultures.

Jesus has passed on the task of being a blessing to the nations to the Church. We have not yet reached the New Creation described in Revelations 21 and 22. The biblical story is not in the past, we are still living out the biblical story; we are part of the story of the followers of Jesus, the Church, being a blessing to the nations.

# What is mission?

> *What is mission? Write down your understanding of the word - we will return to your answers later*

So we, the followers of Jesus - the Church, are called to be a blessing to the nations. Being a blessing sounds very positive and affirming, but what does it really mean? What do we need to do to be part of that blessing? The answer lies in the task of putting right what has gone wrong in the first eleven chapters of Genesis. The biblical shorthand for the thing, or things, that have gone wrong is the word Sin. I always feel that Sin is one of those words that we are meant to understand but which no one explains properly.

> *Read: Genesis 3 about Adam and Eve; Genesis 4. 1 - 16 about Cain and Abel; Genesis 11. 1 - 9 about the Tower of Babel.*
>
> *What relationships are being broken in each narrative? Which one breaks first each time?*

As we look at the stories of Adam and Eve, Cain and Abel and the tower of Babel, in the first eleven chapters of Genesis, we see that they all have the same starting point. There is a breakdown in the relationship between God and the individual person. This breakdown has various causes: disobedience and thinking that we know better than God (Adam and Eve); half-hearted offering to God (Cain and Abel); pride of wanting to be like God (tower of Babel).

This breakdown, in turn, is always followed by the breakdown in relationship between different people. As soon as God challenges Adam, he responds by blaming Eve for giving him the fruit. He also goes on to blame God for creating Eve in the first place! By blaming Eve, rather than himself, Adam falls out with Eve. Eve, meanwhile, responds by blaming the serpent. We see in the fourth chapter of Genesis that Cain is envious of Abel and this leads to the ultimate breakdown of human relationships, when Cain murders his brother. In the Babel story, the breakdown of relationship with God leads to the breakdown of communication. The lack of communication leads on to social separation and to the different language groups being scattered and further separated from each other.

We also see the breakdown of our relationships with ourselves. As Adam and Eve gain knowledge they no longer feel at peace with themselves, as they have been created by God, and feel the need for clothes. They break their relationship with God but cannot cope with the guilty feelings that this gives them. Cain's poor relationship with God makes him envious of Abel and after the murder of Abel, Cain cannot face up to the consequences of his own actions. Blaming others and blaming God leads ultimately, to further separation from other humans and also from God. The breakdown of relationships, that we call Sin, is like a cancerous growth, eating away at all that it touches.

Finally this breakdown in relationships leads to a breakdown in the relationship between God, humans and creation itself. Not only does Eve fall out with the serpent, and there is an enmity between her offspring and the serpent's offspring, but from this point onwards the earth produces thorns and thistles and will need excessive toil. There will be "natural" disasters and other disasters, like the consequences of global warming that are caused by humanity's greed and sinfulness. No longer does creation co-operate with humanity. Creation itself rebels and becomes fallen.

# Four aspects of mission

While the consequences of these broken relationships are felt in all the families of the earth, God's loving response is to keep taking initiatives to bring restoration. And we as the Church are caught up in this task which includes four different elements: -

**Personal** - the theme running through the whole of the Bible is God's love for the people that he has created; his constant willingness to offer us new opportunities for restored relationship with him. The prophet Hosea, through his own experiences of having his love rejected, is able to gain a glimpse into the heart of God and begin to understand the depths of this love and forgiveness. Hosea 11.1 – 3, tells of God's compassion despite Israel's ingratitude: 'When Israel was a child, I loved him, and out of Egypt I called my son. The more I called them, the more they went from me; they kept sacrificing to Ba'als, and offering incense to idols. Yet it was I who taught Ephraim to walk, I took them in my arms; but they did not know that I healed them.'

The events of the Jesus' death and resurrection show us the price that God is prepared to pay, and how much he is willing to suffer, in order to reconcile us to him.

As part of being a blessing to the nations, we need to be involved in restoring the relationship between God and individual people. We are the bridges between God and his people that allow the rebuilding of relationship. We need to point to what Jesus did upon the cross and how it is Jesus, the new Adam, who by dying upon a tree undoes the damage that the old Adam caused through his disobedience over a tree in the Garden of Eden. We must proclaim the incarnate, crucified and resurrected Christ as our redeemer, saving each of us individually. The task is not just to proclaim but, as Jesus indicates within the Great Commission in Matthew 28. 18 – 20, make disciples, baptise and teach everything he has commanded us.

**Social and political** - we also need to be involved in restoring the broken relationships between people, communities and nations. The early chapters of Genesis end with the breakdown in communication at Babel and the scattering of the peoples. The Holy Spirit heralds the beginning of the Church's mission at Pentecost when we read, in the second chapter of Acts, of the apostles finding themselves understood in different languages. In Matthew 19.19, Jesus says that we must love our neighbours as ourselves. This means that we must address all the evils and injustices that divide people and separate them from each other. We can never be fully in communion with God if we do not try to tackle the issues that separate us from our brothers and sisters, and our brothers and sisters from each other.

**Healing** – our task includes spiritual, physical and psychological healing. Some Christians will fulfil a healing ministry through medical service as doctors, nurses or paramedics. A minority of Christians have a spiritual physical healing ministry. But healing is more than just responding to physical symptoms. If people do not love themselves, then they cannot love their neighbours. The nature of our healing ministry will probably be different from that of Jesus but we are still called to help within the healing process as people discover that God loves them and accepts them. If people cannot accept and love themselves then they will, like Adam, project their guilt and dis-ease upon others and upon God.

**Environmental** – we also need to work to restore the relationship between God, humanity and creation. In Eden, human beings were given stewardship over the animal kingdom and the natural world. Stewardship does not mean exploitation, nor does it mean meeting the wants of one generation at the expense of the needs of future generations. Politicians are only just beginning to come to terms with the fact that excessive use of fossil fuels, in recent decades, has damaged the ozone layer at the poles and caused 'global warming' causing severe changes to climatic conditions. The rain forests of South America, and Central Africa, moderate the climates of those continents. As they are exploited the resultant deforestation, too, has a disastrous impact upon climate. Elsewhere the exploitation of the earth's resources has resulted in pollution and poisoning of the environment. Generally

with these trends, it is the wealthy who are taking advantage of the planet's resources and the poor who suffer most as a result of the climatic changes. Whilst it is hard to influence the multinational companies, and governments, who are main offenders, we can all consider the impact of our own lifestyle.

All four of these elements have been seen as part of our task but, sadly, different groups have often been polarised in their understanding, and emphasised one aspect to the exclusion of others. This trait is, of course, part of the breakdown of relationships that we see in the Fall; a breakdown of communication.

The calling, given to the Church, is a holistic ministry. It will include all four of these different elements. It is important to remember that, in each of the Genesis stories that we have considered, the first relationship to fracture is that between God and the individual. This implies that our priority must always be the restoration of this relationship because if it is not restored, then whatever else is achieved will probably break down again before too long. It is only when the relationship between people and God is restored that they can truly be in harmony with others, themselves and creation.

*How does this understanding compare with your own understanding of mission?*

*By considering the bible as made up of five distinct sections: Genesis 1 - 11; the rest of the Old Testament; the Gospels; the rest of the New Testament until Revelation 20; Revelation 21 & 22, try to write, in your own words a five paragraph summary of the bible.*

# HOLISTIC MISSION

The previous unit suggested a biblical basis of mission; this unit explores what such an understanding might mean for one part of the world church at the present time. The term holistic mission reminds us that there isn't just one facet to mission; sometimes the term integrated mission is used instead. When we considered conversion, in the section on Faith, we noted that conversion often occurs because people are challenged by the values and lifestyle of the Christian community. Proclamation without service is unlikely to be very successful and service without proclamation won't bring people into the Kingdom; mission needs to be holistic.

Most of what follows reflects what is going on within the Anglican Church; this is not because this Anglican understanding is considered better than any other understanding, but is the context that the author is familiar with and the issues explored would be typical of those that are important for many different churches.

## CONTENTS

The Five Marks of Mission
A Survey of Mission and Evangelism
Ten key mission contexts:
- Other Faiths
- Migrants, refugees and displaced people
- HIV and AIDS
- Response to emergencies
- Young people
- Reconciliation
- Response to decline
- Growth
- Economic viability
- Christian values

Millennium Development Goals (MDG's)
Challenges and Lessons
The Fifth Mark of Mission

# SECTION FIVE

# The Five Marks of Mission

The different autonomous, but interdependent, churches around the world that make up the Anglican Communion have explored together what their common mission is. This was first defined in 1984 with four Marks of Mission and the fifth mark was added in 1990; the five marks are:

- To proclaim the Good News of the Kingdom

- To teach, baptise and nurture new believers

- To respond to human need by loving service

- To seek to transform unjust structures of society

- To strive to safeguard the integrity of creation and sustain and renew the life of the earth

**Brothers' grim tale has happy ending**

Two young brothers have been saved from a rubbish life – thanks to a Christian project helping homeless youth in Brazil. Rodrigo and Gabriel no longer endure abuse or pick through a garbage dump for food – after prompt action by staff from My Father's House in Olinda. Gabriel was four when he was found abandoned in the dump. 'He had bite marks and cigarette burns all over his body from his mother abusing him,' said Andy Roberts who works at My Father's House with his wife Rose.

'When we went to her to see if we could help, she grabbed Gabriel and threw him against the wall, shouting, "He's my son and I can do what I want with him!" So we took him to My Father's House.' At first, Gabriel recoiled from any human contact. He didn't know how to eat properly or control his bladder. But four years later, the transformation is remarkable. 'It's amazing to see how God has changed him,' said Andy. 'He's one of the happiest boys and he loves school.'

Gabriel's older brother Rodrigo also bears scars from their mother's abuse. 'He was 12 and about to join a drug gang when we first met him,' Andy recalled. Rodrigo's first year at the safe house was difficult, but he overcame his violent past. Now 16, Rodrigo is a committed Christian and a hard worker. 'He's doing a computer course now and dreams of going to England one day as a missionary,' said Andy. The boys' mother is receiving help for psychological problems

This article first appeared on the CMS/SAMS website and is used with permission

# A Survey of Mission and Evangelism

In 2008, the Anglican Communion published the results of a survey about mission and evangelism that had taken place amongst the 38 Provinces that make up the worldwide Anglican Communion. The full text of this can be found at http://www.anglicancommunion.org/ministry/mission/resources/documents/holistic_mission.pdf

This survey identified ten key mission contexts:

## • Other Faiths

A common theme was that of mission within an Islamic context, 'Christianity is perceived as a Western religion creating negative feelings among those who do not like the intrusion of Western values'; some went so far as to say that in their Muslim context 'Evangelism in this part of the world is becoming not just difficult but fatal.' In this context holistic mission was seen as vital, 'people are taking the gospel and the church seriously when the church is interested in their holistic wellbeing – spiritually, socially and physically.' 'People need not to just hear words but see Jesus 'going around doing good.' Recognising that many converts would be disowned by their families, the church was also involved in setting up rehabilitation and vocational centres for new converts as well as considering their pastoral and spiritual needs.

## • Migrants, refugees and displaced people

Recent decades have seen huge movements of people and the terms immigrants, migrants, asylum seekers, displaced people and returnees have all been used. Reasons for being displaced and the contexts and situations vary, but often there are similar problems of being uprooted, marginalised and living with uncertainty and anxiety about the future. There can be the need for counselling, support and joint advocacy against war and abuse of human dignity. Often there has been the need for the receiving church to deal with difference and tackle

Although Britain is generally seeing a decline in church going, many urban areas are seeing real growth. Anecdotal evidence suggests that not only have church numbers been boosted by Christians coming from the Caribbean, Africa and elsewhere, but these resulting multi-cultural churches have offered a form of church that has appealed to the indigenous community encouraging further growth. Although many Christian migrants have not integrated into the existing churches and have established their own Diaspora churches, many of these are becoming active in reaching out in mission to the indigenous community.

prejudice and express a genuine welcome. Although often those moving have been non Christians moving amongst Christians and having opportunities to be exposed to the gospel, those moving might well be Christians bringing a new understanding of faith and mission into the host community and being involved as a Diaspora in mission to the receiving community and bringing new life into receiving churches.

## • HIV and AIDS

A common theme is to respect the dignity of all people by: securing the human rights of those infected by HIV and AIDS, and giving unconditional support; improving the health and prolonging the lives of infected people; accompanying the dying, those who mourn and those who live on; celebrating life; nurturing community, and advocating for justice. Programmatical responses include: awareness-raising, abstinence workshops; dealing with stigma, shame and denial; testing, treatment and counselling services; care, support and empowerment; vocational training and income generation projects; hope and transformation. HIV and AIDS also result in an increase in the number of widows and orphans and the importance of responding to their needs.

## • Response to emergencies

Situations such as tsunamis, earthquakes and hurricanes have provided opportunities for the church to show the love of Jesus in their response to those of all faiths, and none, through helping to rebuild people's lives and infrastructure and through trauma counselling and helping people to come to terms with loss. Flooding and drought has led the church to draw attention to the issue of global warming and the Fifth Mark of Mission.

> When an earthquake caused devastation in the North West Frontier of Pakistan, the local Christian community responded to the physical needs of one particular village. In doing so it overcame the ever growing hostility and hatred that was being shown to the Christian community and has shown that it is possible to cross dividing barriers when the church reaches out with love to service the afflicted and suffering.

## • Young people

Many parts of the world have seen huge changes in the age distribution of their population with far more young people than before. Young people are both those reached out to and also as those doing mission. Generally in the West they are being seen as an unchurched generation: 'Young people are uninterested in the church ... yet interested in spirituality and life-encouraging values'. Generally the Church is investing much time and money into initiatives with children and young people. There are many examples of young people being encouraged to take on responsibility within church: leading services and being appointed to church positions, choir groups etc, as well as gaining short experiences of mission.

## • Reconciliation

There are examples of the need to deal, first, with the problems that the Church is part of before being able to reach out to others; a need to address the wrongs in the way that an incoming group treated the indigenous people in the past or the poverty amongst indigenous people, and apologies for the part played, in the past, in discriminatory government policies.

There are also reconciliation initiatives being taken by Christians working with other communities in war and post-war contexts and mention of the specific role of young people, who don't carry the same 'baggage' in reconciliation initiatives.

## • Response to decline

The assumption of the Christendom countries was that everyone was a Christian leading to an emphasis upon the wellbeing of the population, rather than a need for active evangelism. This assumption was challenged by the Churches of the Global South, leading to a 'Decade of Evangelism' during the nineteen-nineties. Many Churches in 'The West' are questioning whether the existing church structures are effective for the kind of evangelism needed and express the need for new mission strategies. For any evangelism to be effective there is the need to change

> The British colonial enterprise to places like New Zealand, Australia and Canada led to terrible treatment of the indigenous people and attempts to marginalise their culture. Often the church was part of this policy and has needed to repent of its behaviour. In Canada, where Church Schools were used to try to get indigenous people to reject their culture, repentance has led to reconciliation and the Church realising how much it has to learn from the indigenous culture. Not only has spirituality and liturgy been enriched but also the Christian understanding of the environment has been enriched by the insights of people who are used to living in harmony with God's creation.

the mindset of existing congregations and to realise the importance of new initiatives and to try to both attract people back to existing forms of church and also to create new forms of church.

'Fresh Expressions' initiatives, as the name suggests, are not about bringing people into traditional forms of church, but creating different expressions of a worshipping Christian community that are appropriate for the cultural context. They are aimed at attracting both those who are unchurched and those who have previously rejected traditional forms of church. It is possible for 'Fresh Expressions' and traditional forms of church to co-exist and talk of a 'mixed economy' of fresh and traditional expressions of church. Process Evangelism courses, such as Alpha, have proved to be a helpful tool.

## • Growth

The Alpha course is now used in many parts of the world to reach the unchurched and new forms of church exist such as 'church on the streets' and other such urban initiatives. Elsewhere growth comes from the founding of new dioceses. Nigeria has

There has been increased research to help identify the need for different forms of church. In *Gone but not Forgotten,* Philip Richter and Leslie Francis (DLT 1998), there is an analysis of English society that shows: 10% regular worshippers; 10% occasional worshippers; 20% de-churched, but open to church; 20% de-churched, but closed to church; 40% unchurched. Obviously, different strategies are needed to try to reach these different groups. The 40% who are unchurched would be likely to find most churches a totally alien experience. Many of the 20% who are de-churched but open, might be brought back by personal invitation and by tackling some of the reasons why they left. Many of the 20% who are de-churched but closed, will have been damaged by previous experiences of Church.

In response there have been different and diverse approaches. The Church of England initiative of Back to Church Sunday, with personal invitations and follow up of those who have left, has certainly shown considerable success with the de-churched but open sector. Those who have been damaged by church are less likely to enter a church building but might try something like café church, or a cell group within a house. Those who are un-churched might be attracted to something that has a more contemporary approach using music, colour, media, film, drama or discussion rather than the traditional form and language of most church services.

The term Emerging Church has been used during the last decade referring to 'that which is coming to the surface'. The Church of England speaks of a mixed economy of Fresh Expressions of church as well as traditional expressions of church. But aiming services at specific groups is not just an issue in the north. All Saints Anglican Cathedral in Nairobi, Kenya offers 17 different services on a Sunday to make sure that it caters for different age groups and language groups.

Stories from around the Anglican Communion can be found in the *Evangelism and Church Growth Newsletter* http://www.anglicancommunion.org/ministry/mission/ecgi/newsletters/index.cfm

created specifically missionary dioceses, in the rural unreached areas where the gospel had not yet taken root; these are supported for their first three years by individuals or church sponsors. There is also non-geographic mission in Nigeria to the 10 million nomadic Fulani who have not yet been reached by the gospel.

Stories of growth speak of 'church planting', 'incarnational evangelism', 'a ministry of presence', 'evangelistic crusades' and through 'healing and deliverance ministries' suggesting a variety of different approaches. The key role of women in evangelism is often noted and of using the enthusiasm of youth. Throughout, there is a strong emphasis upon holistic mission. There is the underlying assumption that the motivation for evangelism is the 'Great Commission' or, pragmatically in the previous section, as a response to decline. There is also a reference to a shift away from fear of 'hell and condemnation' to a desire to communicate the different facets of the fullness, joy and hope of the gospel.

## • Economic viability

There are examples of initiatives to attempt to tackle the local problems of poverty, churches working towards self-reliance, through stewardship and income generation, and also income generation to fund mission. Social and community transformation is taking place through schools, vocational training small businesses and other income generating programmes and economic empowerment and the importance of micro-finance schemes.

In some parts of the world Christians have introduced micro-finance schemes to help boost economic viability. The Five Talents website gives information about some such initiatives http://www.fivetalents.org.uk/

The traditionally wealthy provinces of the West, facing decline of numbers, are seeing income reduced and financial challenges and all are realising the importance of stewardship and of become self-sustaining.

## • Christian values

Mission and evangelism includes standing up for Christian values; this includes challenging social and moral decay as well as work tackling drug abuse, family breakdown, loss of respect to elders and corruption. Mention was made of work amongst street children who are caught up with prostitution and drugs. Mothers' Union initiatives have seen men value their women more, leading to an increase in Christian weddings and God-fearing families. Consultations have been run on violence and the family.

There are challenges for Western agencies finding that balancing a faith-based charter with a host of employment and contractual obligations is rarely straightforward. There is also 'the challenge of secularism, conservatism and cowardice of our elected political leaders, the challenge of enormous far-reaching corporate agendas in public policy'. The tension of clarifying what are specifically Christian values within rapidly changing cultures, and how mission initiatives should be modified in a changing world, is an issue facing all countries

**Millennium Development Goals (MDG's)**

The eight Millennium Development Goals form a blueprint agreed to by all the world's countries and all the world's leading development institutions. They have galvanized unprecedented efforts to meet the needs of the world's poorest people. The Church has also seen a response to the MDG's as part of its mission.

The MDG's are:

1   Eradicate extreme poverty and hunger

ii   Achieve universal primary education

iii   Promote gender equality and empower women

iv   Reduce child mortality

v   Improve maternal health

vi   Combat HIV and AIDS, malaria and other diseases

vii   Ensure environmental sustainability

viii Develop a global partnership for development.

---

*What surprised you about the ten key mission contexts mentioned above?*

*Which of these mission contexts are ones that your church responds to?*

*Which are ones that your church could be responding to?*

*What could your church learn from the examples mentioned above?*

# Challenges and Lessons

The survey identified that apart from the financial challenges, the main challenges include pluralism, living with different worldviews, and the need to adapt to rapidly changing worldviews. Rapidly changing worldviews provide challenges in identifying and implementing vision and also in inspiring and motivating people to put the new vision into practice.

The biggest lesson that those responding to the survey commented upon was the importance of working with others. This might be other denominations or with Anglicans from other parts of the world, who had different insights and experiences, or with Non Government Organisations (NGO's) or governments. But it is in responding to new forms of mission appropriate to different contexts that people are finding that they learn more about God; 'by partnering God in God's mission, new insights are being gained; God is alive and at work in unexpected ways inside and outside the church.'

# The Fifth Mark of Mission

Many Christians assume that the fifth mark of mission ('To strive to safeguard the integrity of creation and sustain and renew the earth') is listed as the last of the five marks either because it is the least important, or because it is an afterthought added so as to be relevant to our current ecological crisis. Nothing could be further from the truth. In many ways the fifth mark of mission is both the starting point and the ultimate goal for all biblical mission.

Such an assertion needs justifying. Firstly, 'creation care' is quite literally the starting point for mission in that God's very first words to human beings in Genesis 1.26-28 are about reflecting God's image in ruling over the earth and its creatures. This first 'Great Commission' that God gives is effectively a job description for what it means to be truly human. Our primary mission as the human species is to image God's character in seeking the flourishing of all that God declared 'very good'. As spelt out in Genesis 2.15 it is to 'till and keep' or 'serve and preserve' the garden of creation. The tragedy of humanity's rebellion against God and the consequent dislocation of the delicate ecology of relationships throughout creation do nothing to take away this primal mission. In fact, in the light of Christ's saving work as the second Adam, who restores humanity into right relationship with God, fellow humans and all creation, the bible is clear that redeemed humanity is to take up its original mission again. In Romans 8:19 we read that the whole created order is waiting 'in eager expectation' for God's children to be revealed – for the Church to take up its mission of wise and gentle stewardship of God's earth.

Secondly, human mission is always within the context of the Mission Dei - God's mission. At the cosmic level the ultimate goal of God's mission is 'to bring all things in heaven and on earth together under one head, even Christ' (Ephesians 1.10). Jesus is the purpose and destiny of the whole created order – all things are made 'for him', hold together 'in him', and are redeemed through his death on the cross (Colossians 1.16-20). Whilst theologically orthodox Christians would agree with this, few seem to have reflected adequately on its enormous missiological implications. As Dr Jane Williams puts it 'the whole glorious broken world that God loves is our project too' (transcribed from talk at 'The Holy Spirit and the World Today' conference at Holy Trinity Brompton, 21st May 2010) and as Bishop N T Wright states, 'God intends his wise, creative, loving presence and power to be reflected, 'imaged' if you like, into his world through his human creatures. He has enlisted us to act as his stewards in the project of creation.' (Tom Wright, *Surprised by Hope*, SPCK, 2008, p.218)

This reframing of mission does not simply include 'creation care' as one amongst five Marks of Mission but rather gives coherence to all the other marks too. They are not a disparate list of objectives, but God's one over-arching reintegrating mission in his world in Christ and by the Spirit, characterised by a vision of the earthing of God's Kingdom – in redeemed individuals, transformed societies and a restored creation. Your kingdom come on earth as in heaven.

**Dave Bookless**
**Director for Theology, Churches &**
**Sustainable Communities**
**A Rocha UK**

(For a fuller development of the themes contained here see also, Dave Bookless 'The Fifth mark of Mission - Ecological Concern from a Praxis Perspective' in *Mission in the Twenty-first Century*, eds. Prof. A Walls & Dr C Ross, Darton Longman & Todd, London, 2008)

# Where to? Where from?

Mark Oxbrow Faith2Share Network

## SECTION FIVE

'The wonderful thing about being here in Kampala', writes a missionary from Lincolnshire, 'is the vibrancy of the worship, the great Bible studies we have and the way you get into conversations about Jesus at the bus stop and in the market.' After two years of training and raising thousands of pounds from her family, friends and the tiny village church she attended, this missionary nurse had left one of the least evangelized corners of Europe to work in a Christian hospital in a country where more that 85% of the population attend church. No one could deny the good work she is doing as an orthopaedic nurse in that hospital, but can we really call her a missionary? What if she had left her hospital job in Lincolnshire and spent her days sharing the gospel with the young people in her home village and with the immigrant workers from Eastern Europe working in the fields and the potato factory less than a mile from her house – would she be a missionary then? Would those generous family and church members who are supporting her in Uganda have been just as generous?

If you go into your garden and see that the cabbage seedlings are dried up and withering you do well to give them some water. But what do you do the next day, and the next, and the next? Do you continue watering the cabbage and neglect the rest of the garden? No, day by day, you see new needs; new plants that need water, weeds that need pulling out, and trees that need pruning. It's the same in God's world – mission moves on, changing day by day.

*Discuss*

*Where do you need to be to be called a 'missionary'?*

*Why is the Christian engineer who goes to Nigeria called a 'missionary' and the Nigerian nurse who comes to work in a Birmingham hospital called a 'migrant worker'?*

*What makes a person on the move a 'missionary'?*

Here is one example of a group that are often ignored

## Cross-Cultural Mission at Home: Deaf People in London by David Flynn

Sometimes local churches and members have to hold up their hand and admit 'we have failed specific people groups in the mission God gave us.' Whether that mission is seen primarily as the proclamation of the good news of God's forgiveness for individuals in Christ, or as promoting justice in wider society or a mixture of these, one people group on our doorsteps often overlooked is the UK Deaf community, at the core of which includes around 60,000 or so profoundly Deaf people who use British Sign Language as their preferred method of communication. When we add friends and family member of this core and those who have learned BSL at various levels up to the interpreter stage then this figure trebles or perhaps quadruples.

There are some notable exceptions of course but by and large churches and members unconsciously follows the medical model of dis-ability used by the wider society which requires that in any interaction the Deaf adapt to hearing methods of communication and follow the cultural norms of hearing people.          However, if the alternative social or cultural model of different-ability is accepted and the Deaf community is recognised as a linguistic and cultural minority then it becomes clear that a cross-cultural mission approach to reach these people is legitimated. Practically, the same amount, if not more, of language preparation and cultural orientation is required as for any other overseas mission.

Of course the statistics show that in an average village of 6000 people we are likely to have only half a dozen Deaf and therefore hard-pressed churches with limited resources find it difficult to justify devoting precious time and energy to such numbers but didn't Jesus make a point of saying leave the ninety-nine who are safe and concentrate on the vulnerable and lost – even if it is only one? Obviously though there needs to be a creative and flexible mission structure to accommodate this community. In the London area where granted there is a much larger target community one such initiative is the recently started, peripatetic Tabernacle Mission.

Meeting bi-monthly at various venues in and around the London M-25 such as Rickmansworth, Billericay and Epsom with a varied program of worship, teaching, intercessory groups and outreach this ministry provides an 'indigenous' response to the Deaf community's needs. Services and seminars are sign-language, usually but not exclusively by Deaf people, led but with voice over provided for those who are unable to sufficiently follow BSL.

Another missionary challenge to face is how can this group develop its own leadership? Where are the Bible and theological training courses to equip Deaf Christians as pastors, leaders and missionaries? Again with one or two notable exceptions the medical model's influence is pervasive and Deaf people are expected to adapt and sign up for hearing courses, listening to everything from an alien perspective rather than having the curriculum designed by and for them and having teaching delivered in BSL and being able to hand in a filmed rather than written response for exams and essays.

One attempt to fill this training gap is The Deaf Discipleship course run jointly by Christian Deaf Link and the LST (London School of Theology) Open Learning Department. Recently groups of Deaf people have been trained directly in BSL for short-term overseas mission work but more initiatives are required. As a cross-cultural mission perspective is brought to bear on such issues the inadequacy of the current provision for Deaf people is highlighted. Ultimately of course Deaf Christians are the best people to reach out to their own community but they cannot do it alone - neither should they - they are an essential part of the Body of Christ.

**Bibliography: Literature on Contemporary Deaf Theology**

*Deaf Perspectives: Challenging Dominant Christian Thought*, Conference Papers: Open Learning Department, London School of Theology and Christian Deaf Link, 23rd Nov. 2003.

Hitchin, Roger: *The Church and Deaf People*, Carlisle: Paternoster, 2004.

Lewis, Hannah: *Deaf Liberation Theology*, Aldershot, Ashgate, 2007.

Linderman, Albert, 'Deaf Society: Issues of Training and Contextualization,' *Missiology*, XXVII, 3, (Jul. 1999), 363-375.

McCloughry, Roy and Morris, Wayne, *Making a World of Difference: Christian Reflections on Disability*, London: SPCK, 2002.

Morris, Wayne, *Theology Without Words*, Aldershot, Ashgate, 2008.

In the late eighteenth and early nineteenth centuries European explorers in Africa correctly identified the great need for missionaries to go to that continent to evangelise, plant churches and demonstrate the love of God through medicine, education and in many other ways. Thousands responded, God blessed their work, and today we see the fruit – some of the most Christian countries in the world are on the continent of Africa. There is still much to be done in Africa but that must not blind us to the fact that the world has changed and there are now new priorities in mission.

One useful measure which is used by mission strategists is to divide the world into three parts according to its response to Christ.

**World A** is the unevangelised world, or those individuals who have not yet heard of Christ, Christianity or the Gospel.

**World B** are those who have heard the Gospel, but have not yet responded.

**World C** are those who are professed members of a Christian church.

Applying this measure to whole countries, peoples, cities, or provinces

World A = less than half evangelized;

World B = over 50% evangelized but less than 60% Christian

World C = over 60% Christian or over 95% evangelised

**Now for the shock statistic!**

In 2010 more than 70% of Christian mission and ministry is concentrated in World C and less than 5% is committed to World A!

Test this out yourself. In the box below put one tick in the middle column for every missionary you know about in that country. Then in the last column estimate whether that country is in World A,B or C. (Answers at bottom of page.)

| Country | Missionaries you know of | World A, B or C |
|---|---|---|
| Kenya | | |
| Cambodia | | |
| Japan | | |
| Uzbekistan | | |
| Philippines | | |
| India | | |

World A : Cambodia, Uzbekistan; World B: Japan, India; World C : Kenya, Philippines

# Where is God calling me?

What does all of this mean for me as I consider my own Christian discipleship and where God has called me to be?

Some years ago I interviewed a couple who clearly knew that God was calling them into mission in a different culture. As we spoke they confessed that they were not clear where their calling would take them but they were convinced it would be a hot place and probably in Africa. A year later, after months of prayer and preparation, they began their mission service – in St. Petersburg, in January! I'm sure they would have done a good job in Burundi or Malawi but actually God needed them in St. Petersburg, to support and encourage Russian Christians at the moment when they were emerging from years of communist domination and had real opportunities to build the Kingdom of God on Russian soil. Looking back I am so grateful that couple were not blinded to God's call by the romantic pull of African sunsets.

As we each consider where God is calling us to serve we need to be open to His surprises. Maybe God needs us where we are right now, or in a school in Middlesbrough. Or perhaps the call will come to go to Kazakhstan (once you've found it on the map) or to work alongside Muslims in Lebanon, or with a business school in Japan.

**Don't forget Europe**

**The continent of Europe has some of the lowest church membership rates in the world. Highly secularized populations know about Jesus, have Bibles in their homes, ignore both and have no idea how Christian discipleship could transform their lives. Your cultural background might make you just the right person to serve as a missionary in France, the Czech Republic or Croatia.**

# The healing hand of Jesus

David Innes – Arab World Ministries

It's one thing believing that Jesus loves people; it's another thing realising that He is passionate about you and your family. For one Arab Muslim, it was this revelation of Christ's personal concern – expressed through the practical medical care of believers – that transformed her life.

Like any mother would, Um Ahmed* became concerned when her youngest son fell seriously ill. Her distress increased when all their herbal medicines failed to bring down the fever, or decrease the coughing. In sheer desperation the son, Omar*, was taken to a Christian hospital in the region. The medic who treated Omar was initially impressed by the Bedouin family's commitment to do all they could to save his life. Um Ahmed is the second of four wives and has eight children (not including the other wives' children who wander in and out of her tent!). Her husband is very poor and every day is a struggle: not knowing if there will be enough milk for the baby, enough wood gathered to make a fire, or enough rice to cook with. Her husband had heard rumours about our Christian hospital. People said that our medicine was good and that the sick returned home healed. So, they borrowed a neighbour's pickup truck and came to our clinic.

On arrival, Omar was diagnosed with pneumonia and stayed in hospital for two weeks; Um Ahmed hitchhiked into town and visited him every day. Her love and devotion for her son was visible to all the staff. The medic discussed with the mother the details of Omar's condition, the treatment plan, and tips on preventing the infection returning. At times, the medic also sat with her and Omar in the TV room, where the Jesus film played every morning. The medic couldn't help notice that the re-telling of Jesus' miracles was stirring faith in Um Ahmed.

As we talked day by day, I saw her pay more attention to the movie. One day she asked me, 'Do you think Jesus can heal my son, like he does in the movie?' 'Yes!' I exclaimed. I then explained to her the whole story of Jesus' love for us and His desire to heal us, to save us, and to give us eternal life. She had never heard a story like that before.

Once Omar returned to health, Um Ahmed took him home. The medic continued to visit their home and developed a relationship with the family. On Christmas day, Um Ahmed repaid the honour by visiting the medic at the hospital on the Christian holiday. As part of the celebration a speaker explained the significance of Christ coming into the world to save mankind from their sins. Again, the medic realised that Um Ahmed was deeply affected by these Bible truths.

When it was over I asked her, 'Do you believe this story? Do you accept that Jesus is your Saviour?' And this time it was she who exclaimed 'Yes! with all my heart.' Now Um Ahmed regularly brings her children to our hospital when they're sick. She brings the other wives' children too. They usually come a little late, and are the last ones to see the doctor. Um Ahmed does this on purpose. She takes them to wait in the TV room. She wants them all to see the movie so they'll know about Jesus too.

*Names have been changed.

# Where from?

As we consider where God might be asking us to go in mission we also need to notice who we might be working with? In the past a British missionary in Egypt might have found himself working alongside Australian, American and German missionaries. Not so now. His fellow missionaries today are just as likely to be Korean, Kenyan or Armenian.

The chart below illustrates this very significant change over a period of 100 years

| Countries sending most cross-cultural missionaries | | |
|---|---|---|
| **1950** | **2000** | **2050 (projected)** |
| USA | USA | China |
| Britain | Brazil | USA |
| Germany | India | Brazil |
| Italy | Korea | India |
| Ireland | Nigeria | Philippines |

In 2050 many of these cross-cultural missionaries will not only come from different places (Europe in particular being eclipsed by Asia) but they will also adopt very different methods in mission and ways of crossing cultural barriers. Churches in the Philippines, for example, have developed a whole strategy and training programme to equip migrant workers, often travelling into Muslim and Hindu countries, to be effective Christian missionaries.

*Discuss*
*What do you see as the major implications of the changes outlined in the above table?*

*What challenges does this present for European missionaries?*

*What do you see happening if large numbers of Chinese and Brazilian missionaries come to your home town? (Just as large numbers of Europeans went to Bangalore and Mombasa a hundred years ago.)*

# Collaboration in Mission

The picture of mission we get from the Bible is one of intense collaboration. The Father does not send the Son and leave Jesus to get on with it. Throughout the Bible we see Father, Son and Spirit in deep collaboration as God seeks to restore his creation, and above all human beings, to true fellowship with him. In building his mission team Jesus called together a really odd group of people – a Zealot and a Roman sympathiser, four fishermen and women from a range of backgrounds. He taught them to work together. Moving on into the first decades of the early Church we again see collaboration between Peter and Paul, Silas, the young man Timothy, and a host of others. Each brought their own particular gifts and insights.

Today, in a world shrunk by the Internet, air transport and a global economy, we have the most amazing opportunities for collaboration in mission. Brazilians run training centres in Spain to prepare Nigerian businessmen for outreach in Tunisia. Mission teams in Mongolia include Koreans and Indians working alongside Swedes and New Zealanders. These mixed teams in mission are, of course, a witness themselves to a God who 'unites all in all' and in whose kingdom there is 'neither Jew nor Greek'.

As you consider your call into God's mission you need also to consider who you might work with and how you can prepare to collaborate with those of a very different culture and background from your own.

*Final Thought*

*What most excites you, and what most concerns you, about the possibility of working in mission with Christians from many different cultures and backgrounds?*

## For Further Study

**Web Resources**
World Christian Database  http://www.worldchristiandatabase.org/wcd/
Joshua Project  http://www.joshuaproject.net/
Perspectives Course http://www.perspectives.org
Lausanne World Pulse on-line magazine http://www.lausanneworldpulse.com/

**Books**
Samuel Escobar *The New Global Mission* IVP 2003
Trev Gregory *Mission Now* Authentic 2003
Michael Pocock, Gailyn van Rheenen & Douglas McConnel *The changing face of world missions: Engaging contemporary issues and trends* Baker 2005
Philip Jenkins *The Next Christendom: The coming of global Christianity* Oxford University Press 2002
Enoch Van and Michael Pocock *Missions from the majority world* William Carey Library 2009
David Smith *Mission After Christendom* Darton Longman & Todd 2003
David J Phillips *Peoples on the Move* Piquant 2001

# MISSION PARADIGMS - 1

## CONTENTS

## SECTION FIVE

# What is a paradigm?

We noted in the introduction to this section on Missiology that the Church's understanding of mission had changed between the beginning of Acts 10 and Acts 11.18; originally they had not intended to take the gospel to the Gentiles, but the action of the Holy Spirit had convinced Peter and then the Church that they should do this. We are also aware that initially the Church took one approach to what rules applied to Gentile Christians but that it took some time before this was fully accepted by the Jewish believers and even Peter went back upon his original decision about eating with Gentiles. Circumstances change and there is change in how mission is understood and practiced, but it can take a while before everyone has agreed that the change has really occurred and accepted the new practices.

Some other examples may help to better understand the concept. In the world that the New Testament was written in, Christians were a tiny persecuted minority, they were generally made up of the poor and many were slaves and they lived in fear of their lives. By the time of the Edinburgh 1910 Mission Conference (mentioned in Section 4) there was an assumption that the world would be completely evangelised, primarily by western Protestant missionaries, within a generation.

Four years after the Edinburgh 1910 Mission Conference came the First World War; the European nations, who saw themselves upholding Christian values, tore themselves apart with a war that saw the greatest slaughter of people ever experienced. This war was followed by a huge economic depression leading to a Second World War that was followed by the Cold War. A hundred years after Edinburgh 1910, Europe has lost its confidence in the Gospel and the Church has to work out its mission agenda against an increasingly hostile secular agenda. Meanwhile the Churches of Africa, Asia and South America generally grow and gain confidence in their role in God's mission. There were obviously some very big changes in how mission was perceived during both of these periods.

In the onion model of culture that we considered in the section on Culture, we explored how worldviews change and considered some of the factors that impact upon worldview and how beliefs, attitudes and then behaviour and customs change to reflect the modified worldview. This is not an instant process. Basically some people begin to realise that their beliefs, behaviour and customs don't feel as comfortable as before and that their worldview has changed to some extent and begin to work out the implications of this to the outworking of God's mission.

With many, but not all, such changes of worldview the new understanding eventually becomes the view accepted by the majority. Such a change, which reflects a leap in how the worldview and values and attitudes and customs and behaviour are perceived, is referred to as a paradigm. The word paradigm was originally used in the scientific community, by Thomas Kuhn, and its application to missiology was first seen by Kung but has been increasingly used in missiology since the publication of *Transforming Mission – Paradigm shifts in the theology of mission* by the late David Bosch (Orbis Books 1991). A paradigm isn't a sudden change of understanding and usually, as an increasing number of people accept the new view, there is increased tension between those holding the different views. Often it is possible, for different reasons, for different paradigms to exist at the same time, so there isn't a clean break between one paradigm and another and it is suggested that paradigms never completely disappear and so we will encounter different mission paradigms.

Looking at the two examples given above, the shift from New Testament times until 1910 and from 1910 until now, it is far easier to make sense of the first changes than the second, because they are clearly 'history'. Any recent paradigm might well still be 'change in progress' and might need to be re-evaluated at some point in the future. Bosch helpfully identifies four missionary paradigms before considering current trends.

- The missionary paradigm of the Eastern Church

- The Medieval Roman Catholic missionary paradigm

- The missionary paradigm of the Protestant Reformation

- Mission in the wake of the Enlightenment

The first two paradigms are dealt with very briefly in what follows and the final two paradigms and some thoughts towards a postmodern mission paradigm are considered in the next unit. To explore these further a full exploration can be found in *Transforming Mission* by David Bosch or a briefer exploration in *Christian Mission* by Stephen Spencer (SCM Press 2007).

# The missionary paradigm of the Eastern Church

In *Gospel and culture in a changing world*, in the section on Culture, we noted that after the time of the apostles, the Church continued to grow and spread into Asia Minor and Greece and so developed within a Greek thinking and speaking culture very different from that which had given birth to Christianity. Greek religious and philosophical insights gave them new understanding of what had been revealed to them through Christ. The Christian concepts, of God appearing in human form and of salvation being achieved through Jesus dying and of resurrection and new life, made more sense within a Greek worldview than within a Jewish worldview and so Christianity became distanced from its Jewish roots.

It was against this background that they felt the need to express who the person of Jesus Christ was and so the understanding of the divinity of Christ and of the Trinity were shaped by this culture during the third to sixth centuries. Eschatology, the understanding of the end-times, was shaped by the fact that Jesus had not in fact returned during the lifetime of the apostles. This led to an understanding that the end times have begun, with the events of the crucifixion and the resurrection being signs of the universal fulfilment that is still to come; with the Holy Spirit being a pledge.

Through the early centuries of the Church, until medieval times and the increasing divide between the Church in the East and the West, the Church was synonymous with the Eastern Church. It would now be identified with the Greek Orthodox and the Russian Orthodox. Because of the schism with the Western Church and the rise of Islam cutting the Eastern Church off from the West, the Eastern Church never engaged with the issues raised by either the Reformation or Enlightenment, and this is only just beginning in some parts of the Eastern Church. This means that this mission paradigm is still true for much of the Eastern Church.

The following are characteristics of this paradigm:

- Christianity identifying more closely with the Greek worldview than the Hebrew worldview

- Emphasis upon right doctrine

- Christendom leading to a blurring of the edges between Church and State with the Church being granted huge privilege within the life of the State, but also needing to compromise its views in the interest of the State

- An understanding that 'the purpose of mission is the Church' rather than 'the purpose of the Church is mission'

- Salvation can only be achieved through the Church

- Missionary activity can only happen through being sent and supported by the Church

- A centripetal, rather than centrifugal understanding of mission; that is bringing people into the Church rather than going out to where people are

- A theology that is based more upon John 3.16 – 17, 'For God so loved the world that he gave his only Son, so that everyone who believes in him may not perish but may have eternal life. Indeed God did not send the Son into the world to condemn the world, but in order that the world might be saved through him.' than on Paul's Epistles and 'the Sin of Man'

- A theology that puts greater emphasis upon 'the Incarnation' and the Resurrection', than on 'the Crucifixion'. For instance, the historic sites of Christ's crucifixion and burial lie within a large church that is managed by different denominations and known by the Eastern Church as the Church of the Resurrection but by the Western Church as the Church of the Holy Sepulchre.

Note how the Eastern name emphasises Christ's resurrection and the Western name the death and burial!

- A dualistic world-view consisting of 'the material world' of sin and shadows passing away and 'Eternal life' as union with God; but the teaching and liturgy of the Church comprising the area where the two worlds overlap. The Church being an open door through which Eternal life can be reached

- Seeing themselves as the Church that others have broken away from throughout the history of the Church, there is particular pain from the disunity of the Church and the question of how a disunited Church can witness to the world

- The worshipping community is, in itself, an act of witness. An understanding that worship can give an experience, or taste, of heaven and that worship, or the Liturgy, is the primarily tool of mission. (According to tradition Vladimir, Prince of Kiev during the 10th century, sent his followers to look for the true religion. They found no joy within Muslim worship and no beauty within the Christian worship of Germany and Rome but their experience of the beauty and splendour of the Eastern Liturgy in Constantinople convinced them that God dwells amongst men, leading to Russia becoming Christian in the 10th century.)

*Which aspects of this mission paradigm exist in churches that you are familiar with?*

*Which aspects exist in the church of any other country that you know about?*

# The Medieval Roman Catholic missionary paradigm

Although this paradigm is identified as lasting from about 600, with the collapse of the Roman Empire, until 1500 and the launch of the age of discovery, traces of it will be found still within Catholicism. Its origins can be traced back to the beginning of the 5th century when St Augustine took a stand against the Pelagian heresy that suggested that Christ was merely an example or ideal to be strived towards. To counter this, St Augustine developed a strong emphasis upon Christ dying for our sins. St Augustine's classic work, *The Heavenly City*, underpins the theology of this paradigm there is an overlap of the 'Heavenly City' and of the 'Earthly City'; the overlap is the combination of the Catholic Church and the State.

The following are characteristics of this paradigm:

- An emphasis upon Christ dying for our sins based on Paul's writings (although this emphasis would need to be rediscovered with the Reformation)

- The individualism of salvation with the need for individuals to repent and join the Church in order to be saved

- The development of Christendom, with the close relationship between Church and State. In theory with the Church dominant but, at times, with the Church being compromised by the State

- Mission as the establishing of Christendom with all people within Christ's Church for their own salvation

- With Christendom came the concept of the 'Just War' contrary to the pacifist understanding of the early Church Fathers

- Christendom also led to the acceptance by the Church of the 'status quo' within society and that people should accept their social standing and not try to improve it.

- There was a move away from the God who 'didn't come to condemn the world' John 3.17 to an emphasis upon 'compel them to come in' Luke 14.23

- This sense of compelling, coupled with the understanding of a 'Just War' and the question of how Christian rulers could rule amongst those who were not Christian, meant that pressure could be exerted upon those who were 'reluctant to come in'. Initially, there was bad treatment and financial pressures to make life impossible for those who did not convert. It then became acceptable to use force on 'heretics' to convert and eventually it became acceptable to use force and torture on those who were heretics, or not Christians, and acceptable to kill them. An example would be the Crusades where it was not just the Muslims who were killed, but also Eastern Christians who were considered heretics.

- The relationship with Jewish people was severed and often they would be persecuted and seen as responsible for the crucifixion of Christ.

- Another aspect of Christendom was that Christianity was associated with civilisation; those who were not Christian were considered as uncivilised.

- The colonial period was seen as an opportunity for mission and the Pope happily divided the unconquered world between the Spanish and the Portuguese for their colonial and missionary endeavours.

- At one level, the colonial endeavour was an extension of the Crusades and, because those on the receiving end were of a different colour and, as a consequence of their cultural differences, were not perceived to be 'civilised', they were considered inferior leading to slavery being considered as acceptable resulting in the slave trade.

- A positive dimension was the monastic movement. Unlike the individualism of the monastic movement of the Eastern Church, Western monasticism was communities. These monastic communities were famous for their:

    o agricultural endeavours redeeming and cultivating much land that had previously been considered un-farmable

    o care of local communities

    o scholarship, gaining reputations as centres of learning

    o tenacity and faith in not succumbing to persecution.

*Which aspects of this mission paradigm exist in churches that you are familiar with?*

*Which aspects exist in the church of any other country that you know about?*

# MISSION

# PARADIGMS - II

## CONTENTS

# SECTION FIVE

# The missionary paradigm of the Protestant Reformation

This paradigm begins with Martin Luther, an Augustinian monk, rediscovering the theology of Augustine that had long been forgotten by the Roman Catholic Church. Central to the Reformation were five tenets:

1. Justification by faith

2. An understanding of the Fall that meant that all needed to be saved

3. The need for personal salvation

4. The priesthood of all believers

5. Centrality of the Scriptures

Initially the Reformation saw little missionary activity. This was caused by the combination of trying to define right doctrine and the expectation that the Second Coming was imminent. As the Reformation embraced the theology of Calvin, St Augustine's understanding of predestination was emphasised. Initially this led to the understanding of the saved being the elect, chosen for privilege, with those not saved being outside of God's plans and open to exploitation by colonial movements. Later it was understood that God might have chosen to save them as well and mission was affirmed.

Calvin also stressed pneumatology, not only the role of the Holy Spirit in renewing the inner life but also in renewing creation, leading to a greater emphasis upon Christ's role in society at large. Persecution of Puritans in Europe led them fleeing to North America and establishing socio-economic communities, where God was seen as ruler, that would be a manifestation of the Kingdom of God on earth.

This paradigm reflects the pre-Enlightenment stage of Protestantism, and some traits of this paradigm are still encountered. The following are characteristics of this paradigm:

- An emphasis upon Paul's understanding of salvation outlined in Romans 1

- The importance of right doctrine

- A continuation of the Christendom model of the relationship between Church and State, except amongst the Anabaptists, who rejected and challenged this understanding

- Initially, a number of religious wars established which branch of the Christian faith would be the Christendom expression in that area

- Initially, there was an indifference to mission, except amongst the Anabaptists, who were keen to baptise both Roman Catholics and those Reformers who still practiced infant baptism

- Monasticism was abandoned and, with it, the positive missionary endeavours that had stemmed from it

- There was a reaction against forced conversions

- Scripture was affirmed for verbal inspiration, but not understood as inerrant. In the same way that The Church had replaced God in the Roman Catholic Church, there was a tendency for Scripture to replace God within the Reformation

- Justification by faith led to an understanding of the urgency of mission, tempered by the realisation that it was God that takes the initiative

- An understanding of the Fall affirmed the sovereignty of God but a pessimistic attitude to humanity

- The need for personal salvation affirmed the worth of the individual

- The understanding of the priesthood of all believers emphasised the role of all believers in God's plans

- Pietism, an early movement associated with the Reformation, emphasised life, rather than doctrine. Although narrow in its outlook, it had an emphasis upon personal conversion and was missionary in its outlook.

Which aspects of this mission paradigm exist in churches that you are familiar with?

Which aspects exist in the church of any other country that you know about?

# Mission in the wake of the Enlightenment

The *modern* or *Enlightenment* era or the age of reason is considered to have begun in the 17th century and began to impact upon Protestant thought; in contrast the Roman Catholic Church withstood its influences until the 20th century. The medieval worldview was based upon an undisputed hierarchy of God; Church; Kings and Nobles; the people; animals, plants and objects. Each was in its God-ordained position, which could not be challenged. The Enlightenment led to this worldview being undermined in a number of ways:

1.  The Reformation destroyed the unity of the Church and its power. The Age of Revolution, in the 18th century, undermined the power of kings and nobles and started a process that would eventually lead to democracy. The Age of Science meant that people could understand why things happened and, although the early scientists didn't question God's existence, began to take God out of the hierarchy. With the role of God, Church and Royalty undermined humanity could derive its validity from considering the subhuman level of animals, plants and objects.

2.  Nature ceased to be considered as Creation, but the object of study. The mysteries of creation were increasingly understood. The study of individual parts took precedence over the study of the whole. Humans, for instance, were no longer solely defined theologically, but could be understood through philosophy, sociology, religious studies, medicine and the sciences and cultural anthropology.

3.  Related to the above is the elimination of purpose. No longer was the emphasis upon the place of someone or something within God's plans, but understanding was identified by cause and effect.

4.  People were excited by progress and gained a new confidence in humanity. There were countries to be discovered and colonised, with progress and civilisation brought to their inhabitants. There were scientific discoveries to be made. Through development programmes, there was poverty to be overcome. Power could be used for the common good, rather than to support the status quo; although this didn't stop it being misused.

5.  Scientific truth was factual, value free and neutral. It was Objective Truth, determined by facts rather than values that are shaped by opinions. Religion, on the other hand, was considered to be about values that were subjective and couldn't be proved. Religion, therefore, belonged in the private realm of opinion and not in the public realm of provable facts.

6.  All problems were ultimately solvable and all facts ultimately knowable; the horizon was limitless. The power of nature could be overcome and harnessed.

7.  People were considered emancipated, autonomous individuals. Individuals took priority over communities. Human beings could be seen as more important than God but equally, with no imposed hierarchy of values, as being no more important than animals and things. Without any supernatural reference both Capitalism and Marxism would be derived from this understanding of the individual.

The Church responded to these challenges in different ways. The Enlightenment coincided with the colonial era and a time when the gospel was being taken to different parts of the world. The Enlightenment led people to compartmentalise life. This meant that through foreign missions a worldview that was divided into the religious and the secular was being presented to cultures that still had a holistic worldview.

Many of the traits of this paradigm are still encountered. The following are characteristics of this paradigm:

- Christianity ceased to be the benchmark by which all values, institutions and academic disciplines were judged

- Theology became a separate academic discipline, rather than the starting point that embraced all other academic disciplines

- Christianity was no longer synonymous with religion, but just one of the religions. Religion was about values, not facts; we are free to choose which set of values, that is which religion, we wish to follow

- Christianity, realising that it was operating in an alien and sometimes hostile environment, lost its self-confidence and sometimes compensated for this by over emphasising itself

- Human optimism replaced an understanding of Sin. Sin, as a theological understanding of fallen humanity, became replaced with sins; moral codes and disobedience

- Faith was replaced by reason, although some would keep the two separate and restrict religion to feelings and experience

- Another response was the privatisation of religion, keeping it out of the public domain; the divide between the religious and the secular

- Academically, much theological study embraced the tools of the Enlightenment, trying to make sense of what biblical texts meant then, and how they should be understood now. Reaction to this approach led to others declaring the inerrancy of Scripture, claiming every statement of Scripture as factually true

- As cause and effect were better understood and the world viewed as a perfect and predictable machine, increasingly there was no room for surprise, mystery, miracles or the supernatural within religion

- Increasingly during this era, the Christendom relationship between Church and State broke down and they went their separate ways; this would occur at different speeds in different European countries. Colonial expansion, that had begun within a Christendom paradigm, began to reflect this change

- Countering the picture painted above, there were different renewal movements that weren't considered to be opposed to the evolving scientific view of the age. These included the Great Awakening in the American colonies, Methodism and the English Evangelical Revival. These, although not missionary themselves, did lay the foundations for later missionary endeavours that developed in the 19th century as the result of further renewal movements. Some renewals were able to learn from the lessons of previous ones, but such renewals were seen to be temporary phenomena

- For various, complex, reasons, the British churches retained an emphasis upon foreign mission that was largely lost by the churches of the rest of Europe that succumbed to Rationalism

- The Victorian era saw evangelicals well represented within politics in Britain

- Although Church and State became more distinct, missionaries were seen to reflect colonial values and were often paternalistic

- As the 20th century approached, evangelicalism, which had been able to hold together social reform with revival, split into two distinct streams; one combining an ecumenical emphasis with social reform and the other with an emphasis upon evangelism and a clear confessional orthodoxy. As the 20th century developed, the divide became more distinct between social gospel and fundamentalism

- An interesting development was that mission was carried out by missionary societies rather than by the Church. Missionary societies, in the spirit of the age, represented like minded individuals banding together for a common task. They could be denominational, interdenominational or non-denominational.

- Different understandings of the end times, eschatology, evolved depending upon different understandings of Revelation 20 and the thousand year reign of Christ on earth. It is because of that reference to a thousand years that the word millennialism appears within each of the different understandings. Some view this as literally a thousand years, and others view it figuratively as representing a long period of time.

o **Premillennialism** – is the understanding that Jesus will return and defeat Satan before his thousand year reign on earth. It stresses the importance of personal rather than structural sins and so focuses upon personal conversion rather than any other aspects of mission. The growth of Communism, after the First World War, was seen as a particular threat and premillennialism became particularly associated with the defence of middle class American values and the New Religious Right.

Premillennialism is based upon an understanding that before Jesus returns the fullness of the Gentiles needed to be brought into the Church. As the gospel has been taken throughout the world this moment could be seen as imminent. Another precondition would be that the Jews needed to be converted. A strand of premillennialism is Christian Zionism that views the creation of the State of Israel as being part of this, with a special dispensation given to the Jews, who will convert when they finally recognise Jesus as Messiah on his return.

o **Postmillenialism** – sees the millennium as already begun with a gradual defeat of Satan and his powers and the gradual establishment of the Kingdom with Christ coming when this is complete. As such, it looks towards establishing Kingdom values and emphasises a broad understanding of mission and tackling structural sin.

o **Amillenialism** – sees the millennium as having begun with Pentecost, but representing a spiritual reign by Jesus, with Satan bound, but not totally

defeated. It sees that there will be a mix of good and evil, both in the world and the Church, such as indicated in the parable of the wheat and tares, and that we have no idea when Jesus will return to finally defeat Satan and establish his earthly reign.

*Which aspects of this mission paradigm exist in churches that you are familiar with?*

*Which aspects exist in the church of any other country that you know about?*

# Towards a Postmodern Paradigm

Enlightenment thinking assumed that Christianity and all other religions would die out. Not only is Christianity still around and growing rapidly in many parts of the world, but there has been a resurgence in other religions such as Islam, Buddhism and Hinduism.

The theory of relativity and quantum mechanics have challenged the traditional Newtonian understanding of physics and shown not only that what was considered as scientific fact was only opinion, but also the gap between religion and science might not be as big as previously thought.

It was assumed that Enlightenment thinking would lead to peace, justice and the eradication of poverty and an era of hope ushering in a man-made Utopia. Instead, the twentieth century saw the devastation of two world wars and many regional ones, the Holocaust, terrible injustices, increased gaps between rich and poor and the lack of hope. Modern technology meant that far greater numbers of soldiers and civilians were killed in wars than ever before and led us to live under the shadow of both nuclear destruction, with the Cold War, and the destruction of the planet in response to human greed.

Pursuing wealth and increased production has enslaved rather than liberated workers, taken away much job satisfaction and left people vulnerable to global recessions. It has also diminished the available resources for future generations.

The move away from holistic thinking, to the focus on separate parts, has proved unsatisfactory for many and the emphasis upon cause and effect has taken purpose out of life and left people seeking wholeness and purpose.

A consequence of the above has been to begin to develop a new worldview, to follow the modern one. As such, until it has been established long enough to develop a different title, it is know as postmodern.

Much was said in the section on Culture about postmodernity and its impact upon our worldview, but it is impossible to give a neat list of characteristics for a paradigm that is still emerging. Instead I can only offer a few pointers.

- One aspect has been the rediscovery of the Missio Dei, the realisation that it is God's mission, not ours, that God invites us to take part in.

- Dietrich Bonhoeffer, the German theologian who was killed for resisting Hitler during World War 2, concluded that the Christian life, if taken seriously, is not easy. He felt that the church was often guilty of offering cheap grace to its members and describes the costly nature of following Christ in his book *The Cost of Discipleship*. (Re published by different publishers).

- Bonhoeffer was a student of Karl Barth (1886 – 1968) who has shaped recent theology with his writing. As with both St Augustine and Martin Luther, this began with his understanding of the book of Romans, that challenged liberal assumptions, but also by taking the Christ event, his life, death and resurrection, as central to everything. He challenged the prevailing view of trying to understand Christianity from the perspective of religions to understand religions, including Christianity, from the perspective of Christ's existence.

- Barth also brought a new emphasis to the understanding of the doctrine of the Trinity. The importance of the Trinity had been down played within the Western Church since the break with the Eastern Church, but the Trinity and the relationship between the three persons of the Trinity is becoming increasingly emphasised in recent theology. Many in the West have recently been moved by Rublev's icon of the Trinity that makes the connection between Abraham's

three visitors (Gen 18) and the three persons of the Trinity. This icon makes the viewer aware of the dynamic and relationship between the three persons of the Trinity, but also draws the viewer into the relationship. In *The Open Secret* by Lesslie Newbigin (Revised Edition - William B Eerdmans Publishing Co 1996) the Trinity is the starting point for developing a contemporary understanding of mission.

- A rediscovery of elements of Celtic Spirituality has not only re-awoken an interest in the Trinity but, at a time of increased concern about both our planet and the separation of different aspects of life, has affirmed creation and wholeness.

- The break with the Eastern Church also saw the Western Church down play the importance of the Holy Spirit; this has been rediscovered by the Western Church in various ways. Recent engagement with the Eastern Church has given insights into the Spirit's importance within their doctrines that had been lost by the West, but Pentecostal and Charismatic movements have brought different insights. *The Go Between God* by John Taylor (SCM Classics) gives an understanding of mission taking the Holy Spirit as its starting point.

- Vincent Donovan, in his book *Christianity Rediscovered - An Epistle to the Masai* (SCM 1982) tells how the traditional approach of Christian institutions, such as schools and hospitals, had made no impact at all with the Masai. Instead he follows the approach of St Paul; visiting the Masai just to share about Jesus. His approach not only bore much fruit, but through this vulnerability, in dialogue with the Masai, he found himself having to answer questions that his own culture had not prepared him for and to rediscover who Christ was for him within his own culture.

- The theme of religious dialogue has been referred to in the section on Faith and how we should go into any dialogue not only confident in the revelation of God that we have through Jesus Christ, but through being vulnerable and open to what else we can learn about the God revealed in Jesus Christ through our listening to and understanding the religious experiences of the person of a different faith.

- Another important theme is that of the local community and what it means to be the Body of Christ within the local community; Christians feeling that they are there to serve the local community and to share their faith through their sense of servanthood.

- In many parts of the world there has been the realisation that different denominations are the product of European history and a barrier to effective mission; this has led to united churches or post denominational churches. Increasingly, in a broken world, Christians need to be able to show their ability to work together across denominational and other differences.

- Stuart Murray in his books *Post-Christendom* (Paternoster 2004) and *Church after Christendom* (Paternoster 2005), helpfully identifies certain characteristics from the pre-Christendom era that we should expect of the Church in the post Christendom era. These include a move:

  - From centre to margins
  - From majority to minority
  - From settlers to sojourners
  - From privilege to plurality
  - From control to witness
  - From maintenance to mission
  - From institution to movement

- Flowing from much of the above is the whole issue of power and an attempt to move away from the power associated with Christianity as a result of Christendom or the economic power and wealth of the traditional Christian countries; to explore what appropriate models of authority should be within the church. This means exploring ways in which we can reach out with the gospel as equals. A strong emphasis has been the way that God converts Peter, and not just Cornelius. Often Christians are working closely with those of other faiths, or of no faith, in the tasks of serving the poor and marginalised, transforming unjust structures or for the benefit of the planet. It is through being involved in God's mission with others that the belief in the God, revealed through Jesus Christ, is shared. Many feel more comfortable in speaking of mission **with** others, rather than mission **to** others. Mission **to**, implies a hierarchy within the relationship and that it is the other person who should change, not us. Being involved in God's mission **with** others, acknowledges that God can change both parties through the experience.

The previous unit, on Holistic Mission, identifies a number of themes presently current in mission around the world: The Five Marks of Mission; Other Faiths; Migrants, refugees and displaced people; HIV and AIDS; Response to emergencies; Young people; Reconciliation; Response to decline; Growth; Economic viability; Christian values; Millennium Development Goals (MDG's); concern for the environment expressed within the Fifth Mark of Mission.

- Mention was made in the section on Church of the Edinburgh 2010 Mission Conference. Those planning for this Conference, reflected on what they saw as the key mission themes for the coming decades. As well as the expected themes, these included issues related to women, youth, the marginalised and voiceless and the whole issue of mission and power.

All of these can be considered as part of the current paradigm. Other aspects hinted at, but not explicit in the above, are gender issues and the empowerment of women, increased urbanisation, globalisation, post-colonialism and neo-colonialism.

But what text should represent this paradigm? In the spirit of postmodernity, I can feel free to choose the text that is valid for me. I choose a story of God taking the initiative in mission though his Holy Spirit to enable the gospel to be shared with a group of migrants who have a minority worldview in the country that they are living in. But there are also interesting issues of power and vulnerability around, as they are the household of a member of a colonial occupying army, so it is the one who is politically powerless who is sharing the gospel with the one with political power. God speaks to the believer in a strange way to encourage him to share his faith with a people of a different culture that the Church had previously not tried to share the gospel with. This believer becomes vulnerable, not only in engaging with a different culture and the member of an occupying army, but also to the church that he is part of.

He shares the narrative of his belief, rather than his doctrines; this results in the setting up of a different part of the church for a different people group, with some different practices. The believer who shared his faith then has problems in convincing the wider church about the rightness of his actions and this debate lasts for many years. In the end, through the Holy Spirit, the new understanding is accepted and a way of understanding the relationship between the new believers and the wider church is worked out.

This is, of course, the story of Peter and Cornelius; what better biblical narrative at this stage for this emerging mission paradigm?

Hopefully the above give some pointers to the emerging mission paradigm. But what issues would you add to this paradigm?

Which of the issues mentioned do you see in your local mission context?

Which would you expect to be important in the situation you intend going into?

# SECTION 6: ENDPIECE

**CONTENTS**

This section is designed to be used after you have returned from your cross-cultural experience.

# ENDPIECE

Like Peter, in Act 10. 1 – 11.18, you have:

- moved as a Christian from one culture to another and will have become more aware of your own culture

- experienced a different lifestyle and made choices about your own lifestyle

- probably experienced miscommunication and reflected upon how both good communication and miscommunication occur

- experienced some wonderful times and some difficult times, and found out more about yourself and about God

- found, like Peter in Cornelius's household and Cornelius and his household within the early Church, what it is like to be the outsider; the one who is different

- found that your faith has changed in some ways and, like Peter, this may not have been an easy or straightforward process

- had different experiences of church and probably come to different understandings of what it means to be church

- been involved within God's mission and gained new understandings of what mission is and how God wants his Church to respond to his mission.

You may have a journal where you have recounted some of these experiences and feelings, or it may just be memories.

> *Reflect upon these experiences and offer them to God in prayer. There may still be hurts and confusion and strong feelings; offer these to God so that you may experience his healing, enlightenment and peace.*
>
> *Re-read Acts 10. 1 - 11.18*

Write down your thoughts about the following:

1.   Culture

What have you learnt about your own culture?

What have you learnt about how you are shaped by your culture?

In what ways is your understanding of how you interpret the bible shaped by your culture?

How is your understanding of Christianity shaped by your culture?

## 2.    Living

*How did your lifestyle change while you were in the different culture?*

*What implications does this have for your lifestyle now that you have returned?*

*What have you learnt about cross-cultural communication?*

*What implications does this have for the future?*

3.    Faith

How has your faith changed?

What have you learnt about how your faith grows?

What have you learnt about your spiritual resources?

What have you learnt about other faiths?

What have you learnt about sharing your faith?

## 4. Church

What, from your experiences, do you want to share with your church?

How are you going to effectively communicate this with your church?

What have you learnt about your own denomination and other denominations?

What have you learnt about working with others and about partnership?

What new understanding do you have of being part of the church, both locally and globally?

5. Mission

Having had experience of being an 'outsider', who are the 'outsiders' in the situation that you have returned to?

What has the gospel to say to them? How can they be reached?

How has your understanding of mission changed?

What form of mission might God be preparing you for in the future?

How can you explore whether you are being called by God into this mission?

## 6.   Action points

*In the light of the above, make a list of action points that you intend following up.*

*If there are any hurts that need healing or any unresolved issues, note how you are going to try to move forward with these.*

*Reflect on what God may be calling you to do next, and how you are going to explore this.*

7.   Sustaining the vision

Who can help you sustain this vision?

Who can you discuss it with?

Who can encourage you?

Who will provide you with prayer support?

Make a note of when you are going to check back and monitor progress on your action points.

# Certificate in Christian Studies
## Strengthening the roots of your faith

The Certificate in Christian Studies (CCS) is a practical course in applied theology, designed to equip people in every local church for ministry and mission. It is equivalent to one year of full-time study, spread over several years on a part-time basis. As a distance learning course, it is accessible throughout the UK and abroad.

The module **Cross Cultural Christian**, if studied with a distance learning tutor, may be offered as part of the Certificate in Christian Studies.

## A course to rely on

The CCS was established in 1978. Our current courses draw on over 30 years of experience – and it shows in the quality of our study materials, tutorial help, administration and other support. Almost 10,000 people have completed all or part of the programme.

## A course of Christian development

For many different kinds of people, the CCS has been a dependable way of developing their Christian learning and discipleship.

- Many have continued to serve God where they are – giving leadership to house groups, children's and youth work, and other roles in the church.

- Others have deepened their faith and witness in the world, living out a more thoughtful Christianity in the complexities of today's society.

- Others again have been enabled to progress to further studies, sometimes for formal ministries in the church.

## University validated courses

St John's Extension Studies also offers distance learning courses in Theology to BA Honours level. A range of part-time Counselling courses is also available, including a Postgraduate Diploma and MA in Pastoral Counselling.

---

**For a Distance Learning prospectus:**

| | |
|---|---|
| **Phone**: | 0115 925 1117 |
| **Write**: | St John's Extension Studies, Bramcote, Nottingham NG9 3RL |
| **E-mail**: | ext.studies@stjohns-nottm.ac.uk |
| **Web**: | www.stjohns-nottm.ac.uk |

# Registering for tutorial support

If you would like help and support in exploring the material in this book, we will be very pleased to link you with one of our tutorial staff. The tutor will answer your queries about the material, and comment on some written work which you will be asked to prepare. Please fill in the form below (photocopy it if you prefer).

I want to study **Cross Cultural Christian** with tutorial support.
I enclose a cheque for £100.00 (in 2010) to cover the cost of distance learning tuition.

| |
|---|
| Name |
| Address |
| Postcode          Telephone |
| Email |

Please use the space below to tell us about yourself: something about your background and why you are interested in doing this course. It will be useful to your tutor to have this information.

| |
|---|
| |

Send this form, with your remittance, to: St John's Extension Studies, Bramcote, Nottingham NG9 3RL. Telephone 0115 925 1117 for enquiries and credit card payments.